ULYSSES

by

JAMES JOYCE

IS NOW READY
~~will be published in~~
~~the Autumn of 1921~~

by

"SHAKESPEARE AND COMPANY"
— *SYLVIA BEACH* —
12, RUE DE L'ODÉON, PARIS — VI

ULYSSES

BY

JAMES JOYCE

ONE HUNDRED YEARS
OF JAMES JOYCE'S
ULYSSES

EDITED BY COLM TÓIBÍN

PUBLISHED BY

The Pennsylvania State University Press, University Park, Pennsylvania
and The Morgan Library & Museum, New York, New York

Published to accompany an exhibition at the Morgan Library & Museum, New York,
3 June–2 October 2022

One Hundred Years of James Joyce's "Ulysses" is made possible by The Pierre and Tana Matisse Foundation, the Government of Ireland, and the Lucy Ricciardi and Family Exhibition Fund.

Rialtas
na hÉireann
Government
of Ireland

Library of Congress Cataloging-in-Publication Data
Names: Tóibín, Colm, 1955– editor. | Pierpont
    Morgan Library.
Title: One hundred years of James Joyce's Ulysses /
    edited by Colm Tóibín.
Other titles: Penn State series in the history of the
    book.
Description: University Park, Pennsylvania : The
    Pennsylvania State University Press ; New York,
    New York : The Morgan Library & Museum,
    [2022] | Series: Penn State series in the history
    of the book.
Summary: "A collection of essays commemorating the
    1922 publication of James Joyce's Ulysses. Includes
    contributions by preeminent Joyce scholars and by
    curators of his manuscripts and early editions"—
    Provided by publisher.
Identifiers: LCCN 2021061268 | ISBN
    9780271092898 (cloth)
Subjects: LCSH: Joyce, James, 1882–1941. Ulysses.
Classification: LCC PR6019.O9 U68466 2022
LC record available at https://lccn.loc.
    gov/2021061268

Printed in Lithuania by BALTO print

Published by The Morgan Library & Museum,
225 Madison Avenue, New York, NY 10016, and
The Pennsylvania State University Press,
University Park, PA 16802–1003

The Pennsylvania State University Press is a member of the Association of University Presses.

It is the policy of The Pennsylvania State University Press to use acid-free paper. Publications on uncoated stock satisfy the minimum requirements of American National Standard for Information Sciences—Permanence of Paper for Printed Library Material, ANSI Z39.48–1992.

Front cover: Berenice Abbott, photograph of James Joyce, 1928 (fig. 7.1, p. 88).
Page i: Shakespeare and Company prospectus for *Ulysses*, 1921, annotated by Sylvia Beach (fig. 11.9, p. 142).
Frontispiece: First edition of *Ulysses*, 1922. The Morgan Library & Museum, New York. Gift of Sean and Mary Kelly, 2018.
Page vi: James Joyce at age six with his mother, father, and maternal grandfather, 1888. The Poetry Collection of the University Libraries, University at Buffalo, The State University of New York.
Page viii: Patrick Tuohy, portrait of James Joyce, ca. 1924. Oil on canvas. The Poetry Collection of the University Libraries, University at Buffalo, The State University of New York.
Page 144: National Library of Ireland, between 1880 and 1900. National Library of Ireland.
Page 150: James Joyce, last page of the "Penelope" episode, 1921. Autograph manuscript. The Poetry Collection of the University Libraries, University at Buffalo, The State University of New York.
Page 169: Shakespeare and Company, *Ulysses* notice annotated by Sylvia Beach, detail. The Poetry Collection of the University Libraries, University at Buffalo, The State University of New York.
Back cover: Sylvia Beach and James Joyce in the Shakespeare and Company bookshop, ca. 1926, detail (fig. 5.5, p. 67).

CONTENTS

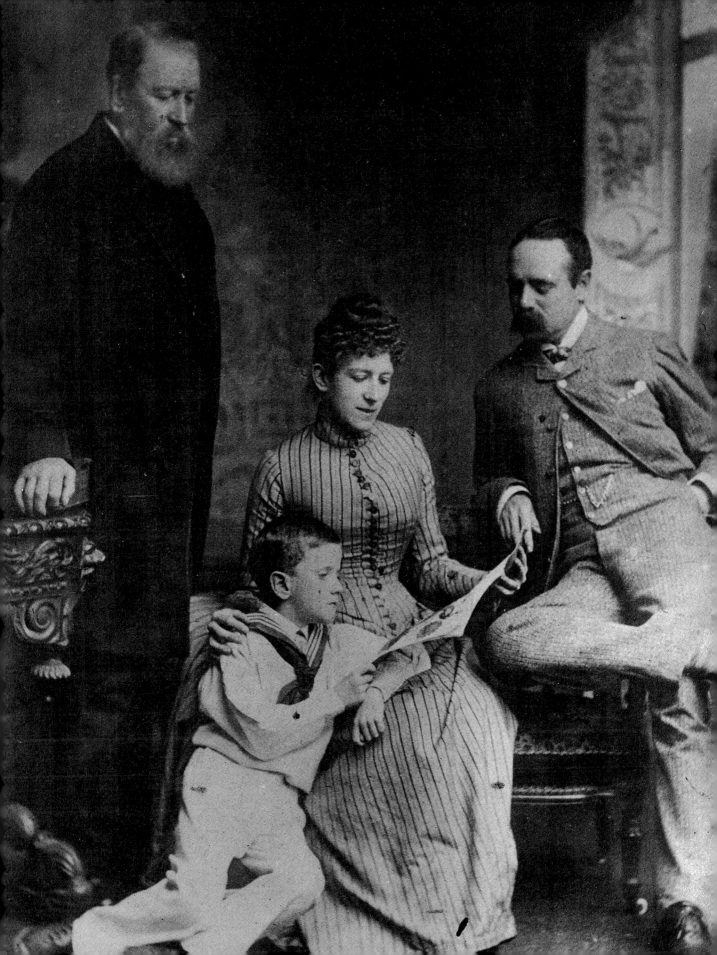

UACHTARÁN NA hÉIREANN
PRESIDENT OF IRELAND

"We are still learning to be James Joyce's contemporaries."

Richard Ellmann's striking assessment, written in 1959, remains true one hundred years after Sylvia Beach collected the first copies of the first edition of *Ulysses* from the Dijon-Paris Express on 2 February 1922.

This exhibition marks the centenary of the publication of *Ulysses* in a scholarly and comprehensive way, bringing together some of the most important texts of Joyce's creative life, his circle, and changing circumstance wonderfully curated and introduced by Colm Tóibín.

Joyce had a critical curiosity, courage, and creative daring rarely matched in his own time or since. That creativity crossed borders of time and discipline in a way that reflected a unique genius. But those qualities alone would not have sufficed to bring *Ulysses* to print. That required the belief, friendship, support, and raw courage of many others—his family, friends, patrons, benefactors, and collectors—Irish, English, Italian, French, and American.

This exhibition draws these supporters from the shadows: those who befriended him, believed in his genius, and sought support for his work. The exhibition recalls the vital role that a handful of collectors and institutions have played in protecting and caring for his papers, making them available to specialists and public alike.

The exhibition will remind us of the enormous impact that great art can exert on our lives and in our communities—and the importance of the cultural space in guaranteeing and promoting the creative, independent, and inclusive thought that underpins our democracies. It does so, too, at a time when the creative arts in all of our societies have been facing an increasingly uncertain and precarious financial future.

Most important, perhaps, is that this exhibition may usher us in to the intimate presence of James Joyce himself, one of the most original and indeed seminal creative voices of the twentieth century.

Michael D. Higgins
Uachtarán na hÉireann
President of Ireland

DIRECTOR'S FOREWORD

The Morgan has several reasons to celebrate the centenary of *Ulysses*. First published in 1922, it is the preeminent modernist novel of the twentieth century, a literary masterpiece of epic proportions with daring innovations in subject matter, style, and structure. No other work of fiction has been so inspiring and controversial. The Americans who were brave enough to publish it had to contend with the enormities of the text, the obstacles of censorship, and the obstinacy of the author. Their struggle is a story in itself—and a recurring theme in these essays.

Members of the Morgan community have played a part in the history of the book. Junius S. Morgan, a nephew of our founder, supported its publication by subscribing for a copy in advance (his subscription form is illustrated in fig. 5.6). A prescient bibliophile, he had advised his uncle on acquisitions and played an important part in the formation of the Morgan Library & Museum—but then went off to live in Paris, where he must have heard about *Ulysses*. Somehow it piqued his interest, although his taste ran more to early editions of the classics. What he thought of it we will never know, but we can see in this transaction a shrewd investment, a desire to stay *au courant*, and a sense of adventure.

The Morgan's longtime curator of literary manuscripts Herbert T. F. Cahoon wrote the bibliography of Joyce in association with John J. Slocum. In 1948, Cahoon followed in Joyce's footsteps to do research in Trieste, Zurich, and Paris, seeking information on the author's earliest publications as well as the origin story of *Ulysses*. Published on Bloomsday, 16 June 1953, the bibliography was a milestone in Joyce scholarship and a step forward in Cahoon's professional career: he was hired here a year later and presided over our literary holdings until 1989.

Other Americans joined in the quest for Joyce books and manuscripts. Just as they took the initiative to publish *Ulysses*, they were the first to collect it in depth. Although the Morgan received significant gifts and bequests, it did not make an institutional commitment to Joyce until Sean and Mary Kelly donated their collection in 2018. Sean and Mary Kelly's vision, connoisseurship, and generosity are recognized elsewhere in this volume, but I should note the extent of their contributions. Their collection contains all the best-known publications described by Slocum and Cahoon, including the first forays in print, the forerunners of *Ulysses*, and four copies of the first edition. With their advice and encouragement, we continue to build on their accomplishments and explore the implications of their ideas. They hoped that their gift would help others appreciate the novel—that we would use it to guide readers through the intricacies of the text and show them its pleasures and rewards, its humor, pathos, vivid characterization, compelling narrative, and encyclopedic references to ancient myths, politics, religion, folklore, music, and popular culture. That is a tall order, but I believe that we have made a good start with this publication, the exhibition it accompanies, and a monograph catalogue of their collection.

The editor of this publication and the guest curator of the exhibition is Colm Tóibín. He took on similar assignments in 2017 when we presented *Henry James and American Painting*. An acclaimed novelist, journalist, and critic, he is the Irene and Sidney B. Silverman Professor of the Humanities at Columbia University, where this spring he taught a seminar on *Ulysses*. He has frequently written on Joyce, most recently an account of the author's relationship with his father in *Mad, Bad, Dangerous to Know: The Fathers of Wilde, Yeats, and Joyce* (2018). I am very grateful for his work on this volume, including his introductory essay and the other essays he commissioned with the goal of producing an enticing and authoritative commentary on *Ulysses*.

The essays trace the evolution of the text through notebooks, manuscripts, and proofs to the published versions, the serialization in the *Little Review* (1918–1920), the first edition (1922), and the precedent-setting first American edition (1934). They sketch the political and social background with special reference to the four cities that mattered most to Joyce: Dublin, Trieste, Zurich, and Paris. Dublin is the point of departure, but each of these cities influenced the author's worldview and artistic outlook. The essays also cover the aftermath in America. A chapter on censorship takes place in New York, where a sympathetic judge heard the case *United States v. One Book Called "Ulysses"* and handed down a landmark decision that allowed the novel to be published in this country. An account of a collector's literary patronage and a bookseller's acumen at auction explains why the manuscript of *Ulysses* has resided in Philadelphia since 1924. We learn how a Joyce study center in Buffalo was founded on archives acquired through the foresight of librarians, donors, administrators, and an intrepid English professor. The volume concludes with an overview of the Sean and Mary Kelly Collection and an interview with Sean Kelly, who speaks about his encounters with *Ulysses*, the origins of the collection, and his family's reasons for donating it to the Morgan.

The Joyce industry has suffered, in general, from a shortage of illustrations. At best they make a token appearance in the standard commentaries, although they are essential for understanding the author's intentions and the publication process. I thank Sean Sweeney, trustee of the James Joyce estate, for permission to reproduce copyrighted material here, as well as the Consulate General of Ireland, and Ciarán Madden in particular, for assistance with the pictorial content. At the Morgan, Marilyn Palmeri and Eva Soos obtained the illustrations, many of which are from photographs by Graham S. Haber and Janny Chiu. We were fortunate to get a head start on the picture research while we were planning the exhibition. John Bidwell, formerly Astor Curator of Printed Books and Bindings, devised the original concept in consultation with Colm Tóibín and two members of the Morgan staff: Sheelagh Bevan, Andrew W. Mellon Associate Curator of Printed Books and Bindings, and Philip Palmer, Robert H. Taylor Curator of Literary and Historical Manuscripts. Sheelagh Bevan and Philip Palmer took over the *Ulysses* project after John Bidwell retired, but he stayed on to prepare the text and see it through the press. Karen Banks, Publications Manager, was the liaison with Penn State University Press, which has overseen the production and distribution of this volume. Laura Reed-Morrisson was the copyeditor, and Jennifer Norton coordinated production with Jo Ellen Ackerman, who designed the page layout and the dust jacket. The photograph reproduced on the jacket is, by the way, by Berenice Abbott and was featured in a 1930 *Vanity Fair* article that declared *Ulysses* to be "the most important single volume of fiction written in our time"—albeit still illegal in America. Donated by Sean and Mary Kelly, our print of the photograph was the one used by *Vanity Fair*. Portraits of Joyce helped make Abbott's reputation, although the writer would later remember in *Finnegans Wake* that he had flinched at his first sitting: "girl with coldblooded Kodak shotted the as yet unrenumeranded national apostate, who was cowardly gun and camera shy."

Several institutions generously agreed to lend to the exhibition. Not all of the loans are illustrated here, and some of the illustrations are not represented in the exhibition, but the thematic interchange will be obvious to those who can see *One Hundred Years* in print and in person. When we started on our wish list, we knew that we should first explore the holdings of the University at Buffalo and the Rosenbach Museum and Library. James Maynard, curator of the Buffalo collection, and Derick Dreher, former director of the Rosenbach, provided invaluable advice and extraordinary opportunities to display the makings of *Ulysses*. Ralph Ellison and Vladimir Nabokov documents loaned by the Pennsylvania State University and the Berg Collection, New York Public Library, helped demonstrate the novel's influence on the modern movement. Columbia University, Cornell University, Harvard University, Princeton University, the Metropolitan Museum of Art, and the American Irish Historical Society gave us the means to show the cultural milieu and the writer at work. At the end of the exhibition we address the artistic impact of the novel, and here, too, we look into the creative process. The Dedalus Foundation and The Pierre and Tana Matisse Foundation loaned preliminary studies for *Ulysses*, a proof etching by Robert Motherwell and a chalk drawing by Henri Matisse.

Winona Packer, Registrar, coordinated the loans and arranged the logistics with the lenders.

Elizabeth Abbarno, Director of Exhibition and Collection Management, supervised the installation of the exhibition, which was designed by members of the IKD firm in Boston. As always, Maria Fredericks, Frank Trujillo, and their colleagues in the Thaw Conservation Center have ensured that the Morgan's books and manuscripts are displayed to their best advantage. The graphics were produced by Miko McGinty Inc., and the gallery lighting was provided by Anita Jorgensen.

We have had to deal with a multitude of moving parts, like the to-and-fro of Dubliners in the "Wandering Rocks" episode. The exhibition and the publication projects were large and complex, all the more reason to be grateful for the major funding we received from The Pierre and Tana Matisse Foundation, the Government of Ireland, and the Lucy Ricciardi and Family Exhibition Fund. I have already mentioned the good offices of the Consul General. I should also acknowledge the continuing support we have received from the Matisse Foundation, which encouraged us to investigate the artist's engagement with *Ulysses* in our 2015 exhibition *Graphic Passion: Matisse and the Book Arts*. Alessandra Carnielli, Executive Director of the Matisse Foundation, helped us select hitherto unrecorded artwork for that exhibition and this one as well.

Joyce was a great writer of IOUs. He exasperated friends and family, but he also inspired patrons to support him while he endeavored to make a living in literature. His two most selfless benefactors were Harriet Shaw Weaver, who paid the bills and edited his work, and Sylvia Beach, who published *Ulysses* on generous terms and relinquished it after he received better offers elsewhere. Beach deserves credit for her contributions to the cause, which is why this book begins and ends with her annotated

Sylvia Beach and George Antheil, ca. 1923. Private collection.
Courtesy of Stéphane Briolant.

publication announcements, signs of her personal commitment and hands-on business methods. We celebrate Joyce's genius in this centenary year, but we also recognize what made it possible: his Dublin–Trieste–Zurich–Paris cultural itinerary, his coterie of loyal allies, and a legion of readers, renewed in every generation, responsive to new ideas and new ways of expressing them.

Colin B. Bailey

ACKNOWLEDGMENTS

The editor and the project managers are grateful to the following colleagues for their assistance with this publication: Patrick H. Alexander, Claire Altizer, Kelsey Scouten Bates, Stéphane Briolant, Christopher Cahill, Nicholas Caldwell, Kate Carlin, Gerald W. Cloud, Catriona Crowe, Carmen Alonso Diego, Josie DiNovo, Eugene Downes, Clara A. Drummond, Hedi El Kholti, Jack Flam, Benoît Forgeot, Alison Fraser, Elizabeth E. Fuller, Declan Kiely, Jennifer B. Lee, John T. McQuillen, Julic Mellby, Leslie A. Morris, Ed Mulhall, William G. Noel, Helena Nolan, Janice North, AnnaLee Pauls, Ryan Peterson, Nik Quaife, Katherine Reagan, Michel Scognamillo, Joelle Seligson, Lauren Stakias, Carolyn Vega, and Jobi Zink.

Fig. 1.1. Paul Darby, photograph of James Joyce, graduation from Royal
University (later University College Dublin), 1902. The Poetry Collection of the
University Libraries, University at Buffalo, The State University of New York.

COLM TÓIBÍN

1.   The Music of the Future

When Henry James came to Dublin in March 1895, he wrote to his brother William that "the whole landlord and 'nobility and gentry' class" was boycotting social events in Dublin Castle. James stayed for some of the time with the Lord Lieutenant, Lord Houghton. "He means well," he wrote, "but he doesn't matter; and the sense of lavish extravagance of the castle, with the beggary and squalor of Ireland at the very gates, was a most depressing, haunting discomfort." Houghton was reduced to entertaining "a very dull and second-rate, though large, house party from England."[1]

At the time of James's visit, Ireland was undergoing a slow revolution. A series of Land Acts, beginning in 1870 and culminating in the Wyndham Land Act of 1903, the year before James Joyce's *Ulysses* is set, meant that many tenants became landowning farmers, while many landlords were paid compensation by the government to divide their estates among their tenants. The power of the gentry in Ireland was greatly reduced.

Half of the Irish land surface, at the time of *Ulysses*, was used for the raising of livestock. The largest weekly livestock sale in Europe took place in Dublin. Cattle were brought to market in the area around the North Circular Road, Hanlon's Corner, Prussia Street, Aughrim Street, and Stoneybatter, where the Misses Morkan and their niece in Joyce's story "The Dead" had lived, as the story tells us, before they moved to Usher's Island. Well-to-do traders stayed at the City Arms Hotel in Prussia Street, where Leopold Bloom and his wife live early in their marriage. Mrs Riordan, who has strong anti-Parnellite views in Joyce's *A Portrait of the Artist as a Young Man*, is also a guest at the hotel. In the "Ithaca" episode of *Ulysses*, when it is asked if Leopold Bloom and Stephen Dedalus can find another connecting link between them, the reply reads:

> Mrs Riordan (Dante), a widow of independent means, had resided in the house of Stephen's parents from 1 September 1888 to 29 December 1891 and had also resided during the years 1892, 1893 and 1894 in the City Arms Hotel owned by Elizabeth O'Dowd of 54 Prussia street where, during parts of the years 1893 and 1894, she had been a constant informant of Bloom who resided also in the same hotel, being at that time a clerk in the employment of Joseph Cuffe of 5 Smithfield for the superintendence of sales in the adjacent Dublin Cattle market on the North Circular road.[2]

In the "Hades" episode, as Bloom and Simon Dedalus and others make their way to Paddy Dignam's funeral, they are forced to stop when a "divided drove of branded cattle passed the windows, lowing, slouching by on padded hoofs, whisking their tails slowly on their clotted bony croups. . . . Emigrants, Mr Power said."[3] Bloom speculates about alternative methods that the cross-city transportation of cattle could use, favoring the creation of a tramline from the cattle market to the Dublin quays paid for by the more affluent cattle farmers. Stephen Dedalus, who worries that he will be known as "the bullockbefriending bard,"[4] also has a concern with livestock in the novel, since Mr Deasy, his employer as a teacher, has strong views on how to deal with an outbreak of foot-and-mouth disease. He wants Stephen to use his influence to have a letter on the question published in the press.

The image of cattle in the novel, like much else, must be treated ambiguously. As a result of the Land Acts, many of the farms on which cattle were raised were run by Irish farmers, but the cattle, when we see them in Dublin, are on their way to the English market that controlled the prices and ran the abattoirs and processing factories. When Bloom and his companions see the cattle, the novel reads: "For Liverpool probably. Roastbeef for old England. They buy up all the juicy ones."[5] The cattle are caught between what seems like benign reform and an age-old economic dependence that Joyce would deplore in his essay "Ireland: Isle of Saints and Sages."

If the line of cattle—the cattlecade—in the book represents an uncertain sort of stability, there is a cavalcade in the "Wandering Rocks" episode that shows, perhaps by default, by a lack of eventfulness, another form of uncertain stability. In that episode, the Lord Lieutenant and his entourage make their way by carriage from Phoenix Park to Ballsbridge, passing through the city center.

William Humble Ward, the second Earl of Dudley, was Lord Lieutenant in Dublin from 1902 to 1905. His wife appears first in the "Aeolus" episode, where it is reported that "Lady Dudley was walking home through the park to see all the trees that were blown down by that cyclone last year and thought she'd buy a view of Dublin. And it turned out to be a commemoration postcard of Joe Brady or Number One or Skin-the-Goat. Right outside the viceregal lodge, imagine!"[6]

Skin-the-Goat, a name used for the cabman James Fitzharris, who was implicated in the Phoenix Park Murders, haunts *Ulysses*. He was part of a group known as the Invincibles who in May 1882 stabbed to death the new Chief Secretary and an Under-Secretary in Phoenix Park. The assassins were betrayed by James Carey, one of their colleagues, who is mentioned first in *Ulysses* when Bloom, thinking about Catholic rituals, notes that Carey received "communion every morning."[7]

Soon, it is reported that Skin-the-Goat, who was released from prison in 1899 and toured America before returning to Ireland the following year, "has that cabman's shelter, they say, down there at Butt bridge."[8] Toward the end of *Ulysses*, in the "Eumaeus" episode, Bloom and Stephen will visit the shelter: "Mr Bloom and Stephen entered the cabman's shelter, an unpretentious wooden structure, where, prior to then, he had rarely if ever been before, the former having previously whispered to the latter a few hints anent the keeper of it said to be the once famous Skin-the-Goat, Fitzharris, the invincible, though he could not vouch for the actual facts which quite possibly there was not one vestige of truth in."[9]

Ulysses lives in the shadow of Irish rebellions, especially the 1798 Rebellion in Wexford, Robert Emmet's Rebellion in Dublin in 1803, the Fenian movement, and the Phoenix Park Murders by the Invincibles. The image of the hapless Lady Dudley, so concerned about trees, wanting to buy "a view of Dublin"—only to find that the postcards on sale outside her very own house commemorate the knife-wielding men who murdered two representatives of the Crown in Dublin—has a bitter humor that would be appreciated by most of the characters in *Ulysses* but would make no sense to Lady Dudley herself.

The Lord Lieutenant makes a brief appearance at the end of the "Lestrygonians" episode, when Bloom sees a placard advertising a bazaar in Ballsbridge in aid of Mercer's Hospital to be opened by His Excellency. Two episodes later, the journey of Lord Dudley and his entourage is dramatized. In this episode, "Wandering Rocks," the action, such as it is, takes place in the center of Dublin. Nineteen different scenes show what various characters, some of them new to the narrative, are doing at three

o'clock in the afternoon. The chapter opens with an image of undisputed, ordinary power as Father Conmee, a Jesuit, wearing a silk hat, meets Mrs David Sheehy, the wife of a member of the Irish Parliamentary Party at Westminster. They greet each other effusively, Father Conmee noting that Mr Sheehy himself is "still in London. The house was still sitting, to be sure it was."[10] While Joyce allows the "ee" sound in Conmee to reverberate comically against the name "Mr David Sheehy M.P.," whose name is spelled out in full three times, this is a mild play on sounds rather than an effective mockery of the easy, friendly encounter between these two pillars of power.

When Father Conmee hands a schoolboy a letter to post, it is noted that the boy does so in a "red pillarbox," and later "a bright red letterbox," red being the color of postboxes in the British Isles.[11] The redness of the postbox is not a subject for dispute. Father Conmee does not see it as a symbol of foreign dominance. In his thoughts during his walk, he accepts what he finds. Since he represents authority, he has no reason to argue with its manifestations. If he has problems with the administration, they are minor ones, such as his view that there should be a tramline on the North Circular Road.

The episode uses a system of spliced narrative, with some characters appearing a number of times in the chapter, and others only once. There are moments when one scene clearly happens after another, such as when Stephen meets his sisters, who have just been with their father. But some scenes stand alone. What is most notable about the chapter is its ordinariness. Nobody says anything especially interesting. Nothing dramatic occurs. The drama arises from the way that time and city space are handled, how experience is edited, chopped up, and put back together again as an image of a peaceful city.

Fig. 1.2. Hely's Limited, *Viceroy's Entrance into Dublin*.
Postcard. Courtesy of Aida Yared.

The account of the quotidian is interrupted by a single sentence about a third of the way into the episode: "The gates of the drive opened wide to give egress to the viceregal cavalcade."[12] The gates are those from which Lady Dudley had earlier ventured to look at the trees and buy a "view of Dublin." This is the cavalcade on its way to the bazaar in Ballsbridge, earlier noted by Bloom. Six pages later, we meet the cavalcade again: "The viceregal cavalcade passed, greeted by obsequious policemen, out of Parkgate."[13] Two pages later, in another brief section, we see the cavalcade once more. Soon, a "clatter of horse-hoofs sounded from the air,"[14] a number of Dubliners witness it, and one asks what the sound was: "The lord lieutenantgeneral and general governor of Ireland, John Wyse Nolan answered

from the stairfoot."[15] Immediately, the narrative cuts away from this scene.

What is significant here is that, in a novel filled with quips and sour remarks, John Wyse Nolan has nothing smart or funny or disrespectful to say about the cavalcade. Unlike other events in *Ulysses*, such as the Ascot Gold Cup, this cavalcade did not, in fact, take place on 16 June 1904. Joyce chose to invent it and place it there. It was needed not as the dramatization of a display of power but as the dramatization of a display of weakness. No one in the novel feels anything much at the sight of the king's representatives in Ireland. It is as though their day has passed.

While the most humble citizen is allowed to speak in this episode, the novel does not enter the carriage itself. The English people being transported across the city are silent. The Dudleys are not described. It is as though a ghost wandered by carriage through a busy city on an ordinary afternoon.

At the end of the episode, Joyce finally depicts the response to the procession in some detail, showing how citizens, many of whom appear elsewhere in the novel, either miss it, ignore it, or pay quiet homage to it. The ones who pay homage include Tom Kernan, from the story "Grace" in *Dubliners*, and Simon Dedalus, who "stood still in midstreet and brought his hat low." Dedalus's homage is not presented simply, however. He is "steering his way from the greenhouse" at the time, the "greenhouse" being a public urinal. His standing "in midstreet" echoes his being in midstream not long before.[16]

It is interesting that neither Bloom nor Stephen witnesses the cavalcade. Excluding Bloom and Stephen from having to respond to it frees them both from taking a position on these pale representatives of British power in Ireland. If they were to bow or doff their caps, we would see them as subservient, or nonchalant about British power in Ireland. If they were, on the other hand, to have bitter thoughts about the cavalcade, or if Bloom were to ruminate about its meaning, then they would be pinned down: they would represent some Irish faction, and their fate would be dictated by how they reacted to the carriages.

It might have been tempting to make this scene into one of high drama, in which nationalist tempers flared at the sight of the cavalcade. Soon, in the "Cyclops" episode, we will see the Citizen and his nationalist friends, but for the most part, they are absent from the streets as Lord Dudley and his entourage pass. Their presence would ruin the air of quietness and aftermath that the scene evokes. Yet the lack of patriotic response to the cavalcade in the novel is not sociological; it is not a way of telling the reader how passive Dubliners were in 1904. Rather, it is a way of freeing the novel and its characters from the constraints of fixed response.

Joyce had watched parades in Dublin. He could easily have created different images had they been required. As an eighteen-year-old, he had witnessed a visit by Queen Victoria that he recalled in a lecture he gave in Italian in 1907:

> The queen's carriage passed by, tightly protected on all sides by an impressive bodyguard with bared sabres, while inside a little woman, almost a dwarf could be seen, hunched and swaying in movement with the carriage, funereally dressed with horn-rimmed glasses on her ashen vacuous face ... the crowd watched the sumptuous procession and its sad central figure with eyes of curiosity, almost pity. When the carriage passed by, they followed its wake with ambiguous glances ... the queen of England entered the capital of Ireland in the midst of a silent people.[17]

While Joyce in "Wandering Rocks" was careful to make no political drama and portray those who saw the cavalcade as quiescent rather than silent, nothing comes simply in *Ulysses*. Clearly, the spectators in the episode do not express any objection to the cavalcade, but there is one sentence that represents another perspective as the party goes by: "From its sluice in Wood quay wall under Tom Devan's office Poddle river hung out in fealty a tongue of liquid sewage."[18] Thus, while the citizens have been loyal, the river, using its "tongue," gets to speak. It expresses its disloyalty in a way that could not have been mistaken. It could not have been lost on Joyce how close "fealty" is to "filthy." As Michael Rubenstein has written, "The river gives a raspberry to the cavalcade, announcing its subversive 'fealty.'"[19]

The image is all the more subversive and powerful for its isolation. But there is another image hidden in the text that also adds to the ambiguity of the episode: "On the steps of the City hall Councillor Nannetti, descending, hailed Alderman Cowley and Councillor Abraham Lyon ascending."[20] Nannetti was an M.P. and a member of the City Council, becoming Lord Mayor of Dublin in 1906. While there is no record of any Cowley on the City Council, Abraham Lyon was a member for Clontarf West. Around these figures are others, including John Howard Parnell, Long John Fanning, and Tom Devan, who were involved in local government at a time when the power and reach of local government were radically expanding.

The Local Government Act of 1898 was as important as the Wyndham Land Act in changing power structures in Ireland. The Act expanded the franchise, allowing women to vote for the first time and abolishing property qualifications for candidates, which meant that politicians from poorer backgrounds could run for office. In Dublin, the number of eligible voters rose from almost eight thousand to almost thirty-eight thousand, including many from the city's poor. Matthew Potter has written about the effect of these reforms: "The rising Catholic bourgeoisie gained control of a significant aspect of the administrative machine for the first time. . . . The result was the overthrow of Protestant ascendancy, and by 1900 the Catholic/nationalist propertied classes were firmly in command of boroughs, town councils and Poor Law unions all over the country."[21]

As James Fairhall has pointed out, Joyce was in Dublin for the 1902 and 1903 municipal elections.[22] Joyce's story "Ivy Day in the Committee Room" takes place during elections in 1902. At the time, the possibility of a labor movement coming into politics posed a genuine threat to the old opposition between nationalist and unionist. Since Joyce himself, as we know from his brother's writings, had socialist sympathies, this would have interested him. The Joyce family was also close to one of the main players in this enhanced game of local politics, Timothy Harrington, who was Lord Mayor of Dublin from 1901 to 1904. Before he left Ireland, Joyce got a character reference from Harrington that he carried with him in both 1902 and 1904.

These changes in local government and the novel's interest in cattle culminate in the "Circe" episode when Bloom, in a phantasmagoria, is elected Lord Mayor of Dublin and makes a speech to his electors, saying, "better run a tramline, I say, from the cattlemarket to the river. That's the music of the future. That's my programme." The former Lord Mayor Timothy Harrington seems to support the bullockbefriendingbloom, demanding that "alderman sir Leo Bloom's speech be printed at the expense of the ratepayers. That the house in which he was born be ornamented with a commemorative tablet and that the thoroughfare hitherto known as Cow Parlour off Cork Street be henceforth designated Boulevard Bloom."[23]

Dublin was a city without a large manufacturing base. The two biggest employers were Guinness's Brewery and Jacob's Biscuits. Out of a male labor force of around forty thousand, as Fairhall writes, "only a quarter or so earned relatively adequate wages in skilled trades. . . . Unemployment among unskilled male workers may have been as high as twenty per cent."[24] F. S. L. Lyons has written, "About thirty per cent (87,000) of the people in Dublin lived in the slums which were for the most part the worn-out shells of Georgian mansions. Over 2,000 families lived in single-room tenements which were without light or heat or water (save for a tap in a

Fig. 1.3. Philip Phillips, Guinness barrels. Dublin, Ireland, 1950. Gift of Sayre P. Sheldon and Lady Richard Davies. The Rosenbach, Philadelphia (2006.0004.0139).

chance. Even the ones who have actual jobs seem to have plenty of spare time. They are literate; they are good company; they have original minds.

While they are idle much of the time, this serves to sharpen their wit. While they are ostensibly powerless, they live in a time when power is quickly shifting in their direction. While they live in a city that is maimed by poverty, their response to life is not constrained by the mortality rate. While they make references to British rule and Irish rebellion, they are easily distracted by other, more mundane concerns.

They live in a web of small conspiracies, easy gossip, old associations. Many of them are connected to one another by an interest in music and song.

In an essay on *Ulysses* first published in 1966, Anthony Cronin wrote about the importance of music in the novel.

passage or backyard) or adequate sanitation. Inevitably, the death-rate was the highest in the country, while the infant mortality rate was the worst, not just in Ireland but in the British Isles."[25] Lord Dudley, he of the cavalcade, said that "he had seen the misery of Irish peasants in the West, but nothing compared to what existed at their own doors in Dublin."[26]

Ulysses, however, does not explore social misery in Dublin in any great detail, although it is there in the background, especially in the "Circe" episode. Nor is the novel set among the city's middle classes. None of its people are doctors, bankers, or accountants. Nor are they clerks in offices, people who go to work every morning and stay at their desks all day and receive a regular wage. They are in-between people, often, like Simon Dedalus, down on their luck, or, like Leopold Bloom, in search of the next

> But a common misconception about *Ulysses* is that its characters are a cross-section of middle or lower-middle class Dublin. They are in fact splendidly typical of a certain kind of Dubliner, but not even in a city so small as Dublin could they all, or nearly all, be so well acquainted with each other unless they had a bond or activity in common. That activity is song. With the exception of Stephen's medical friends practically every character is connected with that world of semi-professional, semi-amateur concert and operatic singing which flourished in Dublin. . . . Joyce and his parents belonged to this and, apart from the students, Father Conmee and the company in the library, it furnishes the cast of the book.[27]

It might be easy to see the references to song and the use of singing in *Ulysses* as a side show, or a way, as Cronin suggests, of connecting the characters into a sort of inner world, one that can, in certain moments, soar above class or circumstances, allowing characters to transform a room. But song in the work of Joyce also has a more powerful purpose.

This is explored first in "The Dead," in the description of Aunt Julia's song: "Her voice, strong and clear in tone, attacked with great spirit the runs which embellish the air and though she sang very rapidly she did not miss even the smallest of the grace notes. To follow the voice, without looking at the singer's face, was to feel and share the excitement of swift and secure flight."[28] So, too, Aunt Kate, in her evocation of the singer Parkinson, who had "the purest tenor voice that ever was put into a man's throat,"[29] suggests the power of song to live in the mind over time more powerfully than other memories. The idea that song can carry a shivering power is given greater depth by the singing "in the old Irish tonality"[30] of Bartell D'Arcy toward the end of the story.

Most of the characters in the story are connected through music. It is song that propels the plot of the story and gives "The Dead" its haunted atmosphere.

In these years of change and ferment in Dublin, song took on a special intensity. In a city that partly saw itself as the capital of a nation that was not a state, there were absences and silences. The power of the Anglo-Irish may have waned as the influence of local politicians increased, but there was still no national parliament, no sense that the city was the site for solid government. Mr David Sheehy M.P. went to London to make his speeches, reported by journalists there. Public rhetoric in Dublin was easier to parody than to practice.

The Local Government Act of 1898 and the Wyndham Land Act of 1903 consolidated and destroyed systems of rule, but they also opened a window. Instead of satisfying political needs, these changes allowed some to dream of further change. In these years, the dreams became even dreamier and thus harder to defeat. In the early years of the twentieth century in Ireland, various forms of utterance—a poem, a translation, a play, a story, a novel, a speech over a grave, a song—carried an authority that was all the more powerful because it was often fragile, delicate, melancholy, or had a heightened rhetorical tone.

In his 1922 essay "Ireland After Parnell," W. B. Yeats noted that he had predicted the rise of "an intellectual movement at the first lull in politics." Thus, by 1891, once Parnell was out of the way, Yeats believed that "Ireland was to be like soft wax for years to come."[31] The life of the imagination, he saw, was to replace arguments about politics.

It would be too much to suggest that song replaces politics in the world of the characters in *Ulysses*, yet singing in the novel evokes a high sort of yearning. It is worth looking at the way in which song affected the life of other cities like Dublin, places that believed themselves to be nations but did not have a national parliament or the apparatus of a state.

It is easy to imagine Joyce's story "The Dead," for example, taking place in other cities where two languages, or two cultures, seemed to clash, cities such as Barcelona, Edinburgh, and Calcutta that were, like Dublin, capitals of an emerging nation and not of a solid state, cities in which traditional song or opera or oratorio seemed to lift the argument away from the minutiae of politics or the terms of trade toward some larger exploration of human striving. In these cities, there were dreams of sacred places in the countryside in which the soul of the citizens could be purified. In Bengal, Rabindranath Tagore (1861–1941) exalted the village over the city, using folktale and folksong to nourish his own compositions. His compatriots in British Calcutta were, in his view,

Fig. 1.4. James Joyce with Nora Joyce, John Sullivan, and Mrs. Sullivan at the piano. The Poetry Collection of the University Libraries, University at Buffalo, The State University of New York.

caught between a dull, deadly provinciality and the even duller possibility of cosmopolitanism.

In Dublin in the early years of the twentieth century, musical life was conducted with a peculiar concentration; songs and singers were handed the forceful, ghostly power that Parkinson had for Aunt Kate. In Barcelona, it was not traditional song that became part of the city's culture, but art song and opera. There was a particular reverence for the music of Wagner and, strangely, it was believed that this music had a special place in Catalan culture. In Scotland and in Bengal, the revival of traditional melodies, the efforts to energize a tradition, had much in common with the work of the Literary Revival in Ireland. In *Ulysses*, it is art song and opera but also music hall songs, ballads, and sentimental songs.

In "The Dead," when they discuss singers during the meal, the ones they name and revere are opera singers. But this is not a sign of high cosmopolitan company. The interest in opera and singers is natural here, native. It is a Dublin thing.

Feeling about lost love in a song could become feeling about other things that have been lost, such as an imagined country, or an imagined sense of autonomy. Songs and other forms of music, including opera and traditional music, were, before anything else, an ordinary part of social life in these cities, and all the more powerful for that. But a soaring voice, the hitting of a high note, the use of a grace note moved the mind into the realm of aspiration, pure soul, longing transforming itself to include large and unnamable things such as an imagined country that was unbroken, even free. Or the singer's enduring spirit on transcendent display.

Song connects Molly Bloom with Blazes Boylan, and a possible concert gives him an excuse to visit her. Song also connects Simon Dedalus to the company he keeps and becomes an essential tool for Joyce as he seeks to put his father into the novel without concentrating on his father's drunkenness and improvidence, without using *Ulysses* to work out the set of filial resentments harbored by his brother Stanislaus.

John Stanislaus Joyce, the father of James Joyce, was perhaps unlucky that he lost his job as a rate collector early in his life, and unlucky too that he did not know how to manage his finances, and unfortunate also that he had so many children to feed. But his worst piece of luck throughout his fall from grace may have been the brooding presence in his household of his second living son, Stanislaus, who charted what happened to the family with bitterness and in some detail in two books, both published after his death: *My Brother's Keeper* in 1958 and *The Complete Dublin Diary of Stanislaus Joyce* in 1971. There is a remarkable difference between how John Stanislaus Joyce is treated in the work of Stanislaus and in the novel *Ulysses*, where he appears as Simon Dedalus. Stanislaus's memoir has a raw sense of grievance, at times against both his brother and his father.

There is something radiant and oddly magnificent, however, in James Joyce's deciding that he had other onions to fry besides the onions of grievance. After his father's death, Joyce wrote to his benefactor Harriet Shaw Weaver, "I was very fond of him always, being a sinner myself, and even liked his faults. Hundreds of pages and scores of characters in my books came from him . . . I got from him his portraits, a waistcoat, a good tenor voice, and an extravagant licentious disposition (out of which, however, the greater part of any talent I may have springs) but, apart from these, something else I cannot define."[32] He told his friend Louis Gillet in Paris, "The humour of 'Ulysses' is his; its people are his friends. The book is his spittin' image."[33]

Since we have so much evidence about John Stanislaus Joyce as a father, it is fascinating to watch his son set about making art from the threadbare and often miserable business of what he knew. Simon Dedalus appears or is mentioned in seven of the eighteen episodes of *Ulysses*. In Stanislaus's account of him, he is ostracized by his family, but when we meet him first in the "Hades" episode of *Ulysses*, he is fully socialized. In a carriage with other men on his way to Paddy Dignam's funeral, he is presented in complex ways. Bloom calls him a "noisy selfwilled man" and then says, "Full of his son. He is right."[34] Simon is included in the conversation as one of the company. Twice, when he speaks, he is given a good sharp line of dialogue, establishing him as a man who is witty or has a way with words.

The next time we see Simon Dedalus he is in the offices of the *Freeman's Journal*, and once more he is in company where he feels comfortable, comfortable enough to exclaim, "Agonising Christ, wouldn't it give you a heartburn on your arse" when he is read a piece of overblown writing on the subject of Ireland.[35] Soon he is quoting Byron. And not long after that he is giving "vent to a hopeless groan" and crying "Shite and onions!" before putting on his hat and announcing: "I must get a drink after that."[36]

Soon, however, the real world, or the world of Simon Dedalus's unfortunate family, makes itself felt in "Wandering Rocks," as two of his daughters talk in the kitchen of his house, one of them remarking, "Crickey, is there nothing for us to eat?"

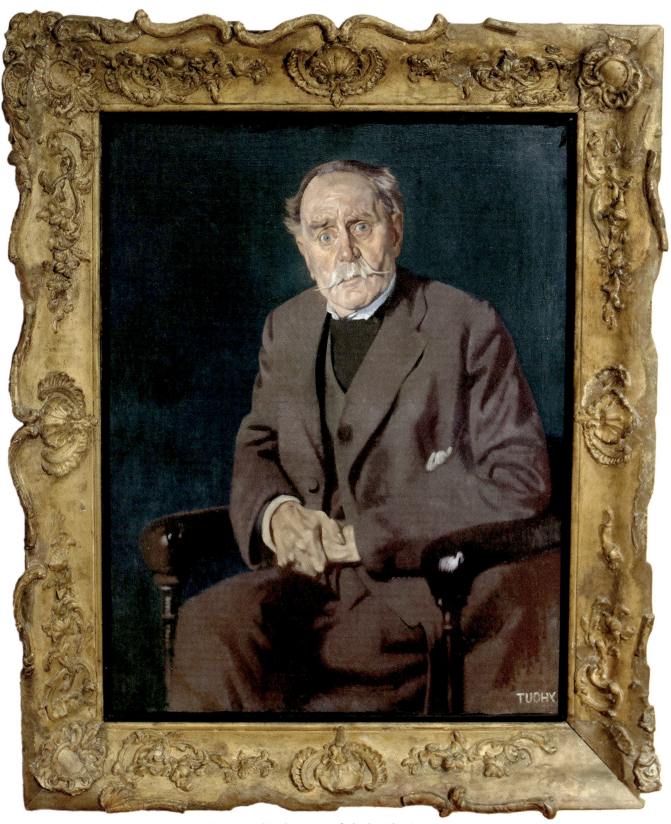

Fig. 1.5. Patrick Tuohy, portrait of John Stanislaus Joyce, ca. 1924.
Oil on canvas. The Poetry Collection of the University Libraries,
University at Buffalo, The State University of New York.

Soon, the other sister asks where their sibling Dilly is. "Gone to meet father," she is told. The other sister replies, "Our father who art not in heaven."[37] And then, close to an auctioneer's house, the afflicted Dilly meets her afflicted father and asks him for money. Eventually, he gives her money and says that he will be home soon. He has been placed in the position of a man whose children do not have enough money for food as he himself moves easily in the city, a man more at home with his companions and acquaintances than with his family.

Up to this point, Simon has been merely part of the day, another figure who wanders in the book, but in the next episode, "Sirens," which takes place at four o'clock in the bar and restaurant of the Ormond Hotel on Ormond Quay, Simon moves toward the center. When his friend Lenehan puts his head around the door, he says, "Greetings from the famous son of a famous father." And when asked who this is, he replies, "Stephen, the youthful bard."[38] Simon's response to news about his son, who is clearly avoiding him, is subdued, almost thoughtful. Joyce wishes to create in Simon a figure of moods, an unsettled rather than a solid presence in the book, a man who often controls himself rather than a figure of easy rages.

As well as possessing a talent for not having money, Simon has, as Joyce's father did, a rich tenor voice. It is courtesy of song that he redeems himself in the book as he sings "M'appari" from Flotow's *Martha*: "Through the hush of air a voice sang to them, low, not rain, not leaves in murmur, like no voice of strings or reeds or whatdoyoucallthem dulcimers touching their still ears with words, still hearts of their each his remembered lives. Good, good to hear: sorrow from them each seemed to from both depart when first they heard."[39] As Bloom listens, "the voice rose, sighing, changed:

loud, full, shining, proud."[40] This is Simon Dedalus at his most exalted. His voice "soared, a bird, it held its flight, a swift pure cry, soar silver orb it leaped serene, speeding, sustained, to come, don't spin it out too long long breath he breath long life, soaring high, high resplendent, aflame, crowned, high in the effulgence symbolistic, high, of the etherial bosom, high, of the high vast irradiation everywhere all soaring all around about the all, the endlessnessness-ness. . . . . . ."[41] Bloom notes the "glorious tone he has still. Cork air softer also their brogue."[42] Joyce, in this portrait of his father as an artist, has made him Simon Hero among his friends.

But Joyce will never let anything happen for long. As Bloom watches Simon, he muses, "Silly man! Could have made oceans of money." And then in one pithy phrase, he returns the soaring singer to earth: "Wore out his wife: now sings."[43]

Simon Dedalus, after his moment of apotheosis in the book, also remembers, for his friend Ben Dollard, Italians singing in Cork: "He heard them as a boy in Ringabella, Crosshaven, Ringabella, singing their barcaroles. Queenstown harbour full of Italian ships. Walking, you know, Ben, in the moonlight with those earthquake hats. Blending their voices. God, such music, Ben. Heard as a boy. Cross Ringabella haven mooncarole."[44] In the "Eumaeus" episode, Simon Dedalus's voice comes into Bloom's mind as he and Stephen walk toward Eccles Street, where Bloom lives. Bloom remembers Simon singing the aria from *Martha* earlier in the day (or the day before, as it now is). It was, he lets Stephen know, "sung to perfection, a study of the number, in fact, which made all the others take a back seat."[45]

In the final episode in the book, known as Molly Bloom's soliloquy, when Molly mentions living in Ontario Terrace, where John Stanislaus

Joyce and his wife first lived after they were married, it is as though she and her husband have all along, throughout the book, been pursuing Stephen—whose mother has died, whose father has been cast aside—to become shadow versions of what his parents might have been, Bloom having taken on some of John Stanislaus's preferences, such as his relishing "the inner organs of beasts and fowls,"[46] and some of his characteristics, such as his interest in reading magazines like *Titbits*. Stephen, in turn, becomes a shadow version of the Blooms' son, Rudy, who died as a baby, just as Stephen's older brother, John Augustine, the first boy in the family, born in Ontario Terrace, had died as a baby. In the soliloquy, Simon Dedalus is remembered by Molly, singing a duet with her:

> Simon Dedalus too he was always turning up half screwed singing the second verse first the old love is the new was one of his so sweetly sang the maiden on the hawthorn bough he was always on for flirtyfying too when I sang Maritana with him with him at Freddy Mayers private opera he had a delicious glorious voice Phoebe dearest goodbye sweetheart *sweet*heart he always sang it not like Bartell DArcy sweet *tart* goodbye of course he had the gift of the voice so there was no art in it all over you like a warm showerbath O Maritana wildwood flower we sang splendidly though it was a bit too high for my register even transposed and he was married at the time to May Goulding but then hed say or do something to knock the good out of it hes a widower now I wonder what sort is his son he says hes an author and going to be a university professor of Italian[47]

Simon is redeemed by a voice that allows him to soar above his own circumstances. If his character is bad, then his voice is his personality and it is capable of exquisite moments. This sense of the voice as soul, or of some element in the self that erases dull circumstance, takes on a special importance when it emerges on the walk to Eccles Street that Stephen has inherited his father's singing voice: "A phenomenally beautiful tenor voice like that, the rarest of boons, which Bloom appreciated at the very first note he got out, could easily, if properly handled . . . command its own price where baritones were ten a penny and procure for its fortunate possessor in the near future an *entrée* into fashionable houses in the best residential quarters."[48]

Once more, it is song that has narrowed the distance between Simon and Stephen; it is song that connects them, just as, in Bloom's mind, as they approach his house, it is song that will make Molly become interested in Stephen. His wife, Bloom says, "would have the greatest of pleasure in making your acquaintance as she is passionately attached to music of any kind."[49]

Like movements in a sonata or a symphony, the episodes in *Ulysses* often respond to one another or, indeed, repudiate one another. Each style adopted or narrative texture explored sets out to exhaust itself; the novel is reenergized as each new episode begins. Yet the novel has characters and events that run from episode to episode. For much of it, for example, there is a bar of soap in Leopold Bloom's pocket that has to be credibly registered. The novelist has to remind us regularly that this is the day of the Ascot Gold Cup, and much depends on the outcome for several of the characters, not least Bloom, whom some believe has money on the winning horse.

But while objects and events anchor the book, there is great emphasis on style itself—and often with parody of style. In a letter to Harriet Shaw Weaver in 1919, Joyce referred to his method of changing styles: "The word *scorching* . . . has a peculiar significance for my superstitious mind not so much because of any quality of merit in the writing itself as for the fact that the progress of the book is in fact like the progress of some sandblast . . . each successive episode, dealing with some province of artistic culture (rhetoric or music or dialectic) leaves behind it a burnt up field."[50]

"Oxen of the Sun," for example, is written as a set of parodies of systems of English prose, leaving a "burnt up field" as the episode moves from pastiche and parody of one author to another. The episode takes its inspiration from a schoolbook or an anthology, such as Saintsbury's *A History of English Prose Rhythm*, used by Irish students as much as English ones, since both share the same language. Jennifer Levine has written that "Oxen of the Sun" is "clearly a bravura performance of some kind," adding that it is "a moment of exhilaration and power on the part of the author." She quotes the novelist Anthony Burgess on this episode, "the one he would have most like to have written": "It is an author's chapter, a dazzling and authoritative display of what English can do. Moreover, it is a fulfilment of every author's egotistical desire not merely to *add* to English literature but to *enclose* what is actually there. But it is a pity that Stephen and Bloom have to get lost in the process of glorifying an art that is supposed to be their servant."[51]

For an Irish reader, the term "servant" as used by Burgess is not stable. The word appears a number of times in the opening pages of *Ulysses*. For example, Stephen says, "It is a symbol of Irish art. The cracked lookingglass of a servant."[52] In the same episode, Haines the Englishman tells Stephen, "You are your own master, it seems to me." And Stephen replies, "I am a servant of two masters . . . an English and an Italian."[53] The word "master" also appears in *Portrait*, when Stephen responds to the English Jesuit: "The language in which we are speaking is his before it is mine. How different are the words *home*, *Christ*, *ale*, *master*, on his lips and on mine! I cannot speak or write these words without unrest of spirit. His language, so familiar and so foreign, will always be for me an acquired speech. I have not made or accepted its words. My voice holds them at bay. My soul frets in the shadow of his language."[54]

While the English and Italian masters mentioned by Stephen are the British Empire and the Roman Catholic Church, the real master here is irony. Stephen's argumentative tone and his easy contempt have to be examined carefully. He enjoys announcing that he is a servant, but he doesn't mean it. No words, not least the words that signify power, can be taken here at their face value.

In "Oxen of the Sun," Joyce puts on a virtuoso performance to show what the English language can do with him as its master. He displays what he himself can "enclose," as Burgess would have it, and seeks to be playful with prose history, to make a game out of it, to lighten its load. Taking Stephen's feeling about language, so filled with anxiety, Joyce removes the anxiety and undermines the feeling.

The question, then, is if "Oxen of the Sun," in its mastery of prose history, represents an Irish response to the history of English writing, or if Joyce, by displaying his command of the language, is, in fact, arguing with the Irish Literary Revival's insistence on a Hiberno-English vernacular as the natural tone for Irish writers. His mastery of something whose servant he once was can be read as itself an ironic form of reconquest, if a term such as "reconquest" is not too heavy-handed. If Joyce's "own work is itself part of the history of Ireland's complicated linguistic condition," as Seamus Deane has written,[55] then using the history of English

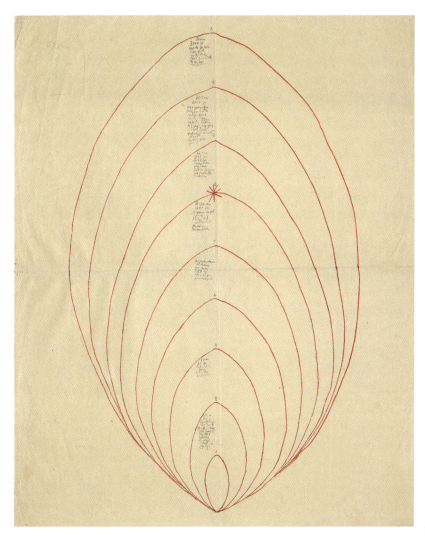

Fig. 1.6. James Joyce, embryological chart for the "Oxen of the Sun" episode, 1920. Autograph manuscript. Division of Rare and Manuscript Collections, Cornell University Library. © The Estate of James Joyce.

prose to further his narrative, to move it from twilight into darkness, taking the novel from Sandymount strand to Nighttown, is a way for Joyce to treat the history of English prose as a linguistic circus, of which he is emphatically the ringmaster. At the very end of the episode, in what Terence Killeen calls a "breakdown of style into a babel of conflicting voices,"[56] Joyce moves out from the shadow of Caliban into the realm where words, as

Eliot would have it, "strain / Crack and sometimes break." From the breakdown at the end of "Oxen of the Sun," he moves into further narrative fragmentation in the "Circe" episode.

As with "Wandering Rocks," it is difficult to read "Oxen of the Sun" without considering Joyce's intense relationship both with Ireland and with Dublin. Nonetheless, critics from Ezra Pound to Terry Eagleton have suggested that *Ulysses* could easily be set in any city. Pound wrote, "Erase the local names and a few specifically local allusions, and a few historic events of the past, and substitute a few different local names, allusions and events, and these stories could be retold of any town."[57] Eagleton wrote, "Joyce's compliment to Ireland, in inscribing it on the cosmopolitan map, is . . . distinctly backhanded. The novel . . . deploy[s] the full battery of cosmopolitan modernist techniques to recreate it while suggesting with its every breath just how easily it could have done the same for Bradford or the Bronx."[58]

Joyce is writing about a city that is on the cusp of change, a place where many battles are being fought, not least between insularity and cosmopolitanism, religion and the secular, restriction and the carnal, the nation and the empire, the nation and the parish, reality and mythology, earnestness and humor. It is hard to imagine these battles being fought with the same intensity in Bradford or the Bronx, or in any other city much.

One way to differentiate Dublin from Bradford or the Bronx is to look at the shadow figures in *Ulysses*, the ghostly presences that operate as an undercurrent in the text, offering it a powerful energy. These figures include Robert Emmet and Charles Stewart Parnell but also W. B. Yeats, Lady Gregory, and Oscar Wilde. Bloom and Stephen circle a city that is haunted by their presence, by the signs they have made, as it is by the signs made by Sinn Féin and the Irish Catholic Church. It would be hard to summon up such presences in Bradford or the Bronx.

The last words of *Ulysses* are "Trieste – Zurich – Paris, 1914–1921." These seven years include years of European conflagration as well as the 1916 Rebellion in Ireland. *Ulysses* is not a diary of these years; its chapters are not ways of responding to public

events. Yet, as Enda Duffy has written, "By setting his book in a relatively uneventful earlier year, while writing it amid violent, revolutionary and transformative time, *Ulysses* can know the future without admitting to such knowledge."[59]

In the first quarter of the twentieth century, as violence and fanaticism increased in Ireland, as Ireland began to question its relationship to England more intensely and to interrogate and recalibrate its own sense of tradition and its relationship to myth, as Ireland began to summon up in its own imagination a new political reality, Irish writers, including James Joyce, dramatized the relationship between community, including an imagined community, and violence. Poems and novels and plays were not only arguments that the writers were having with themselves but also serious and deliberate interventions in a debate about history, tradition, nationhood, violence, and politics. In Ireland, poems and novels and plays sought to capture, encapsulate, and indeed influence and formulate what the future might be, not merely the future of the imagination or the life of the mind or the spirit but life itself, politics, public memory, the nation, the state.

Thus, placing a novel in a city that seemed detached much of the time from the nation—with a Jewish man of great independence of mind, a born noticer, whose response to life is original and sensuous and intelligent, at its center—is a political act. Creating an Irish hero who is not insular but tolerant, open to life and to modernity in a book to be published in 1922, offers a blueprint for a state-in-the-making about how private life, and perhaps even public life, should be conducted. But the blueprint is subtle and exalts doubleness, contradiction. In *Joyce's Politics*, Dominic Manganiello writes, "In *Ulysses* there is constantly at work a double motive which Joyce is not at pains to make single or crystal clear. The desire to bring Ireland to a new self-awareness is matched by the equally urgent need of preventing its acceptance of any rigid control by Church and State."[60]

While Joyce wrote *Ulysses* in exile, he had deep roots in a changing Dublin. He would have viewed the 1916 Rebellion not as a remote event in a city he had abandoned but as led by people with whom he had associations, some close, including Patrick Pearse, the president of the Republic, as declared in Easter Week 1916. Joyce attended a few Irish-language classes given by Pearse at University College Dublin in the spring of 1899. Joyce gave them up because he found Pearse a bore and objected to his efforts to denigrate English in favor of Irish. Joyce decided to study Norwegian instead so that he could read Ibsen in the original.

The clash between the two young men over ideas of language and cultural identity would make its way into the encounter between Gabriel Conroy and Miss Ivors in Joyce's story "The Dead." When Gabriel tells Miss Ivors that he goes to France and Belgium "partly to keep in touch with the languages," she replies, "And haven't you your own language to keep in touch with—Irish?" To which Gabriel replies, "Well, if it comes to that, you know, Irish is not my language."[61]

In Joyce's *Stephen Hero*, a figure whose ideology is close to that of Pearse roundly denounces Stephen Daedalus when he delivers a paper on "Drama and Life" to the University College Literary and Historical Society: "Mr Daedalus was himself a renegade from the Nationalist ranks: he professed cosmopolitanism. But a man that was of all countries was of no country—you must first have a nation before you have art."[62]

Both Pearse and Joyce wrote for the theatre and wrote poetry and fiction, Joyce rather more success-fully than Pearse. Both, as the soft wax hardened around them, needed to throw stones at the Irish Literary Revival, which was led by Yeats and Lady Gregory.

In the front hall of St Enda's, the school that Pearse founded, were written up the words ascribed to the legendary hero Cuchulainn: "I care not though I were to live but one day and one night provided my fame and my deeds live after me."[63] This idea of living a heroic rather than a domestic or an ordinary life is alluded to at the end of Joyce's story "The Dead," when Gabriel is pondering death. The sentence "One by one they were all becoming shades" is followed by: "Better pass boldly into that other world, in all the full glory of some passion, than fade and wither dismally with age."[64] It was this same idea, which for Gabriel was merely a passing thought, that would animate Pearse and inspire some of his followers in the years leading up to the 1916 Rebellion.

During the Rebellion, one of Joyce's oldest friends in Dublin, Francis Sheehy Skeffington, was shot dead by firing squad on the orders of an officer who was later declared guilty but insane. Sheehy Skeffington and Joyce had published a pamphlet together, and Sheehy Skeffington inspired the character of McCann in *Portrait*.

The 1916 Rebellion came as a shock not only to the British authorities but to many in Ireland. Yeats's poem "Easter 1916" is filled with questions and uncertainties. Like Joyce, who has Leopold Bloom invoke "love" in the "Cyclops" episode, Yeats uses the word in a question about the level of emotion in the politics of the leaders of the Rebellion: "And what if excess of love / Bewildered them till they died?"[65] The playwright Sean O'Casey, whose play *The Plough and the Stars* is set during Easter Week, found himself outside the nationalist fold by the

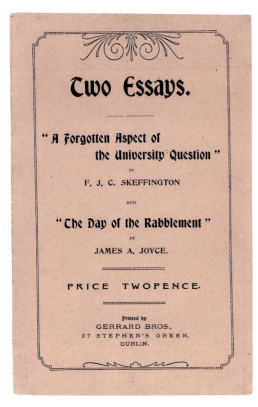

Two Essays.

"A Forgotten Aspect of
the University Question"

BY

F. J. C. SKEFFINGTON

AND

"The Day of the Rabblement"

BY

JAMES A. JOYCE.

PRICE TWOPENCE.

Printed by
GERRARD BROS.,
87 STEPHEN'S GREEN,
DUBLIN.

Fig. 1.7. F.J.C. Skeffington and James Joyce, *Two Essays*,
1901. The Morgan Library & Museum, New York.
Gift of Sean and Mary Kelly, 2018.

Fig. 1.8. *Poblacht na hÉireann. The Provisional Government
of the Irish Republic to the People of Ireland*, 1916. Courtesy
of the American Irish Historical Society.

POBLACHT NA H EIREANN.

THE PROVISIONAL GOVERNMENT

OF THE

IRISH REPUBLIC

TO THE PEOPLE OF IRELAND.

IRISHMEN AND IRISHWOMEN : In the name of God and of the dead generations from which she receives her old tradition of nationhood, Ireland, through us, summons her children to her flag and strikes for her freedom.

Having organised and trained her manhood through her secret revolutionary organisation, the Irish Republican Brotherhood, and through her open military organisations, the Irish Volunteers and the Irish Citizen Army, having patiently perfected her discipline, having resolutely waited for the right moment to reveal itself, she now seizes that moment, and, supported by her exiled children in America and by gallant allies in Europe, but relying in the first on her own strength, she strikes in full confidence of victory.

We declare the right of the people of Ireland to the ownership of Ireland, and to the unfettered control of Irish destinies, to be sovereign and indefeasible. The long usurpation of that right by a foreign people and government has not extinguished the right, nor can it ever be extinguished except by the destruction of the Irish people. In every generation the Irish people have asserted their right to national freedom and sovereignty ; six times during the past three hundred years they have asserted it in arms. Standing on that fundamental right and again asserting it in arms in the face of the world, we hereby proclaim the Irish Republic as a Sovereign Independent State, and we pledge our lives and the lives of our comrades-in-arms to the cause of its freedom, of its welfare, and of its exaltation among the nations.

The Irish Republic is entitled to, and hereby claims, the allegiance of every Irishman and Irishwoman. The Republic guarantees religious and civil liberty, equal rights and equal opportunities to all its citizens, and declares its resolve to pursue the happiness and prosperity of the whole nation and of all its parts, cherishing all the children of the nation equally, and oblivious of the differences carefully fostered by an alien government, which have divided a minority from the majority in the past.

Until our arms have brought the opportune moment for the establishment of a permanent National Government, representative of the whole people of Ireland and elected by the suffrages of all her men and women, the Provisional Government, hereby constituted, will administer the civil and military affairs of the Republic in trust for the people.

We place the cause of the Irish Republic under the protection of the Most High God, Whose blessing we invoke upon our arms, and we pray that no one who serves that cause will dishonour it by cowardice, inhumanity, or rapine. In this supreme hour the Irish nation must, by its valour and discipline and by the readiness of its children to sacrifice themselves for the common good, prove itself worthy of the august destiny to which it is called.

Signed on Behalf of the Provisional Government,

THOMAS J. CLARKE.

SEAN Mac DIARMADA, THOMAS MacDONAGH,
P. H. PEARSE, EAMONN CEANNT,
JAMES CONNOLLY. JOSEPH PLUNKETT.

time of the Rebellion. Early in 1914, however, he had written the constitution for the Irish Citizen Army, one of whose main principles made its way, using some of the same language, into the Proclamation of Easter 1916 read by Patrick Pearse on the steps of the General Post Office in Dublin.

The Proclamation's opening phrase would have interested Joyce. It began: "In the name of God and of the dead generations. . . ." As he worked on "Cyclops," the episode that deals most intensely with politics, the idea of the dead generations gave him considerable ammunition for parody.

The "Cyclops" episode takes place in Barney Kiernan's pub; it is narrated by a nameless man. Although the narrative in "Wandering Rocks" cuts between scenes and characters, the tone of each scene is relatively stable. It is written, as it were, by the same person in the same place. On the other hand, the narrative in "Cyclops" comes in two guises. The first is pub talk, pub argument, some of it parody, some serious; the second is parody of types of discourse, much of it current in 1904.

At the heart of the pub talk is a set of speeches and rants by the Citizen, who has strong nationalist views. He is more fluent and sure of himself than Bloom, whose voice is hesitant and whose interventions have a tentative sound. Bloom is like a man attempting to say something true in the company of quick-witted men who want to win an argument using tones that are filled with cliché.

Many critics have insisted that "Cyclops" allows us to read Joyce's politics clearly. Some parts do allow this, but not all. But even when his politics emerge, Joyce seems to belong to the disruptive party rather than any more widely followed political factions in Ireland. In this, he has much in common with Yeats and O'Casey, who got energy from disrupting an evolving consensus in Ireland; their

work was nourished by an impulse to provoke. It is unlikely that Yeats's Crazy Jane, O'Casey's Rosie Redmond, or Joyce's Cunty Kate was created to console the authorities in Ireland or win friends for the authors among the faithful.

In sections of "Cyclops," Joyce sought to disrupt his very own opinions, or at least unsettle them. For example, if we are invited to take the Citizen's speeches as the sounds made by a diehard nationalist talking in a pub, then we have to look at the connection between his views on Irish industry and those of Joyce himself, expressed in the 1907 essay "Ireland: Isle of Saints and Sages." In the essay, Joyce writes, "Ireland is poor because English laws ruined the country's industries, especially the wool industry, because the neglect of English governments in the years of the potato famine allowed the best of the population to die from hunger."[66] In "Cyclops," the Citizen says, "Where are our missing twenty millions of Irish should be here today instead of four, our lost tribes? And our potteries and textiles, the finest in the whole world! And our wool that was sold in Rome."[67]

One possibility is that Joyce is parodying himself, finding good use for the opinions he expressed in Trieste to an irredentist audience that supported Triestine withdrawal from the Austro-Hungarian Empire. Joyce gives the Citizen lines to speak that have been heard many times, including in his own iteration. Bloom's tone, on the other hand, is simpler, with shorter, starker sentences. He uses words that have their source in the personal rather than the communal. And there are no verbal flourishes in Bloom's statement: "Persecution, says he, all the history of the world is full of it. Perpetuating national hatred among nations." It feels almost as though Bloom is speaking to himself, or thinking aloud. All around him there are jokes and quips, but

4 Chapter

12.　*B what about to pay the death penalty*

The last farewell was affecting in the extreme. From
the belfries far and near the funereal deathbell tolled xxx
unceasingly, while all around the gloomy precincts rolled the
ominous warning of a hundred muffled drums punctuated by the
hollow booming of pieces of ordnance. The deafening claps of
thunder and the dazzling flashes of lightning which lit up the
ghastly scene testified that the artillery of heaven had lent
its supernatural pomp to the already gruesome spectacle. A torren-
tial rain poured down from the floodgates of the angry heavens
on the bared heads of the assembled multitude which numbered at
the lowest computation five hundred thousand persons. The learned
prelate who administered the last comforts of holy religion to the
hero martyrs knelt in a most christian spirit in a pool of rain
water, his cassock above his hoary head, and offered up to the
throne of grace fervent prayers of supplication. Hard by the
block stood the grim figure of the executioner, his visage being
concealed in a ten gallon pot with two circular perforated
apertures through which his eyes glowered furiously. As he awaited
the fatal signal he tested the edge of his horrible weapon
by honing it upon his brawny forearm or decapitated in rapid
succession a flock of sheep which had been provided by the admirers
of his fell but necessary office. On a handsome mahogany table
near him were neatly arranged the quartering knife, the various
finely tempered disembowelling appliances£ a terracotta saucepan for the reception of the duodenum, colon, blind xxtx in-
testine and appendix etc, when successfully extracted and two
commodious milkjugs destined to receive the most precious blood
of the most precious victim. The housesteward of the amalgamated
cats and dogs' home was in attendance to convey these vessels
when replenished to that beneficent institution. Quite an excellent
repast consisting of rashers and eggs, fried steak and onions, A
delicious hot breakfast rolls and invigorating tea had been
considerately provided by the authorities for the consumption
of the central figure of the tragedy but he expressed the dying
wish (immediately acceded to) that the meal should be divided
in aliquot parts among the members of the sick and indigent
roomkeepers association as a token of his regard and esteem.
The non plus ultra of emotion was reached when the blushing bride
elect burst her way through the serried ranks of the bystanders
and flung herself upon the muscular bosom of him who was about to
died for her sake. The hero folded her willowy form in a loving
embrace murmuring fondly "Sheila, my own". Encouraged by this
use of her christian name she kissed passionately all the various
suitable areas of his person which the decencies of prison garb
permitted her ardour to reach. She swore to him as they mingled
the salt streams of their tears that she would cherish his
memory, that she would never forget her hero boy. She brought
back to his recollection the happy days of blissful childhood
together on the banks of Anna Liffey when they had indulged
in the innocent pastimes of the young and, oblivious of the
dreadful present, they both laughed heartily, all the spectators,
including the venerable pastor, joining in the general merriment.

That monster audience simply rocked with delight.

√ who was in capital spirits and evinced the keenest
interest in the proceedings

├┤ be launched into eternity

Especially supplied by the worldfamous firm of cutlers, Messrs John Barber, Sheffield)

M with an abnegation rare in these our times rose nobly to the occasion and

A, done to a nicety,

12
1 nec and

Z 8100 4

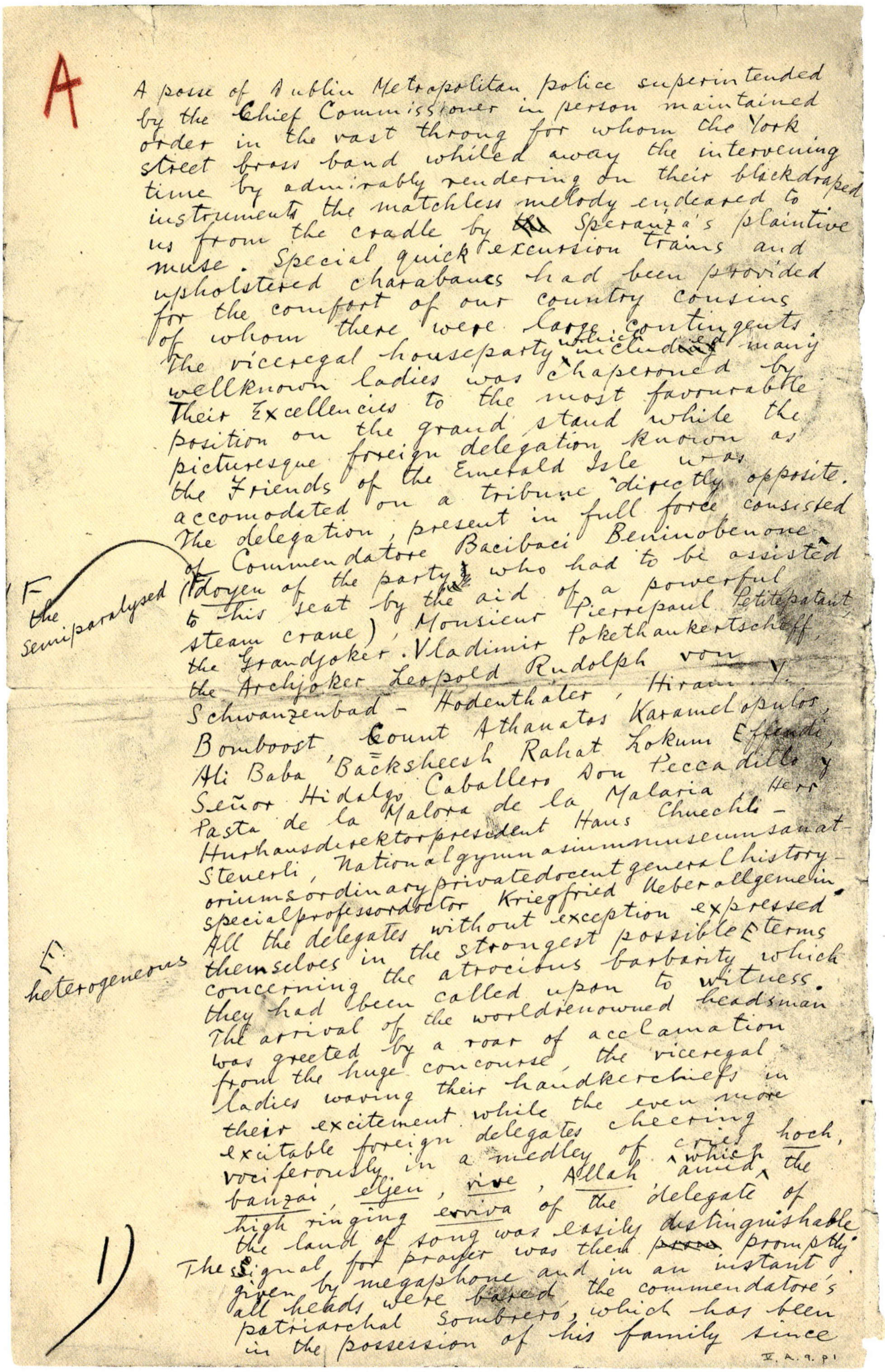

A posse of Dublin Metropolitan police superintended
by the Chief Commissioner in person maintained
order in the vast throng for whom the York
street brass band whiled away the intervening
time by admirably rendering on their blackdraped
instruments the matchless melody endeared to
us from the cradle by Speranza's plaintive
muse. Special quick excursion trains and
upholstered charabancs had been provided
for the comfort of our country cousins
of whom there were large contingents.
The viceregal houseparty which included many
wellknown ladies was chaperoned by
Their Excellencies to the most favourable
position on the grand stand while the
picturesque foreign delegation known as
the Friends of the Emerald Isle was
accomodated on a tribune directly opposite.
The delegation, present in full force, consisted
of Commendatore Bacibaci Beninobenone
(the semiparalysed doyen of the party who had to be assisted
to this seat by the aid of a powerful
steam crane), Monsieur Pierrepaul Petitépatant,
the Grandjoker Vladimir Pokethankertscheff,
the Archjoker Leopold Rudolph von
Schwanzenbad - Hodenthaler, Hiram Y.
Bomboost, Count Athanatos Karamelopulos,
Ali Baba Backsheesh Rahat Lokum Effendi,
Señor Hidalgo Caballero Don Peccadillo y
Pasta de la Malora de la Malaria, Herr
Hurhausdirektorpresident Hans Chuechli-
Steuerli, Nationalgymnasiummuseumsanat-
oriumsordinaryprivatedocentgeneralhistory-
specialprofessordoctor Kriegfried Ueberallgemein.
All the delegates without exception expressed
themselves in the strongest possible terms
concerning the atrocious barbarity which
they had been called upon to witness.
The arrival of the worldrenowned headsman
was greeted by a roar of acclamation
from the huge concourse, the viceregal
ladies waving their handkerchiefs in
their excitement while the even more
excitable foreign delegates cheering
vociferously in a medley of cries hoch,
banzai, eljen, zivio, Allah, amid the
high ringing evviva of the delegate of
the land of song was easily distinguishable.
The signal for prayer was then promptly
given by megaphone and in an instant
all heads were bared, the commendatore's
patriarchal sombrero, which has been
in the possession of his family since

the semiparalysed

heterogeneous

Fig. 1.10. James Joyce, holograph addition to a "Cyclops" placard,
September 1921. The Poetry Collection of the University Libraries,
University at Buffalo, The State University of New York.
© The Estate of James Joyce.

he does not join them. He is the least noisy of men. When asked what his nation is, he answers, "Ireland, says Bloom. I was born here. Ireland."[68] It is not possible to read this as parody; it stands apart from the rest of the talk in the pub, as though orchestral sound were suddenly replaced by single piano notes.

This scene might offer evidence that, writing during the First World War and in the aftermath of the Easter Rising in Dublin, Joyce wanted to rehearse the arguments about violence. When he has Bloom say, "But it's no use, says he. Force, hatred, history, all that. That's not life for men and women, insult and hatred. And everybody knows that it's the very opposite of that that is really life," he will be asked what the opposite is, and he will say, "Love."[69]

This is a major argument being made in a minor key. Bloom's refusal to use a higher rhetorical tone means that his interventions stand apart from the conversation rather than become engaged with it. The others can become angry, or make fun of him, but they cannot speak without approaching self-parody. He, on the other hand, speaks in a tone that is lonely, melancholy, modest. Everything they say has been said before. Bloom speaks as though he is saying these words for the first time.

In this scene, when Bloom speaks, what we see is the importance of being earnest; all of Joyce's playfulness has abandoned him while Bloom is actually speaking. But, as though to compensate, or offer alternate systems, in the elaborate parodies of public speech and writing in "Cyclops," Joyce allows his imagination a soaring, trouble-making freedom. Not only do some of these parodies disrupt the talk in the pub but they disrupt a decorum on how to write about the martyred dead; they are full of mischief and they are desperately funny. Emer Nolan, in *James Joyce and Nationalism*, quotes from a letter Joyce wrote to his

brother at the time of *Dubliners*, saying that his pen "seems to me so plainly mischievous."[70] She also quotes him when, after the 1916 Rebellion, he was asked "whether he would visit an independent Ireland," and he responded, "So I might declare myself its first enemy?"[71]

There is one parody in "Cyclops" that would have especially helped Joyce's candidacy for "first enemy." It occurs just when the Citizen is shouting out some tired slogans. It begins: "The last farewell was affecting in the extreme."[72] It is a parody of a florid description of the execution of Robert Emmet that slowly becomes a parody of the event itself. At the end of the previous episode, Robert Emmet has made a brief appearance when Bloom sees an image of him in a window. The last words of Emmet's famous speech from the dock in 1803 are, "When my country takes its place among the nations of the earth then and not until then, let my epitaph be written. I have done."[73] As Bloom sets out to fart, he uses these words, reserving a broken-up version of "I have done," until the fart has been completed.[74]

Now, having connected a famous Irish hero-martyr with the act of farting, Joyce sets about making fun of his execution, an event that has been commemorated in songs written by Thomas Moore as well as by Hector Berlioz. The memory of Robert Emmet was venerated by many.

While Joyce's version of Emmet's execution is not pious, it is, in all its comic flourishes and deliberate irreverence, glorious. Among those who witness the execution in *Ulysses* are such unlikely Joycean inventions as "Bacibaci Beninobenone . . . Ali Baba Backsheesh Rahat Lokum Effendi . . . Hokopoko Harakiri," an "Archjoker" and a "Grand-joker," and a man whose first name is "Goose-pond."[75] The knife to be used on Emmet is tested first on a flock of sheep, and there is a saucepan "to receive the most precious blood of the most precious victim,"[76] thus making the passage even more offensive by connecting Emmet to Christ, associating God with the dead generations.

Since this was written after the 1916 Rebellion, whose leaders were shot by the British, becoming martyrs in the same tradition as Emmet, the sheer mischief in the passage is even further emphasized. Nothing was more sacred at the time than the names of those who had died for Ireland. By making one such execution into hilarious spectacle, Joyce insists that what is sacred has an even more sacred need to be laughed at.

The description of the execution appears in one very long paragraph, lasting almost five pages, that ends with "the stern provostmarshal, lieutenant-colonel" who oversees the execution speaking in a Cockney accent. He is given a background in India: "he who had blown a considerable number of sepoys from the cannonmouth without flinching."[77] The name given to him is glossed in *"Ulysses" Annotated*, by Don Gifford with Robert J. Seidman, as a "fictional name that suggests extraordinary pretension to 'good family' backgrounds."[78]

The name is "Tomkin-Maxwell ffrenchmullan Tomlinson." It is difficult to see why Tomkin or Tomlinson might have been chosen. The name ffrenchmullan could relate to the revolutionary and labor activist Madeleine ffrench-Mullan, who took part in the 1916 Rebellion, but it is hard to connect her with a man who oversees an execution. The part of the long name that jumps out from the text, for an Irish reader of *Ulysses*, is Maxwell.

Sir John Maxwell, who had served in Egypt and the Sudan, oversaw the execution of the leaders of the 1916 Rebellion, having been sent to Dublin in the week of the Rising as a military governor with plenary powers. He was in sole charge of the trials of the leaders, which were conducted in camera and without any defense. His decision to have so many of the leaders shot was soon questioned by the very British government that had empowered him. In Ireland, his name was associated with the executions.

In evoking his name, Joyce had to be careful. His novel remains set, ostensibly, in 1904. Putting the word Maxwell in the longer name is not an anachronism; rather, it is a sly clue that Joyce is writing "Cyclops" in the aftermath of the 1916 Rising and that his Emmet parody is a sideswipe at Irish martyrology at a time when it had risen to new heights. He does not draw attention to it, but the use of the name "Maxwell" is a small example of Joyce's engagement with events in his own country as Ireland moved toward independence—and as he set about invoking the music of the future.

Fig. 2.1. Constantine P. Curran, photograph of James Joyce, 1904. The Poetry
Collection of the University Libraries, University at Buffalo, The State
University of New York.

ANNE FOGARTY

2. *Ulysses* and Dublin

Ulysses is inextricably, umbilically linked to Dublin, James Joyce's native city. Dublin is not simply a backdrop or a setting in this novel; it is at once a vital "protagonist and co-author," as Peter Barta has contended,[1] and an all-encompassing locus and medium of the imagination. Crucially, *Ulysses* is not simply *about* Dublin. Joyce's artistic ambition was more radically thoroughgoing than merely to furnish us with a fresh fictional milieu. Revolutionizing what the novel can do while ransacking all the resources of Western literature—from Homer to Dante, Shakespeare to Goethe, and ranging Irish writers such as Douglas Hyde, James Clarence Mangan, John Millington Synge, Yeats, and above all himself alongside them—his daring endeavor in creating his modern epic set in Dublin involved staging and embodying it in all its unwieldy, chaotic materiality. If, following the Act of Union in 1801,

the city had been demoted and sidelined when the seat of power moved to Westminster, *Ulysses* determinedly placed it again at center stage.

The objective was not only to reclaim it politically and aesthetically, and to grant it the Home Rule to which much of nationalist Ireland in the period aspired, but also to inspect its history, foibles, failings, and dissipated energies and the profane, beset, and nonheroic lives of its numerous inhabitants, particularly those of Leopold Bloom, Stephen Dedalus, and Molly Bloom. Having left Dublin in 1904, returning only on three occasions between 1909 and 1912—occasions that were marked by increasing personal acrimony and blighted by a fruitless battle with George Roberts to get *Dubliners* published—Joyce wrote about his city as an insider with a limitless local knowledge of its streets and citizens, a scabrous outlier, and a cold-eyed émigré. Nostalgia, disaffection, an unyielding love of place, a fascination with the subaltern and the deviant, and an implacable urge to skewer Dublin and Dubliners form the conflicting substrates of *Ulysses*, as does a plan to rework the novel as form.

Ulysses is literally conceived of as coextensive with the city and not merely a depiction at one or more removes. Due to Joyce's all-involving hyperrealism and his entanglement of his fiction in the infinitesimal aspects of the everyday, the dense minutiae of reality, we can even plausibly surmise things the text does *not* tell us, an impulse that would be a misstep in the case of most other fictions. Hence, we can deduce the route taken by Stephen Dedalus when he walks approximately one mile from the Martello tower in Sandycove to Mr Deasy's private school in Dalkey, at which he holds an early morning class, and how he travels from this south Dublin coastal village to Sandymount strand. We can surmise what might have happened in the nonexistent chapter that would fill the temporal gap between "Cyclops" and "Nausicaa," in which we know that Leopold Bloom visited Mrs Dignam at No. 9 Newbridge Avenue, Sandymount, to discuss her husband's life insurance; we can speculate about who moved the furniture around in No. 7 Eccles Street during the day and why; and we can project forward to the morning of 17 June and debate whether Molly makes breakfast for Bloom, thereby effecting a partial reconciliation between herself and her husband. Joyce does not just transport us to Dublin on 16 June 1904 but insinuates us into its streets, which we experience as if we were locals and intimates. Yet he also recruits us as coauthors who collaboratively enact, spin out, and extend the text. Paradoxically, this means that he bypasses the kind of set-piece visual descriptions

other novelists deploy to build up their fictional realities for their readers.

Such a departure perturbed early reviewers such as Arnold Bennett, who wrongly concluded that Joyce had "no geographical sense, little sense of environment."[2] In fact, the text is saturated with geographical and environmental knowledge as it steers us through the journeys of its characters. Despite the seemingly labyrinthine nature of *Ulysses*, we constantly take our bearings in Dublin topography by name-checking the streets, buildings, and shop fronts. The profusion of detail and spatial coordinates endows the narrative with built-in mapping functions. As readers it is feasible for us to follow the characters as they walk the streets and to track their actions and experiences when (and, above all, where) they occur. Thus, in episode 5, "Lotus Eaters," we follow Bloom's early morning meandering along the quays on the southern bank of the Liffey to Westland Row Post Office, where he picks up a letter from Martha Clifford, with whom he is engaged in a clandestine, erotic correspondence:

> By lorries along sir John Rogerson's quay Mr Bloom walked soberly, past Windmill lane, Leask's the linseed crusher, the postal telegraph office. Could have given that address too. And past the sailors' home. He turned from the morning noises of the quayside and walked through Lime street. By Brady's cottages a boy for the skins lolled, his bucket of offal linked, smoking a chewed fagbutt. A smaller girl with scars of eczema on her forehead eyed him, listlessly holding her battered caskhoop. Tell him if he smokes he won't grow. O let him! His life isn't such a bed of roses. Waiting outside pubs to bring da home. Come home to ma, da. Slack hour: won't be many there. He crossed Townsend street, passed the frowning face of

Bethel. El, yes: house of: Aleph, Beth. And past Nichols' the undertaker.[3]

Bloom's progress is dilatory and haphazard, suggesting the drugged existence of those marooned in the land of Lotus Eaters. To boot, if we follow his movements on a map of Dublin, as several have noted, we ascertain how contorted they are and discover that they approximate a question mark. His zigzag indirection ironically mirrors the furtive nature of his activity. Yet, at the same time, Bloom's "sober" advance from the river to Townsend Street via Lime Street and Lombard Street East serves other narrative purposes and does more than merely convey facets of his personality, sexual makeup, and emotional predilections. His journey is highly contingent and vivid, and through the lens of his involved but roving attention it powerfully but fleetingly realizes these particular streetscapes and the people in them.

By and large, in *Ulysses* Joyce concentrates on the demoralized, disempowered, and indigent lower-middle-class population of Dublin, but here a rare vignette of working-class poverty swims into view. The listless little girl with eczema and the rebarbative boy collecting offal while smoking a salvaged cigarette butt, to whom Bloom imputes an alcoholic father and a downtrodden mother, not only provide a portal onto the bleak social realities of Dublin in 1904—which had the highest rates of urban destitution, child mortality, and disease in Europe—but also point up the communal nature of the city streets. In Joyce's vision and recollection, the streets afford numerous points of intersection, cross-connection, and vivifying empathy, insight, and altercation. Moreover, the view of the city contrived here during Leopold Bloom's first prolonged stroll downtown from his home is of a

space that is at once embodied, affective, and politically charged. Material details graphically highlight the social ills caused by British colonial exploitation and Irish misrule and infighting. The soma-aesthetics of Dublin are foregrounded in the apprehensions propounded in this passage of "Lotus Eaters," as they are throughout the text. Building on the achievements of nineteenth-century writers of the city, particularly Charles Dickens, Victor Hugo, and Gustave Flaubert, Joyce's exactitude and encyclopedism render the sensorial and material aspects of urban life, as well as its psychic and political dissonances, in all their plurality.

Primers to *Ulysses*, such as Don Gifford's volume of annotations and the guides by Jack McCarthy, Frank Delaney, and Robert Nicholson, customarily include topographical maps of sections of Dublin marking the routes followed by the characters; contemporary websites and tourist apps go even further, availing themselves of the resources of geographic information systems (GIS) to create dynamic, interactive diagrams directing us through the narrative. In using such devices, we are duplicating Joyce's own preparations in composing the text. In a letter from Rome dated 6 November 1906 to his brother Stanislaus, Joyce declared that he "would like to have a map of Dublin on my wall," wryly adding that he was "becoming something of a maniac" in his efforts to gather lore on the city.[4] Street plans, both actual and remembered, guided him in the composition of *Ulysses*; he plotted out and calculated the simultaneous movements of the many figures in the nineteen conjoint sections of the "Wandering Rocks" episode on a map of Dublin, for example.[5] But *Ulysses* also preempts and subsumes the orienting functions of any aids we may use to make sense of it. To read *Ulysses* is to be in Dublin in a

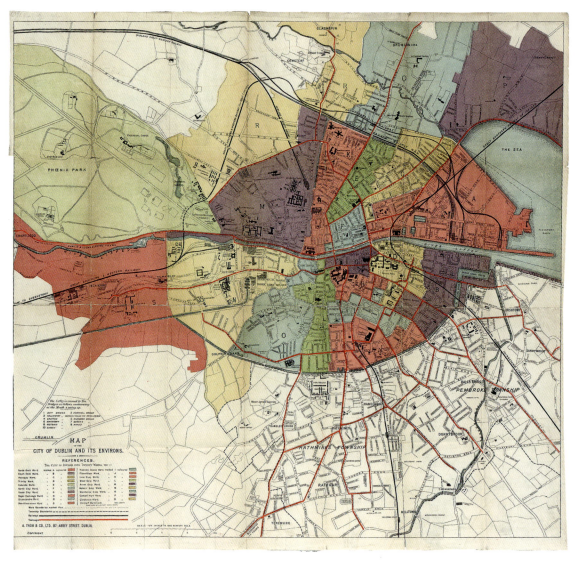

Fig. 2.2. A. Thom & Co., *Map of the City of Dublin and Its Environs,*
1915. New York Public Library Digital Collections.

startlingly immediate fashion. Moreover, since this is a one-day novel, extending from 8:00 a.m. on 16 June to the early hours of 17 June 1904, we can participate, at a stretch, in the diurnal flow of events; our reading time and the temporal flow of the text can be made more or less to coincide.

Any one explication of Joyce's encompassing of Dublin in the novel is necessarily partial. The text is far more than a cartographic rendering of

the city, as prodigious and unreachable as such a goal may be. The Dublin of *Ulysses*, while being an extensive feat of personal and intergenerational memory, is also a meticulous act of re-creation and artistic imagining. Indeed, the most overblown and much-touted of Joyce's pronouncements was his declaration to Frank Budgen that he wanted to "give a picture of Dublin so complete that if the city suddenly disappeared from the earth it could

Fig. 2.3. *Henry Street, Dublin, Looking Towards Nelson's Pillar, After Bombardment*, 1916. Postcard. Special Collections, UCD Library, University College Dublin.

be reconstructed out of [his] book."[6] This is at once a beguiling and chilling objective. The fictional bodying forth and recording of Dublin are predicated on its destruction and demise. Historically, cities rise and fall. The signature dates, 1914–1921, that form the last words of the text remind us, moreover, that *Ulysses* coincides with and is intertwined with the First World War. The mass killings and material wastage of this conflict inflect Joyce's artistic designs and motivations. Additionally, the fact that the center of Dublin— the very area around Sackville Street, present-day O'Connell Street, that features in many of the episodes, especially "Aeolus"—was reduced to rubble during the Easter Rising in 1916 adds a

further urgency and purpose to his narrative. Dublin in *Ulysses* is pieced together through Joyce's aesthetics of salvage and retrieval. It is a virtual city and simulacrum as much as a reality, a ghost town as well as a living entity, a resonant vivification but also a place fading into the past.

Mischievously, Joyce in "Ithaca" includes *Thom's Dublin Post Office Directory, 1886* among the contents of Bloom's bookshelves,[7] thereby obliquely alluding to one of his own chief sources for his re-creation of Dublin. A former employee of Thom's, Bloom in fact owns a shorter directory than those consulted by Joyce. More than any other reference work, the 1904 *Thom's Official Directory of the United Kingdom of Great Britain and Ireland* furnished salient details, such as the times of sunrise and sunset, the tides, an inventory of the ships in the Dublin port, lists of those in trades, and the names and addresses of all the inhabitants, including the shops, hotels, restaurants, and other buildings on every Dublin street. *Thom's* eccentrically and impassively solidified the seeming imperial unity of Great Britain and Ireland through its annual publication of datasets. The information it recorded, however, was at times erroneous and out-of-date or misleading, and Joyce inherits several errors, either unwittingly or by design. He possibly miscalculates, as Ian Gunn and Clive Hart surmised,[8] that No. 75 is opposite Bloom's house on Eccles Street, not Nos. 76 and 77, when he crosses the road in "Calypso"[9] on the way to purchase a pork kidney in Dlugacz's shop. Nonetheless, in not just deploying but imitating the comprehensiveness of *Thom's*, Joyce produces a fictional counter-record rivaling and outshining it. Startlingly, but with winning acuity, his university friend C. P. Curran noted in his obituary for Joyce, published on 14 January 1941 in the *Irish Times*, that Joyce "was certainly the last forty volumes of *Thom's Directory* thinking aloud." In a similar vein, Gunn and Hart pithily argued that *Ulysses* may be seen as "applied Thomism" and that it incorporates, rewrites, and overhauls the well-known directory.[10] In short, Joyce's precise and encyclopedic rendering of Dublin has the aim of upstaging, fictionalizing, quibbling with, and mocking the delineation of the city by *Thom's* as containable within an annual exercise in colonial data capture. Crucially, *Thom's* recorded No. 7 Eccles Street as vacant in June 1904, thereby enabling Joyce to house the Blooms in the interstices of the directory. The teeming details of Dublin life and the inventories of its street addresses anarchically overspill *Thom's* to be bodied forth,

enduringly captured, irreverently dislocated, and verbally transmuted in *Ulysses*.

In *A Portrait of the Artist as a Young Man*, Stephen Dedalus thinks of Dublin as a "new and complex sensation,"[11] in part aligning it with his own febrile development. By contrast, the city in *Ulysses* resists easy categorization or appropriation by any one person. Indeed, the text regularly self-reflexively meditates on the nature of Dublin, thereby emphasizing its protean aspects and lack of fixity. In "Calypso," Bloom muses, "Good puzzle would be cross Dublin without passing a pub,"[12] and an interpolated cross-header in "Aeolus" confers the affectionate but damning moniker "Dear Dirty Dublin"[13] on the city, while in "Ithaca" we learn that Dublin is one of the topics Stephen and Bloom converse about late at night.[14] Dublin in 1904, as social historians and geographers have argued, was marked by many contradictions and divisions. It was a "deposed capital," as Mary E. Daly dubbed it;[15] the grandeur of its wide, central streets and imposing edifices, such as the Customs House and the Four Courts, was a product of an eighteenth-century confidence that had long since faded. However, its secondary role as an imperial backwater was increasingly contested by Dublin Corporation, which was dominated from the mid-nineteenth century onward by tradesmen from the Catholic middle classes, invariably nationalist in persuasion. The conflicted symbolic geography of the city is made manifest in the differing monuments observed by Bloom in "Hades." Statues to the nationalist figureheads William Smith O'Brien, Daniel O'Connell, and Father Mathew and, in June 1904, a still unrealized memorial to Charles Stewart Parnell flank the centrally placed Nelson's Pillar on Sackville Street.[16] Visits by the British monarchs Queen Victoria and Edward VII drew out internal political

Fig. 2.4. Embossed vignette on the binding of *Thom's Official Directory of the United Kingdom of Great Britain and Ireland*, 1904. Rare Book & Manuscript Library, Columbia University.

Fig. 2.5. Philip Phillips, 7 Eccles Street. Dublin, Ireland, 1950. Gift of Sayre P. Sheldon and Lady Richard Davies. The Rosenbach, Philadelphia (2006.0004.0099).

divisions, sparking nationalist protests, on the one hand, and public displays of royalist fervor on the other. Bloom's recollection in "Lestrygonians"[17] of his lucky escape from a charge by mounted policemen on a pro-Boer rally (against the conferring of a degree on Joseph Chamberlain in December 1899) concretizes how the center of Dublin was the frequent scene of political violence.

The modernity of Dublin, evidenced in its well-developed network of trams and the prosperous retail hubs around Grafton Street and Henry Street, was at odds with the pervasive poverty of the city and the unsanitary and overcrowded conditions in the tenements in which most of the working class lived. As Ruth McManus has outlined, an inquiry into the neglect of housing in 1913 established that some sixty thousand people were in urgent need of being reaccommodated. It was estimated that 29 percent of the city population lived in slums; the majority belonged to the laboring class, but a substantial proportion also stemmed from an artisan background.[18] Unlike Belfast or the midland cities in the United Kingdom, Dublin lacked significant indigenous industry and, as a result, there was high unemployment. Charles A. Cameron, the municipal medical officer, in a 1903 report identified the high level of single-room occupancy in Dublin—compared to the situation in Glasgow or London—as a stark indicator of destitution in the city and a primary cause of contagious disease. Additionally, he described the large-scale dependence on pawnbrokers by the poor of Dublin, with clothes among the articles most frequently cashed in for meager monetary advances. The quip that "half the population of Dublin were clothed in the clothes cast off by the other half" was, he noted, substantially true.[19]

Dublin was distinctive for its high social segregation and for the overlapping existences of rich and poor, particularly in its principal urban spaces. While the middle classes increasingly lived in new garden suburbs such as Ranelagh, Rathmines, and Clontarf, prosperous areas, including Merrion Square and Fitzwilliam Square, directly abutted tenements. Cameron observed that in "most cities the purlieus are in a limited number of districts, but in Dublin they are to be met with everywhere."[20] The purlieus, or slums, remain largely unseen in *Ulysses*, but Joyce draws out the peculiar contiguity of rich and poor in the city and the ways in which the differing classes intermingled on the streets. The novel underscores the economic deprivation that characterized Dublin through piercing vignettes, such as those of Dilly Dedalus, Stephen Dedalus's starving and needy sister; the mendicant one-legged sailor; the straitened Gerty MacDowell; the "rainbedraggled"[21] prostitute, Bridie Kelly; and the bereaved Dignam family on the brink of breakup and ruination.

A further peculiarity of Dublin in 1904 was its compactness. Even though the population had grown in the nineteenth century, it stood at only 290,638 in the 1901 census and 304,802 in the 1911 census. Joseph Brady noted the surprising smallness of the city, which could be easily traversed on foot in little more than an hour. He further postulated that Dublin was not a "single city but a number of independent urban entities of quite different character."[22] Indeed, quite how to encapsulate Dublin has long divided Joycean critics. They are torn between viewing Dublin as a village, a conglomeration of dispersed centers, or a quintessential modern city. While Fredric Jameson held that the final episodes of *Ulysses* capture the split between public and private spheres that typifies the alienation of modern life, he also argued that the gossipy exchanges possible in Dublin, given its aspect as "a great village," and the network of cross-references that makes sense of the scattered motifs and fragments of information in the text counter such depersonalization.[23] In his view, *Ulysses* in part "dereifies" the worst effects of urban living because of the particular nature of Dublin and of Joyce's modernist aesthetic.[24]

For Declan Kiberd there is no contradiction in seeing Dublin dualistically as both village and city. In *"Ulysses" and Us*, he has proposed that Joyce conceived of the city simultaneously as a village-like organic community and a metropolis and that the wisdom his novel conveys is rooted in a culture founded on commonality and the shared perspectives and lore of the city's streets.[25] Corroborating Kiberd's contentions, Vivien Igoe has established that many more of the characters of *Ulysses* were based on real-life figures than had long been presupposed, such as "old Troy of the D.M.P.," Denis Troy, alluded to at the beginning of "Cyclops."[26] Her research attests to the intimacy of the city and the multiple familial and social links cross-connecting its citizens. Yet Joyce also "citifies" Dublin and purposefully raises it to the level of a metropolis, emphasizing the peripatetic nature of

urban existence and the overriding sense of dissocia-
tion of many of his figures. In its variousness,
Dublin conforms ultimately to Vicki Mahaffey's
findings about Ireland in Irish modernist writing: it
is malleable and susceptible to "imaginative trans-
formation," on occasion both less and more than a
city, "sometimes a country village and sometimes
the world."[27]

Pointedly refuting Joyce's sweeping claim,
Richard Ellmann has contended that *Ulysses* did not
present Dublin in "reconstructable form"; rather,
the city "rises in bits, not in masses."[28] This is the
case with all of the locations of the novel, which are
created through a tessellation of impressions, the
accumulation of symbolic attributes, and a cross-
referencing of fictional and actual data. We must
immerse ourselves in Joyce's text but also radiate out
from it to check maps, local histories, photographs,
and contemporary sources to make sense of the
Dublin it unfolds. Hence, the tower in Sandycove,
near the Forty Foot bathing area, is rendered only in
half-glimpses in "Telemachus": "Solemnly he came
forward and mounted the round gunrest. He faced
about and blessed gravely thrice the tower, the
surrounding land and the awaking mountains."[29]

The panorama from the tower delineated here
in the description of Buck Mulligan's parody of a
Catholic Mass is suggestive but partial. Its encircle-
ment by the surrounding landscape gestures toward
its centrality but also its one-time role as a defensive
fortification. Other details, such as Stephen's
sighting of the mail boat as it enters the "harbour-
mouth of Kingstown" and a mention of the prospect southward "towards the blunt cape of Bray
Head," a phantom view not actually visible from the
tower, give readers an insight into Dublin's maritime
location and its global connections.[30] The temporary domicile of the ill-assorted friends Buck

Fig. 2.6. Philip Phillips, Martello tower. Sandycove, 1950. Gift of
Sayre P. Sheldon and Lady Richard Davies. The Rosenbach,
Philadelphia (2006.0004.0143).

Mulligan, Haines, and Stephen Dedalus, who have
differing views of how an Irish cultural renaissance
is to be achieved, wavers between the real and the
symbolic: it is the *omphalos* announced by Mulligan,
a site for the translation of Greek culture to Ireland,
Elsinore in *Hamlet*, and an artist's tower reminiscent of the lonely abode of the poet in Milton's "Il
Penseroso," and it anticipates ambiguous edifices in
modernist writing such as Rilke's Duino and Yeats's
Thoor Ballylee. Buck Mulligan's mocking appella-
tion, the "snotgreen sea," is more a jibe at the
pretensions of cultural nationalism than a visualiza-
tion of the sea lapping the nearby shoreline. It also
cruelly evokes Stephen's searing memory of the
"green sluggish bile"[31] vomited up by his mother in
her final illness. Martello towers were built by
British military engineers in imitation of a Corsican
fortification and hence are emblems of militarism

and imperialism. The tower consequently acts as an inauspicious venue for the competing political and intellectual ambitions of these young men. Leased by Mulligan from the British State, it acts as an objective correlative at once of Irish subalternity and of the colonial dispossession of the native Irish. Stephen's insistence, though, that he pays the rent raises the hope that this locus will be transformed through his art and thus recouped from usurpation and betrayal.

In laying Dublin bare, *Ulysses* gravitates toward numerous pivotal loci in the city: Glasnevin cemetery, No. 7 Eccles Street, Sandymount strand, Barney Kiernan's pub, Holles Street Hospital, the cabman's shelter, the brothels of Nighttown, and the Hill of Howth. Ironies and contradictions accrue around each of these places, as well as ramifying symbolic patterns that endow them with meaning. In "Aeolus" Stephen constructs an anticlimactic parable featuring "two old Dublin women on the top of Nelson's pillar." Their ambition to visit this iconic imperial monument seems to nullify itself as they collapse in exhaustion and so never gain ownership of the view they came to enjoy; the plum stones they spit out fall on barren ground instead of leading to new growth. However, on another level, their comedic irreverence and apathy, "too tired to look up or down or to speak," undercut the phallic bravado of the Pillar and query the imperial triumphalism instated in this Dublin thoroughfare.[32]

On his way to lunch in "Lestrygonians," Bloom pauses on O'Connell Bridge to muse and feed the ravenous seagulls:

> As he set foot on O'Connell bridge a puffball of smoke plumed up from the parapet. Brewery barge with export stout. England. Sea air sours it, I heard. . . .
> Wait. Those poor birds.

He halted again and bought from the old applewoman two Banbury cakes for a penny and broke the brittle paste and threw its fragments down into the Liffey. See that? The gulls swooped silently, two, then all from their heights, pouncing on prey. Gone. Every morsel. Aware of their greed and cunning he shook the powdery crumb from his hands.[33]

This pictorial scene renders a further key physical feature of Dublin, the river Liffey. Shorn of any pastoral connections, it is associated here with the episode's overarching themes of hunger, digestion, and cannibalism. Food and drink are ingested by humans and birds alike, just as they, too, are swallowed up in the stolid physicality of the city. Congruent with the movements of peristalsis, perceptions and emotions get broken down and lose any permanence. Thus, Bloom's empathy with and concern for the world around him are turned inside out, as he shifts from thinking about the logistics of the transport of Guinness to dwell on spoiled porter and suddenly fears the rapacity of the gulls, about which he has previously been solicitous. Dublin here mirrors the crudely appetitive drives of its inhabitants; unruly and involuntary organic needs crossconnect the living creatures in this urban space.

The stage directions that preface "Circe" also introduce us to a core aspect of the city, the red-light district around Mabbot Street that Joyce christens "nighttown," known in the era as "Monto": "*(The Mabbot street entrance of nighttown, before which stretches an uncobbled tramsiding set with skeleton tracks, red and green will-o'-the-wisps and danger signals. Rows of grimy houses with gaping doors. Rare lamps with faint rainbow fans. Round Rabaiotti's halted ice gondola stunted men and women squabble.*"[34] Dublin was notorious in the late nineteenth and early twentieth centuries for its thriving sex trade, supported by soldiers from the extensive military barracks throughout the city and sailors landing in the port. The business flourished because, as Maurice Curtis has outlined, there was no regulation preventing the setting up of brothels or "flashhouses."[35] Instead of the poverty that was the primary cause of female prostitution, however, "visibility and containment," according to Maria Luddy, were what most exercised authorities about the infamous square mile that constituted Monto.[36] Defying such propriety and the credo that purity was an intrinsically Irish virtue, Joyce set one of the most avant-garde episodes of *Ulysses* in the area around Mabbot Street, Montgomery Street, and Tyrone Street. The episode combines lurid realism and, as Catherine Flynn has illustrated, extravagant Surrealist effects culled from French modernist texts with the aim of conjoining Dublin with Paris as centers of modernity, consumerist excess, and illicit desires.[37] Above all, it crosses cinematic and theatrical techniques. It restages the novel's events as phantasmagoria, delves into the sexual fantasies and perversions of its characters, foremost amongst them Bloom, and depicts Dublin as an uncontrollable dreamscape and nightmare distortion of reality. In "Circe" everything is upended: Dublin becomes Bloomusalem; demure characters such as Gerty MacDowell reappear in unruly guise; the dead, including Virag, May Dedalus, and Rudy, return as unsettling ghosts; objects, such as the bar of lemon soap, speak; and the prostitutes and madams exact vengeance. The textual unconscious and the repressed life of the city dovetail and coincide. Fittingly, the Mabbot Street entrance mentioned at the beginning of "Circe" has now been renamed James Joyce Street, anchoring the author in the location tied to his most program-

matic utilization of the anarchic energies of Dublin to push against the boundaries of the novel and its aesthetic effects.

Patricia Hutchins has contended that "Howth more than any other place seems to belong to Joyce."[38] Yet it too is obliquely but viscerally rendered, in keeping with the depiction of Dublin throughout *Ulysses*, and transmuted by Joyce's language. Partly concurring with, but elaborating on, Bloom's memories in "Nausicaa,"[39] Molly recollects it as an important site in the couple's romance: "the sun shines for you he said the day we were lying among the rhododendrons on Howth head in the grey tweed suit and his straw hat the day I got him to propose to me yes first I gave him the bit of seedcake out of my mouth."[40]

The erotic, sensorial memory that Bloom and Molly share is linked with clashing affects of happiness and regret. Howth, as envisioned in "Penelope," moreover, is fused with Gibraltar; the Alameda gardens and the hillsides of this Dublin promontory, the Irish Sea and the Mediterranean, intermingle. In her musings, Molly hybridizes people and places, splicing Dublin and Gibraltar and saying yes to Mulvey-Bloom, "as well him as another."[41] But she also, in realigning much of the disparaging gossip about her throughout the novel, questions and talks back to the position of the feminine in this single-day stocktaking of Dublin life. The pillars of Hercules, on either side of the straits of Gibraltar, marked the limits of the known universe in antiquity. In *Ulysses*, they are portals linking Dublin to the world and transfiguring it through the inexhaustible workings of Joyce's imagination.

Dublin is not just lastingly commemorated but made into a living presence in Joyce's *Ulysses*. In the contemporary city, links to the upheavals of early twentieth-century history are forged through

Fig. 2.7. Philip Phillips, Ormond Hotel. Dublin, Ireland, 1950. Gift of Sayre P. Sheldon and Lady Richard Davies. The Rosenbach, Philadelphia (2006.0004.0146).

the fourteen bronze plaques inset in the pavements, installed in 1988, following the footsteps of Leopold Bloom, a wandering Odysseus, an émigré citizen with Austro-Hungarian forebears, and a Jewish Everyman. Joyce's text thus reminds us of the displacements and injustices of the imperial conflicts, nationalist uprisings, and racist exclusions that dominated the early twentieth century as well as the particularities of a single day, 16 June 1904. As people traverse these largely overlooked plaques, Bloom's journeys are renewed in the daily movements of the present inhabitants of Dublin. The restlessness and energy of the text merge kinetically with the city. Notwithstanding, modern-day Dublin is doomed always to be seen as a diminution from Joyce's Dublin and to be measured against it. Proposed changes to the city's historic fabric and moves to demolish, tamper with, or change the function of landmark buildings such as the Martello tower, Clery's department store, Sweny's chemist shop, and the Ormond Hotel are viewed as an assault on the city Joyce built and invented and rendered forever resonant. Even if the Dublin of *Ulysses* is necessarily incomplete and inhabited largely by seedy, venal, and rudderless figures, its integrity, amplitude, and specificity forever overshadow the mutating Dublin of the present.

Joyce declared to Arthur Power that Dublin was his abiding topic: "I always write about Dublin, because if I can get to the heart of Dublin then I can get to the heart of all the cities of the world. In the particular is contained the universal."[42] This indeed is one of the many achievements of *Ulysses*. In overthrowing novelistic tradition, Joyce endowed writers with a new and versatile template for urban fiction and opened up the possibility of fathoming the myriad unknown and unremarkable lives that modern metropolises contain. The Dublin of *Ulysses* is shadowed and figured otherwise in the London of Virginia Woolf and Zadie Smith, the Mumbai of Salman Rushdie and Rohinton Mistry, the Istanbul of Orhan Pamuk and Elif Shafak, the Cartagena of Gabriel García Márquez, the New York of Maeve Brennan and Teju Cole, and the Lagos of Chimamanda Ngozi Adichie. Olivia Laing has identified loneliness as an inescapable aspect of living in a city. Such disconnection and isolation stamp the lives of Joyce's characters, especially those of the central protagonists. What Laing describes as the art of being alone[43] is particularly captured in the fissures created by stream of consciousness and the staccato insistence of interior reflections. Yet through the exactitude and inventiveness of Joyce's language, the characters are also cross-connected, their musings granted significance and woven into the transpersonal but unifying symbolic patterns of his novel.

Dublin, too, is transmuted. Annually, Bloomsday is marked in cities and towns around the world, largely through readings from *Ulysses*. Joyce's recognition that the particularities and eccentricities of his native city can serve as the route to universal truths and apprehensions is thus borne out. His conceit that Dublin can be an everywhere is aptly realized when, on 16 June each year, everywhere becomes Dublin, if only for a short spell but always by dint of the transformative, alchemical force of Joyce's art. In all our Joycean interactions, Dublin features as touchstone, navigational guide and goal, and *omphalos*.

Fig. 3.1. Tullio Silvestri, portrait of James Joyce, 1914. Watercolor on paper.
The Poetry Collection of the University Libraries, University at Buffalo,
The State University of New York.

JOHN MCCOURT

3. Finding *Ulysses* in Trieste

It was no grand plan that took the twenty-two-year-old James Joyce and his even younger partner, Nora Barnacle, on what turned out to be an accident-prone journey across Europe to the far-off and (to them) little-known port city of Trieste in October 1904.[1] Joyce had initially been bound for Zurich, but a promised job at the Berlitz School of Languages there failed to materialize. His borrowed resources dwindling, he decided to travel further east, perhaps more in hope than expectation, following the advice of the school director in Zurich that a position might be available in the cosmopolitan Adriatic city of Trieste. Stepping off the train in what he thought was Trieste, to his dismay Joyce soon realized that they had disembarked too early and that they were in Ljubljana. They had little choice but to spend the night on a bench in the train station, awaiting the first train out the following

morning. When the inevitably bedraggled and exhausted couple did finally arrive in Trieste, Joyce left Nora in the small park in front of the train station with their luggage and set out in search of accommodation. He succeeded, however, only in getting himself arrested, along with a group of British sailors—drunken *ritardatari* (stragglers) who had failed to return to their Royal Navy vessel and were being rounded up by the Austro-Hungarian police. It took the intervention of the British consul to get Joyce released from custody several hours later. Meanwhile, anxious and alone, Nora waited for Joyce, whom she had met for the first time just a few months earlier, to return. The next day Joyce visited the Berlitz School and, after negotiations with Almidano Artifoni, the Neapolitan owner of the school, he was offered a position, not in Trieste but in the small Istrian military port

Fig. 3.2. Stanislaus Joyce in Trieste, 1905. Special Collections Research Center, Morris Library, Southern Illinois University Carbondale.

city of Pola (today Pula). Joyce later borrowed Artifoni's multisyllabic name and surname for Stephen Dedalus's Italian teacher in *A Portrait of the Artist as a Young Man* and *Ulysses*. Pola, in the meantime—in Joyce's words, "a naval Siberia"[2]—became their home for five long winter months before Joyce managed to engineer a transfer back to Trieste in the spring of 1905. By then, Nora was already pregnant with Giorgio.

This litany of accident and incident is reminiscent of the scarcely believable tales told in the cabman's shelter by the "doughty narrator" who is the "globetrotter" in the "Eumaeus" episode of *Ulysses* and who claims, among other things, to have "seen a man killed in Trieste by an Italian chap. Knife in his back. Knife like that."[3] Although this is the only direct reference to Trieste in *Ulysses*, the Joyce reader should not be fooled: the city and its variegated cultures are present in the very sinews of the book and especially so in the rich, complex, multiethnic characters of Leopold and Molly Bloom.

Trieste, by the late 1800s, was the Austro-Hungarian Empire's third-largest city, after Vienna and Prague, and it offered a home to many immigrants arriving from the four corners of the Habsburg Empire but also from further afield. They came, like Joyce and Nora, in search of a living, although the Joyce family would have been a little unusual in their permanently unsettled living arrangements, which saw them making temporary homes in some twenty different, often dingy, always well-located apartments in little over ten years. Trieste was a refuge and an inspiration to Joyce. His children, Giorgio and Lucia, were born there and were brought up to speak the local dialect of Triestino, which was the city's *lingua franca* and which Joyce also mastered. It was also home to Stanislaus, who would spend his entire adult life there, and later to an extended family that included, for a time, Joyce's sisters, Eileen and Eva. Trieste offered Joyce a living as a language teacher and occasional translator of commercial correspondence, but he found little to enjoy in these tasks that, more than anything, distracted him from the only thing that really mattered to him: his writing. Little wonder he would often complain about his "long drudgery and disappointment in Trieste"[4] and write, in *Finnegans Wake*, "And trieste, ah trieste ate I my liver."[5] This was a straightforward translation of the Italian idiom "mi sono mangiato il fegato" (literally "I ate my liver," idiomatically meaning "I wore myself out" or "I was consumed with rage"). The humdrum demands of teaching and making ends meet took their toll on an increasingly frustrated Joyce, and he and Nora would not have made it through his years in Trieste without the significant psychological, practical, and financial help offered by the long-suffering Stanislaus.

Joyce chanced down various paths with a view to supplementing and then finding an alternative to his scant salary at the Berlitz School, which, in any case, he abandoned in 1906 to embark on an ill-fated six-month stint as a bank clerk in Rome. He translated J. M. Synge's *Riders to the Sea* with his multilingual lawyer friend and English-language student Nicolò Vidacovich. Funded by a group of Trieste businessmen, he returned briefly to Dublin to found what is generally considered to be Ireland's first permanent cinema, the Volta on Mary Street in 1909, but this was a short-lived and ultimately (for this group) doomed affair.[6] He worked on and off as a part-time purveyor of Irish tweeds and also dedicated a significant amount of time to having his voice trained at the Conservatorio Tartini, with a view, perhaps, to emulating his fellow Irish tenor John McCormack, who was already enjoying

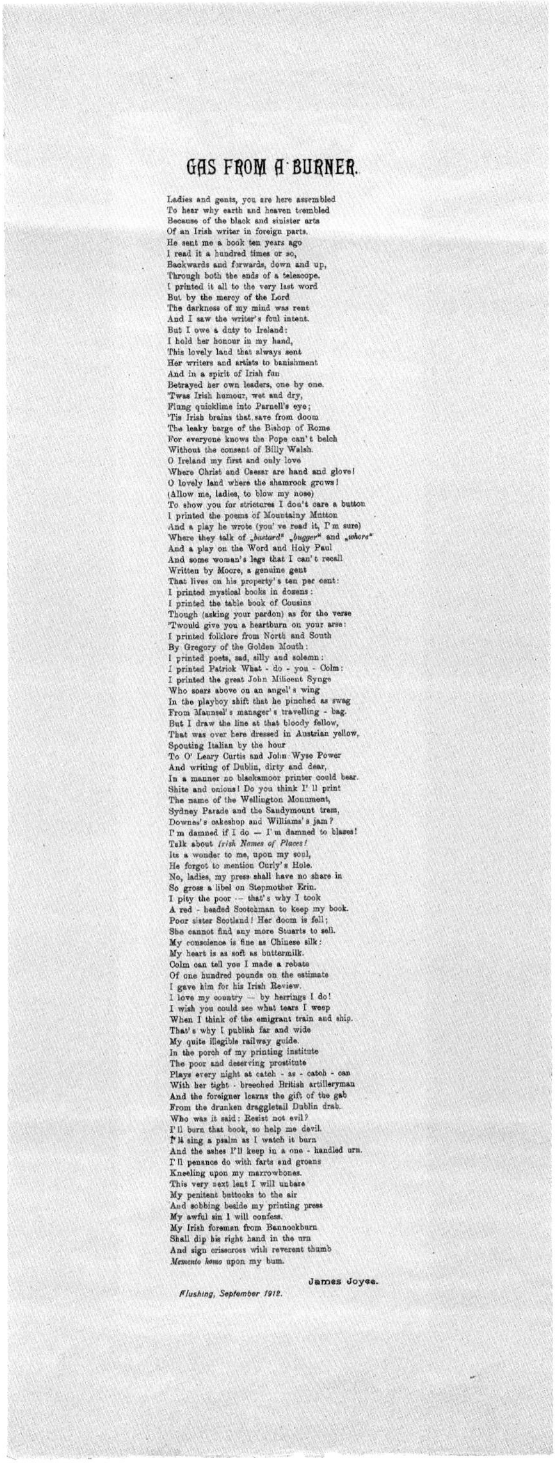

GAS FROM A BURNER.

Ladies and gents, you are here assembled
To hear why earth and heaven trembled
Because of the black and sinister arts
Of an Irish writer in foreign parts.
He sent me a book ten years ago
I read it a hundred times or so,
Backwards and forwards, down and up,
Through both the ends of a telescope.
I printed it all to the very last word
But by the mercy of the Lord
The darkness of my mind was rent
And I saw the writer's foul intent.
But I owe a duty to Ireland:
I hold her honour in my hand,
This lovely land that always sent
Her writers and artists to banishment
And in a spirit of Irish fun
Betrayed her own leaders, one by one.
'Twas Irish humour, wet and dry,
Flung quicklime into Parnell's eye;
'Tis Irish brains that save from doom
The leaky barge of the Bishop of Rome
For everyone knows the Pope can't belch
Without the consent of Billy Walsh.
O Ireland my first and only love
Where Christ and Caesar are hand and glove!
O lovely land where the shamrock grows!
(Allow me, ladies, to blow my nose)
To show you for strictures I don't care a button
I printed the poems of Mountainy Mutton
And a play he wrote (you've read it, I'm sure)
Where they talk of „bastard" „bugger" and „whore"
And a play on the Word and Holy Paul
And some woman's legs that I can't recall
Written by Moore, a genuine gent
That lives on his property's ten per cent:
I printed mystical books in dozens:
I printed the table book of Cousins
Though (taking your pardon) as for the verse
'Twould give you a heartburn on your arse:
I printed folklore from North and South
By Gregory of the Golden Mouth:
I printed poets, sad, silly and solemn:
I printed Patrick What-do-you-Colm:
I printed the great John Milicent Synge
Who soars above on an angel's wing
In the playboy shift that he pinched as swag
From Maunsel's manager's travelling-bag.
But I draw the line at that bloody fellow,
That was over here dressed in Austrian yellow,
Spouting Italian by the hour
To O'Leary Curtis and John Wyse Power
And writing of Dublin, dirty and dear,
In a manner no blackamoor printer could bear.
Shite and onions! Do you think I'll print
The name of the Wellington Monument,
Sydney Parade and the Sandymount tram,
Downes's cakeshop and Williams's jam?
I'm damned if I do — I'm damned to blazes!
Talk about *Irish Names of Places*!
Its a wonder to me, upon my soul,
He forgot to mention Curly's Hole.
No, ladies, my press shall have no share in
So gross a libel on Stepmother Erin.
I pity the poor — that's why I took
A red-headed Scotchman to keep my book.
Poor sister Scotland! Her doom is fell;
She cannot find any more Stuarts to sell.
My conscience is fine as Chinese silk:
My heart is as soft as buttermilk.
Colm can tell you I made a rebate
Of one hundred pounds on the estimate
I gave him for his Irish Review.
I love my country — by herrings I do!
I wish you could see what tears I weep
When I think of the emigrant train and ship.
That's why I publish far and wide
My quite illegible railway guide.
In the porch of my printing institute
The poor and deserving prostitute
Plays every night at catch-as-catch-can
With her tight-breeched British artilleryman
And the foreigner learns the gift of the gab
From the drunken draggletail Dublin drab.
Who was it said: Resist not evil?
I'll burn that book, so help me devil.
I'll sing a psalm as I watch it burn
And the ashes I'll keep in a one-handled urn.
I'll penance do with farts and groans
Kneeling upon my marrowbones.
This very next lent I will unbare
My penitent buttocks to the air
And sobbing beside my printing press
My awful sin I will confess.
My Irish foreman from Bannockburn
Shall dip his right hand in the urn
And sign crosses with reverent thumb
Memento homo upon my bum.

James Joyce.

Flushing, September 1912.

Fig. 3.3. James Joyce, *Gas from a Burner*, printed in Trieste, 1912. The Morgan Library & Museum, New York. Gift of Sean and Mary Kelly, 2018. © The Estate of James Joyce.

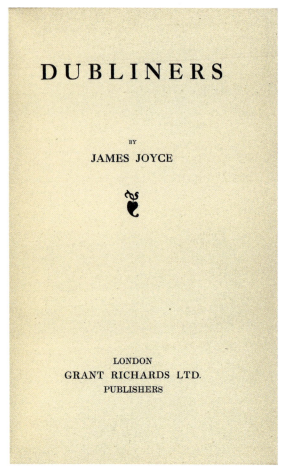

DUBLINERS

BY
JAMES JOYCE

LONDON
GRANT RICHARDS LTD.
PUBLISHERS

Fig. 3.4. James Joyce, *Dubliners*, 1914. The Morgan Library & Museum, New York. Gift of Sean and Mary Kelly, 2018.

articles about the country for Trieste's *Il Piccolo della Sera*, often adopting positions close to those of Arthur Griffith's Sinn Féin, which argued for abstentionism, passive resistance, and economic nationalism following the principles laid out in Griffith's *The Resurrection of Hungary*. The pamphlet showed how this policy had successfully worked in Hungary, which went, in 1867, from being part of the Austrian Empire to being a separate coequal kingdom in Austria-Hungary. Even if his subject matter was unrelentingly Irish, he was, as Giorgio Melchiori pointed out, from 1907 to 1912 "exclusively an Italian writer," and his rather nationalistic articles about Ireland would have resonated in irredentist Trieste.[8]

This period also saw Joyce living through the hugely frustrating seven-year process of wrangling and waiting before he finally managed to publish *Dubliners* on the eve of the First World War (he had completed it in 1907). Whatever hopes he had of making a financial killing were dashed by the war. Despite all this, Joyce's years in Trieste were rich and productive, even if that only became apparent with the benefit of hindsight. Generations of Joyce commentators took excessive heed of Stanislaus's discouraging comment that the "cosmopolitan atmosphere of the Trieste of the early twentieth century did not inspire him at all."[9] His fellow writer and most important Triestine friend, Italo Svevo, was in a unique position to see Joyce up close and gave a more balanced account of both the difficulties encountered and the possibilities offered during Joyce's decade in Trieste: "His inner life was complex but already clear-cut: the elaboration of the subject matter offered him by his childhood and youth. A piece of Ireland was ripening under our sun. But the struggle cost him dear; for the life of a gerund-monger is not an easy one."[10]

significant international success. All of this clearly infuriated Stanislaus, who noted in his Trieste diary, "Now that his writing is 'definitely off', I take little interest in the budding tenorino, that has failed as a poet in Paris, as a journalist in Dublin, as a lover and novelist in Trieste, as a bank clerk in Rome, and again in Trieste as a Sinnfeiner, teacher, and University Professor."[7]

Joyce followed events in Ireland reported in the newspapers very closely and wrote nine front-page

Once he resigned from the Berlitz School in 1906 (leaving Stanislaus to worry about earning enough to pay their bills), Trieste gave him time and space to write about his "piece of Ireland"—Dublin—from, as he puts it in a phrase in *Finnegans Wake*, "the safe side of distance."[11] He was not immune to occasional flights of enthusiasm about Trieste (usually when writing to Nora during one of his two ill-fated trips back to Dublin): "*La nostra bella Trieste*! I have often said that angrily but tonight I feel it true. I long to see the lights twinkling along the riva as the train passes Miramar. After all, Nora, it is the city which has sheltered us. I came back to it jaded and moneyless after my folly in Rome and now again after this absence."[12]

Later he would write with retrospective gratitude and with nostalgia of his time in the principal port of the Austro-Hungarian Empire: "I cannot begin to give you the flavour of the old Austrian Empire. It was a ramshackle affair but it was charming, gay, and I experienced more kindnesses in Trieste than ever before or since in my life."[13] With these words, it was as if Joyce, like Gabriel Conroy in "The Dead," was reaching back to an easier, more graceful time, to more "spacious days": the tail end of the nineteenth century that was wiped away by the Great War, the aftermath of which would see the Trieste that he knew and cherished lose its *raison d'être* and dwindle into a reduced status as a provincial Italian backwater, a port deprived of its hinterland. This latter version of Trieste was the one visited by early Joyce scholars, who struggled to find even the ghost of the city that had so inspired the writer.

It was in Trieste that Europe became, in a very tangible sense, Joyce's home and an extended frame of reference within which to construct and place *Ulysses*. When he came to write his novel, Joyce

Fig. 3.5. *Biglietto d'abbonamento* (subscription ticket) for Joyce's lectures on *Hamlet*, Trieste, 4 November 1912. The Poetry Collection of the University Libraries, University at Buffalo, The State University of New York.

assembled a transnational work that was laden with materials from "all the ends of Europe" (to quote Molly Bloom), from Trieste to Szombathely to Gibraltar to Vienna and Paris, from ancient Greece to contemporary Dublin. Many of these elements he found on the shores of the Adriatic. The French critic Valery Larbaud has, along with Ezra Pound, long been credited with rescuing Joyce from the clutches of provincial Ireland and turning him into a cosmopolitan writer.[14] These influential early supporters appreciated the extraordinary quality of Joyce's writing when Irish readers and critics mostly reacted with hesitation. While they undoubtedly helped early readers see Joyce in the light of international modernism, the real credit for his stepping beyond the confines of Irish literature (or, better, for his expansion of those same confines) belongs to Trieste, a modern, international city by definition, and an unlikely (and long-ignored) hub of European modernism before such a thing had a name.[15] Trieste was home to Italo Svevo, whose name so

Fig. 3.6. Italo Svevo. Svevo Museum, Comune di Trieste.

brilliantly encapsulates his complex identity as the Italian Swabian, to the Jewish poet Umberto Saba (born Umberto Poli), and, for a short period, to the great Bohemian-Austrian poet and novelist Rainer Maria Rilke (at Duino). Much of the city looked north to Vienna, and some of Joyce's students attended university there. The Austrian city was a constant source of new ideas in the fields of literature, art, music, psychology, and philosophy. Innovative ideas and new artistic forms and creations filtered into Italy (and into Joyce's later works) through Trieste from figures such as Theodor Herzl, Richard Wagner, and Gustav Mahler (who conducted in Trieste in 1905); Arthur

Schnitzler, whose short story "Leutnant Gustl" ("None but the Brave," 1900) is often seen as the first to use the stream-of-consciousness technique; Otto Von Weininger; and, most of all, Sigmund Freud, who had even briefly worked in Trieste studying the sexual organs of eels at a marine biology research station in 1876. Joyce was friendly with Freud's Triestine pupil Dr. Edoardo Weiss, who led the way in introducing Freud's work to the city. Even if Joyce supposedly "astonished Svevo by saying that people who feel the need [of psycho-analysis] should stick to confession,"[16] it is not much of a stretch to imagine the presence of Freud somewhere in the mix as Joyce developed his own very particular version of the interior monologue.

Other intellectuals and writers looked south to Italy and were inspired by the Futurist movement. The city was something of a hotbed of Futurist writing, with local figures such as Italo Tavolato, Luigi Crociato, and Teodoro Finzi (who published his volume, *Cannonate*, in 1910 under the pseudonym Fedoro Tizzoni). Marinetti famously referred to Trieste as one of the three capitals of Futurism and was the star, on 12 January 1910, of a spectacular Futurist gathering held in the Politeama Rossetti. The event would have caught Joyce's attention, as many of his acquaintances—such as Roberto Prezioso, the editor of *Il Piccolo*; the journalist and man of letters Silvio Benco; the poet Dario De Tuoni; and his first portraitist, Tullio Silvestri— were all in the audience to listen to Marinetti, Aldo Palazzeschi, Armando Mazza, and Michelangelo Zimolo. Joyce owned or borrowed several Futurist volumes by Palazzeschi and Marinetti[17] but had no sympathy with the aggressive, ultra-male thematic centerpieces of the movement, such as the conquest of time and space, the celebration of war, and the glorification of industry, strength, and speed (all of which the Citizen in the "Cyclops" episode would have valued). At the same time, Joyce was fascinated with Futurism's innovative stylistic features, such as the orthographic revolution, the remodeling of words, the abolition of traditional syntax, meter, and punctuation, the quest to convey simultaneity, and the use of "parole in libertà" (the free placing of words). At one point in Zurich he even asked his friend Frank Budgen whether the "Cyclops" episode struck him as "Futuristic,"[18] a question that could be profitably asked of several episodes of *Ulysses*.

In Trieste, too, Joyce was able to deepen and widen his knowledge of opera and rarely missed a production at the prestigious Teatro Comunale, which the irredentist city council named after Giuseppe Verdi immediately following Verdi's death in 1901. Joyce would queue for a seat in the *loggione* or procure a journalist's pass from his friends at *Il Piccolo* and revel in hearing works by Donizetti and Verdi, by the more contemporary composers of the school of *verismo*, such as Puccini, Leoncavallo, Mascagni, and Giordano (these latter two conducted performances of their own works in Trieste in Joyce's time), or by the local artist Antonio Smareglia, who was his neighbor on via Bramante. He also enjoyed regular performances of works by Richard Wagner and Richard Strauss (whose *Salome* was produced in Trieste in 1909 and was the occasion for Joyce's article "Oscar Wilde: Il poeta di *Salomé*" in *Il Piccolo della Sera*). All of this fed the vast array of material operatic citation in *Ulysses* and deeply influenced Joyce's compositional methods, not only for the "Sirens" episode but for the entire work.

The same could be said of Joyce's involvement with the world of film in Trieste, a city with more than a dozen cinemas at a time that Dublin had none. As early as 1928, Alfred Döblin, the author of *Berlin Alexanderplatz*, drew attention to the

Fig. 3.7. Teatro Comunale Giuseppe Verdi. Civici Musei di Storia ed Arte, Trieste.

cinematic aspects of Joyce's writing when he famously defined *Ulysses* in terms of montage and saw this as a prime example of how cinema had "penetrated the sphere of literature. [. . .] To the experimental image of a person today also belongs the streets, the scenes changing by the second, the signboards, automobile traffic."[19] This was a medium that Joyce fully embraced in Trieste and attempted to export to Dublin; he internalized its techniques, adding them to his stylistic armory for revolutionizing narrative form and technique in *Ulysses*.

Being in Trieste also challenged Joyce in a geopolitical sense, in part by allowing him to achieve the miracle of being in many places at one time. Trieste was uniquely a Middle European city perched on the upper tip of the Adriatic; it was the *Urbs Fidelissima* of Imperial Austria and had, following the Napoleonic Wars, enjoyed the status of an Imperial Free City before becoming capital of the Austrian Littoral region, the *Küstenland*. It was the ancient *città italianissima* of Tergeste, made a colony by Julius Caesar (who mentioned it in his *Commentarii de bello Gallico*). Joyce was well aware of the Roman origins of the city known as Tergeste and later referred to himself as a "*Tergestime Exul*."[20] In Joyce's time in the city, its population was predominantly Italian-speaking and passed up no opportunity to assert its *italianità*, both politically and culturally. For the Slav minority, on the other hand, it was Trst, a city with a notable Slovene and Croat population, especially in the suburbs (26 percent of the total, according to the 1911 census), which might well have a role to play in the formation of a future Slav nation. Aside from these two contending populations, there was also a small Austrian upper crust or ruling class. Trieste, "la porta d'oriente," the gateway to the east or "tarry easty,"[21] was a genuine melting pot, a town where, as George Eliot put it in *Daniel Deronda*, "the garments of men from all nations shone like jewels"[22] or where, as Karl Marx put it rather more soberly in reference to its mercantile vocation, "a motley crew of speculators"[23] held sway. When Joyce has Molly Bloom describe the marketplace in Gibraltar, filled with "the Greeks and the jews and the Arabs and the devil knows who else from all the ends of Europe,"[24] he was aptly remembering what he saw and warmed to in Trieste.

Trieste was also something of an economic miracle. A small fishing port of just a few thousand souls at the start of the eighteenth century, it had grown rapidly into a bustling city, thanks to settlers drawn there by its new role as chief port of the vast Austro-Hungarian Empire. Like other great port cities, such as Marseille and Hamburg, the nineteenth century brought massive growth, and the city that Joyce discovered was living the last days of its golden years as principal port of "old Auster and Hungrig,"[25] a crossroads city of shipping, commerce, insurance, culture. He would witness the crumbling of the empire in which Trieste had enjoyed a vital role and would bemoan the rise of a variety of nationalisms that would replace it.

Hubert Butler, who, like Joyce, had spent time in Trieste, wrote perceptive words about his fellow Irishman's state of exile: "As a young man Joyce had a clearly conceived ideal—he believed that Ireland could realise itself by becoming more European and the choice must have presented itself to him frequently of being a European in Ireland or an Irishman in Europe. The second alternative was chosen only when it was clear that it was the least impossible of the two."[26]

Joyce seems to allude to this state of being an Irishman in Europe in *Finnegans Wake*, although the Irishman here also becomes a Slav-Italian writer, "Shem Skrivenitch," who "caught the europicolas and went into the society of jewses. With Bro Cahlls and Fran Czeschs and Bruda Pszths and Brat Slavos."[27] This suggests the "confusioning of human races,"[28] the social, racial, and religious mixing that was very particular to Middle European Trieste. Being there allowed Joyce to see Dublin from a different perspective and enabled him to frame it in a very different way within the pages of *Ulysses*, compared to the depictions in *Dubliners* and *Portrait*. If the early two books give voice to frustrations, paralysis, and pent-up desires for rebellion or escape, *Ulysses* offers greater space and openness, more European connectedness and, through the varying visions of the three protagonists, a composite alternative vision of a possible

Ireland very different from the one that was actually taking shape in the early years of the Free State. In his 1907 "Irlanda: Isola dei santi e savi" ("Ireland: Island of Saints and Sages") lecture, Joyce introduced his Trieste audience to Ireland, its history, and its links to Europe through Catholicism. Yet he was also careful to undermine attempts to describe the Irish national character as "ancient and monolithic" and to demolish any notions of racial purity at a time when many Irish political and cultural revivalists were claiming the contrary, just as some Italian irredentists were doing in Trieste: "In such a fabric, it is useless to look for a thread that may have remained pure, virgin and uninfluenced by other threads nearby. What race or language (if we except those few which a humorous will seems to have preserved in ice, such as the people of Iceland) can nowadays claim to be pure? No race has less right to make such a boast than the one presently inhabiting Ireland."[29]

The impossibility of national or linguistic purity is a theme in *Ulysses* and *Finnegans Wake*, and that is partly a result of Joyce's immersion in the liminal space of Trieste that at times seemed to belong to everyone and to no one. Few families were able to claim any kind of "pure" racial lineage, be it Italian, Slav, or Austrian, and the city's blood was genuinely mixed as the result of generations of miscegenation. Scipio Slataper, a contemporary of Joyce's and the author of *Il mio carso*—which explains the complex burden of being a Triestine *meticcio*, a "mixed middling"[30]—described the city's dilemma. It was caught between imperial Austro-Hungarian Mitteleuropa and "Illbelpaese,"[31] the promised land that the city's irredentists, against their own economic interests, longed to join while willfully ignoring the fact that Trieste's economic success was due to its role within the larger imperial structure: "It is the torment of two temperaments, the commercial

[Austrian] and the Italian, which collide and nullify each other, and Trieste cannot suppress either of the two: this is the double spirit, otherwise it would kill itself. Whatever is necessary for commerce is a violation of the Italian aspirations, just as any real commercial gain damages the spirit."[32]

Joyce's exasperation with the growing nationalist impulses is caught in his cutting comment in his Triestine poem-in-prose *Giacomo Joyce* (itself a vital transitional text in his development from *Portrait* to *Ulysses*): "Ay. They love their country when they are quite sure which country it is."[33]

The complex nexus of economic, political, and cultural relationships enjoyed and endured by semicolonial Trieste was very different from the one Joyce had abandoned in Ireland. Being Austria's only seaport had brought the city great wealth. In Trieste, the Austrians, along with the Greeks, Jews, Slavs, and Hungarians, all bought their way in, having come to invest in the burgeoning emporium or to seek work there. There was no strong local population to be deposed. Austrian Habsburg Trieste was invented and constructed in an almost empty place, and as a result, it contained multiple identities; it could never be wholly or exclusively identified with any one nation.[34]

Against this very specific Triestine canvas, Joyce formed his theoretical skeleton of ideas (some of which Bloom would later come to represent), including his refutation of "the old pap of racial hatred"[35] in its anti-Irish, anti-English, and anti-Semitic configurations. The influence of Trieste can be seen in Joyce's assertion in his lecture that no race could boast of being pure because none was. In *Ulysses*, both Leopold and Molly Bloom embody the double or even multiple versions of belonging that existed in Trieste and the analogies that Joyce came to see between Ireland and the Adriatic city. Joyce spliced material from home with material from his adopted city, combining a fidelity to his local Irish world with an openness to absorbing what we might call foreign elements, not just as coloring but as constitutive components of his novel. Drawing on what he learned from his Jewish friends and acquaintances—many of whom, like the Budapest-born Moses Dlugacz, had Hungarian roots—and especially from Italo Svevo, Joyce put flesh on the hybrid character, the "mixed middling," that is Leopold Bloom, the most unlikely "hero" for an Irish national epic, who is at once Irish and Hungarian, Jewish and Catholic. Similarly, even if her thinking is Irish and Catholic, Molly is also, as the daughter of Lunita Laredo, a Sephardi (Spanish Jew), and she was born and spent her first sixteen years in Gibraltar. But she is also associated with the Orient and even with Morocco.

Although both Leopold and Molly Bloom are clearly connoted as Dubliners, it is precisely their non-Irish qualities that draw them to each other. Bloom appreciates Molly's being "Spanish, half that is,"[36] her having the "passionate abandon of the south,"[37] while Molly chose him "because you were so foreign from the others."[38] These elements derived from Joyce's reading and his imagination but also from Trieste's variegated and prominent Jewish population, many members of which were well known to Joyce. As Neil Davison has aptly described it, "[Joyce's] first ten years there [in Trieste] represent a [...] very deliberate quest for a well-rounded knowledge about European Jewry, Judaism, and racialist representations of the Jew."[39]

The significant "foreign" elements emerge in *Ulysses* when we read the text through what Joyce calls "doubling bicirculars" and attempt to see this "double densed" work "from a double focus," as a tale of two cities, one front and center, and the second lurking in the shadows.[40] This is not to see

Joyce as a rootless international modernist cut off from his Irish world (as Larbaud and Pound sought to do) but rather to point to *Ulysses* as a work built out of solid, tangible materials gathered in both Dublin and Trieste.

Bloom's definition of the nation is one that Joyce might well have heard from a Triestino and would have been uttered in the true spirit of the city's *municipalismo*—the long-established idea that the municipality of Trieste was capable of embracing different peoples and traditions, of absorbing and offering a future to immigrants from all over Europe and beyond.

—But do you know what a nation means? says John Wyse.
—Yes, says Bloom.
—What is it? says John Wyse.
—A nation? says Bloom. A nation is the same people living in the same place.
—By God, then, says Ned, laughing, if that's so I'm a nation for I'm living in the same place for the past five years.

So of course everyone had the laugh at Bloom and says he, trying to muck out of it:
—Or also living in different places.
—That covers my case, says Joe.
—What is your nation if I may ask? says the citizen.
—Ireland, says Bloom. I was born here. Ireland.[41]

With so many Triestini maintaining strong ties with their countries and cultures of origin, continuing to speak the language of that country while also speaking Triestino, the city was living proof of Bloom's seemingly impossible formulation that a nation was not simply "the same people living in the same place" but also, and essentially, a variegated diaspora of "the same people living in different places." A sense of dual belonging lay at the heart of one of the most important Triestine schools of writing in Joyce's time, that of the group of writers who gravitated toward Giuseppe Prezzolini's avant-garde literary journal *La Voce* in Florence. Often referred to collectively as the Vociani, they included Slataper, Saba, and Angelo Vivante. They rejected political irredentism but gave voice to an alternative form of cultural patriotism, believing that Italian culture should be developed in dialogue with rather than in opposition to that of its neighbors, be their cultures Slav or German. They, like the local socialists, argued for an accommodating version of Trieste, home to different peoples and civilizations. This was very much in tune with the exilic Joyce's vision of the city and in line with the multinational image Joyce superimposes on the Dublin of *Ulysses*, a city prominently populated by "Dubliners" whose names underscore their differences and their foreign origins: Artifoni, Bloom, Nanetti, Rabaiotti, Reuben J. Dodd, Herzog, Moisel, Dubedat, Dlugacz, Purefoy.

Perhaps all these elements help us understand why the Italian novelist Alberto Moravia looked to Joyce at the start of the Second World War, which was to devastate the Continent, as "the incarnation of Europe." Joyce, in his person and in his works, symbolized "a free Europe, where art and literature traveled far and wide like gentle breezes announcing the arrival of spring. A Europe with neither borders nor divisions, where it was legitimate to change places according to the whims of literary inspiration."[42] We should, however, be careful not to idealize. Joyce lived in Trieste in a time of flux and witnessed firsthand its cosmopolitan *raison d'être* being jeopardized and ultimately canceled by rising nationalisms and by a growing distrust of the Other. He uses the pages of *Ulysses* to conjure up the potential of a more open and accepting vision for an alternative Ireland and an alternative Europe—not of strutting nations with their armies at war, but of mixed peoples and languages—while illustrating how difficult this would be to achieve or to maintain. (Bloom's outsider status is the embodiment of this difficulty.) At the same time, Joyce underscores the dangerous potential of unchecked nationalism and the warlike impulse, which he saw rising both in Trieste and from his vantage point at the center of Europe and chose to embody in the cyclopean character of the Citizen. Let us never forget that Joyce wrote *Ulysses* during and after the 1916 Rising and the Anglo-Irish War in Ireland and in the midst of the horrors of the First World War. Although these events receive only occasional, indirect, and peripheral mention in *Ulysses* (it could not have been otherwise in a work set in 1904), Joyce knew all too well the potency of force and hatred to wipe out hard-earned quotidian normality, decency, and justice, and he used the pages of *Ulysses* to illustrate this (among so many other things).

Fig. 4.1. Alex Ehrenzweig, passport photograph of James Joyce in Zurich,
1915. Special Collections Research Center, Morris Library,
Southern Illinois University Carbondale.

RONAN CROWLEY

4. *Ulysses* in Zurich

"Occupied with books, papers, pencils" in Tom Stoppard's comic reimagining, Joyce weathered the war years in neutral Switzerland, at work on *Ulysses*.[1] While the three cities of the novel's dateline receive equal billing, Joyce spent more than half of the 1914–21 time span in Zurich.[2] He arrived in the city in June 1915 a displaced person, just one of some seven million people within Europe uprooted by the First World War. When he left, less than five years later, his personal and professional fortunes had taken a decided turn for the better. The author of four books published on either side of the Atlantic, Joyce was now listed in *Who's Who*, his play *Exiles* had been issued and staged in German translation (albeit as a single poorly received performance), and he set out for Trieste with the freedom of Harriet Shaw Weaver's money in his pocket. More than the scene of

exponential growth in Joyce's social, cultural, and financial capital, Zurich was also the site of major work on *Ulysses*. It was there, in August 1917, that Joyce resolved to "consign [*Ulysses*] serially" for magazine publication, and he completed the first twelve of the novel's eighteen episodes, "Telemachus" to "Cyclops," while in Switzerland.[3] By the time he took his farewell of Zurich in mid-October 1919, the episodes up to and including "Sirens" had appeared in the *Little Review*, Margaret Anderson and Jane Heap's literary journal.

For all the prominence of Zurich, Lausanne in French Switzerland had been the Joyce family's intended refuge when they fled Trieste only to cut short their flight at "the first big city after the frontier," as Joyce told Weaver.[4] He and Nora, with the preteen Giorgio and Lucia in tow, had traveled on an emergency passport issued by the American

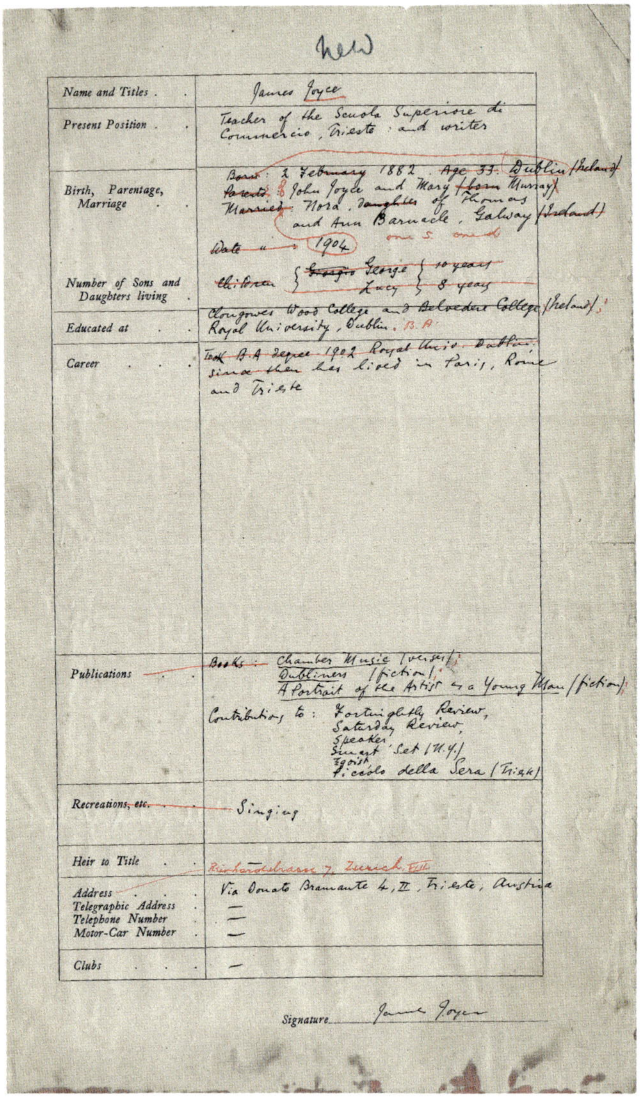

Fig. 4.2. James Joyce, autograph responses to a printed questionnaire from *Who's Who*, 1915. Collection of Pedro Corrêa do Lago. © The Estate of James Joyce.

consulate at Trieste; fighting in Trentino and South Tyrol forced them to undertake a circuitous weeklong train journey of more than six hundred miles through hostile territory before they reached Switzerland. The family traveled light. In the haste of departure, Joyce packed "only a few things and some MSS" as well as a copy of the *Divine Comedy*.[5] He also agreed to serve as go-between for some Triestine associates, an obligingness he came to regret when he arrived at the railway border checkpoint between Austria-Hungary and Switzerland with compromising letters stowed in his luggage. Already subjected to routine state surveillance as an enemy alien resident in the Dual Monarchy, Joyce ran a very real risk of arrest and civil internment. "On those tracks," he would tell Eugene Jolas seventeen years later, "the fate of *Ulysses* was decided."[6]

Stoppard's *Travesties* preserves the gist of Joyce's writing practice but plays freely with specifics. The drama opens in the Zentralbibliothek Zürich (ZB), or Zurich central library, where Joyce, scraps of paper containing snippets of prose in his pockets, dictates the opening lines of "Oxen of the Sun" to an amanuensis. The setting is plausible: Joyce joined the ZB on 3 August 1917, signing himself in the readers' register as a "Schriftsteller," or writer, although there is no record of his ever having paid the library's security deposit of fifty Swiss francs.[7] Notebooks for *Ulysses* include call numbers for works from the ZB holdings that we now know he drew on for the novel. And the scrap-paper approach to composition is corroborated by a single sheet of ruled paper, likely torn from a notebook, that preserves Joyce's tinkering with a paragraph of the "Sirens" episode.[8] Yet, save in exceptional circumstances, he was no dictator.[9] "Oxen of the Sun," moreover, was a Trieste episode, not written until 1920 and the Joyces' return to the Julian March. The details may be off, blamed in the play on the elderly Henry Carr's dodgy memory, but Stoppard captures an essential dimension of Joyce's Zurich experience: the network of associates that he gathered around himself in the city and on whom he relied for friendship, diversion, and professional advancement and as a source of raw material for *Ulysses*.

There is nothing to suggest that either Lenin or Tristan Tzara ever crossed paths with Joyce, but it is telling that within a few weeks of his arrival in Zurich in 1915 he visited another library, the Museumsgesellschaft in the heart of the old city, in order to secure pupils for language lessons. Indeed, one of Joyce's first actions upon landing in Zurich was to reach out to his existing network. He wrote in short order to his literary agent and his publishers, both actual and prospective, for updates on sales, royalties due, and plans afoot to get his writing into print. At the same time, Ezra Pound, tireless puller of strings, was drumming up support for an application to the Royal Literary Fund on Joyce's behalf. Letters crisscrossed London that July between Edmund Gosse, Pound, H. G. Wells, and W. B. Yeats, culminating in a grant of £75 from the benevolent fund (about $10,000 in today's money) and, improbably enough, the promise of a job at the War Office's censorship department.[10] Gosse fretted over Joyce's politics, telling Yeats that he would not have promised "one penny" if he suspected Joyce of harboring any sympathy for the Dual Monarchy; Yeats "pacified" the Englishman, in Pound's recap, by po-facedly replying, "I have never known Joyce to agree with his neighbours."[11] Not only, then, was Joyce an active self-promoter, but he also had a career-long knack for attracting those who would work to advance his interests. During the Zurich years, this activity took on transatlantic scope as

Fig. 4.3. Donald Cooper, color photograph of Lloyd Hutchinson as James Joyce in Tom Stoppard's *Travesties*, Royal Shakespeare Company, 1993.

well-connected backers and barkers in London and New York labored to keep him in the public eye, subsidize his always precarious finances, and unearth professional opportunities.

The typical representation of First World War Switzerland, during the conflict as now, is of an "island of peace" surrounded on all sides by fighting, a safe haven for the citizens and subjects of war-torn Europe's great powers.[12] Switzerland as place of refuge squares with its Dunantist tradition of humanitarianism but belies the degree to which

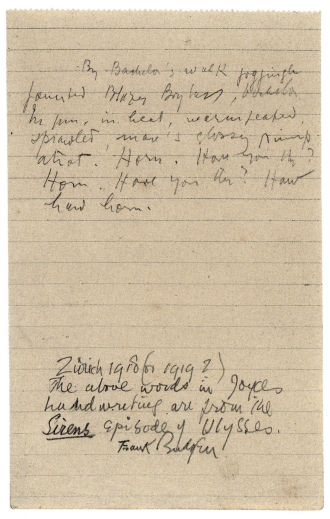

Fig. 4.4. James Joyce, fragment of the "Sirens" episode, 1918 or 1919. Autograph manuscript. The Morgan Library & Museum, New York. Gift of Sean and Mary Kelly, 2018. © The Estate of James Joyce.

outward-facing neutrality was a domestic accommodation, with Romandy leanings toward the Triple Entente canceling and being canceled out by Triple Alliance sympathies in German-speaking eastern Switzerland. Moreover, the Swiss Confederation viewed itself as not so much a destination for those displaced by the war as a point of transit, a temporary stopover or way station en route elsewhere—a role made manifest in the country's strict border controls and inflexible asylum policy. Residency was often a matter of the right contacts or resources. Those who had no alternative but to stay included tens of thousands of deserters and draft dodgers and over 67,000 prisoners of war who, having been injured in the continental theater, were sent to Switzerland to recuperate.[13] So, while wartime Zurich is rightly celebrated as a hothouse for pan-European creative and intellectual talent, the various circles of émigrés and expats in which Joyce moved were not entirely self-selected but took their broad shape from a Swiss immigration policy scrambling to adapt to and keep pace with mass displacement. Exemplary in this regard is his friendship with Frank Budgen, the English painter and socialist activist who served as Joyce's sounding board for difficulties and conceptual breakthroughs in the writing of *Ulysses*. For all Budgen's own creative aspirations, his presence in Zurich in 1918 owed more to his job as a news compiler for the British Ministry of Information. In 1934, with *Ulysses* legally available in the United States for the first time, he published a memoir-cum-handbook to the novel, *James Joyce and the Making of "Ulysses,"* an invaluable account of the latter Zurich years and of Joyce's Paris residency, which Budgen compiled from his own firsthand experience and with input from Joyce.

International mobility was central to Joyce's rising stock in the literary marketplace. Relocation

Fig. 4.5. Frank Budgen, portrait of Nora Barnacle Joyce, ca. 1919. Oil on paperboard. The Poetry Collection of the University Libraries, University at Buffalo, The State University of New York.

caused an effective reset in his social relations each time the family moved country, even as he parlayed success in previous social spheres or networks into advantage in each new milieu. Had the war not intervened and forced the Joyces to flee Austria-Hungary, it is difficult to imagine an event as significant to his career as book publication of *A Portrait of the Artist as a Young Man* breaching the "class ceiling" of Habsburg Trieste. To the city's social and literary elites, the penniless English teacher would have appeared merely arriviste. (Writing to Stanislaus decades later about Italo Svevo, Joyce recalled having never visited the Triestine's home "except as a paid teacher."[14]) In Zurich, by contrast, publication opened numerous doors. Take the association with Claud Walter Sykes, the English actor with whom Joyce cofounded the English Players in 1918 and later a translator of First World War aviation literature and an agent of MI5. On nodding terms at the Museumsgesellschaft, Sykes and Joyce first encountered each other in early 1917 as skeptical parties to a get-rich-quick scheme. A friendship developed, despite the unpromising start, and Joyce lent Sykes a copy of *Portrait*. The Englishman quickly realized that he was "privileged to have the friendship of a very great genius" and, by the end of the year, was fetching reading material for Joyce and overseeing typescript production on the early episodes of *Ulysses*.[15]

In the twelve months after the publication of *Portrait* on 29 December 1916, Joyce inscribed no fewer than half a dozen association and presentation copies of the work, leveraging his symbolic capital to a variety of ends: to solidify his connection with recent acquaintances, such as Edmund Brauchbar, a Swiss-Jewish silk manufacturer; to thank faithful standbys like Pound and Weaver; to

rebuff a nonsupporter, Grant Richards, who turned down the novel after having published *Dubliners*; to woo Gertrud Gradowski, a twentysomething trainee doctor for whom Joyce developed an infatuation late that year; or to reel in a potential benefactor, Edith Rockefeller McCormick. The usual account of Joyce's patronage by McCormick, the socialite daughter of the Standard Oil oilman, is of a largesse as unexpected as it was unsolicited. In Richard Ellmann's reading, the manager of Zurich's Eidgenössische Bank summons Joyce out of the blue in early 1918 to inform him that he is to receive a stipend of one thousand Swiss francs every month for a year. "Dazzled and perplexed by this gift," Joyce sets himself to unmasking his benefactor.[16] The reality is that Joyce had been priming McCormick since at least the preceding December. A week before gifting the Egoist *Portrait* to Gradowski, he sent a copy of the same edition to McCormick "with the writer's compliments" and, once patronage was secured, reciprocated with a steady stream of association copies from his oeuvre.[17] For Budgen, Joyce was "a great believer in his luck," but it is clear that he was also a firm believer in making his own luck.[18] Indeed, for a narrow window in mid-1919, Joyce was simultaneously cultivating no fewer than five benefactors—McCormick, John Quinn, Scofield Thayer, J. S. Watson, and Weaver—all of whom were largely ignorant of each other's contributions, and in whose name letters, inscribed copies, and manuscript materials were dispatched to the Baur au Lac luxury hotel or, further afield, radiated out from Zurich to London and New York in exchange for support, gifts of money, and legal counsel.

Living in Zurich not only retooled the interpersonal networks that sustained Joyce while he wrote *Ulysses* but also profoundly reconfigured the intertextual matrix at the very core of the work. Morton Dauwen Zabel has written appreciatively of Joyce as "a writer so intentionally derivative, affiliations are natural," but Swiss residency in wartime extended the range and character of his reading far beyond the personal pantheon of Flaubert, Ibsen, Dante, et al. that he had erected in late adolescence.[19] In part, this broadening was a function of improved means; in part, it was made possible by both the institutional and everyday resources to which Joyce gained access in Switzerland. His Zurich reading for *Ulysses* ranged from classical (especially Homeric) scholarship to the latest novels by contemporaries; from reference works such as the *Encyclopædia Britannica* and the *Dictionary of National Biography* to British and Irish newspapers from June 1904; and from eighteenth-century rag-paper volumes of Restoration drama sourced at the ZB to the handbills and throwaways of Swiss print culture. To be sure, Joyce took much of the novel from his memories of Edwardian Dublin and from lived wartime experience, but he supplemented direct observation, gossip, and epiphanic showings forth with the proceeds of an altogether more labor-intensive program of reading and note-taking.

As A. Walton Litz has noted, it was in Zurich that the "storytelling Homer" of Charles Lamb gave way to a more scholarly, encyclopedic approach to the *Odyssey*.[20] Joyce first encountered Lamb's *The Adventures of Ulysses* as a schoolboy in 1894 in an edition adapted to late Victorian sensibilities by the same John Cooke who, some fifteen years later, would include three poems from *Chamber Music* in his anthology *The Dublin Book of Irish Verse*. In August 1917, even as Joyce made ready to begin finalizing the early episodes of *Ulysses* for publication, this first exposure to the *Odyssey* was on his mind. He told Georges Borach, one of his English students, "The most beautiful, most human traits are contained in the *Odyssey*. I was twelve years old when we took up the Trojan War at school; only the *Odyssey* stuck in my memory."[21] In the course of the same conversation, he hinted at more recent reading informing his conception of the classical world: "Why was I always returning to this theme? Now *al mezzo del' camin* [sic] I find the subject of Odysseus the most human in world literature. Odysseus didn't want to go off to Troy; he knew that the official reason for the war, the dissemination of the culture of Hellas, was only a pretext for the Greek merchants, who were seeking new markets."[22]

Joyce's suspicion of economic drivers behind the Trojan War was, as Danis Rose and John O'Hanlon first proposed, a neat paraphrase of Walter Leaf's argument in *Troy: A Study in Homeric Geography* (1912): "The ostensible cause of war is almost always some point of honour; the ultimate cause is, almost without exception, economic. Who can say if the abduction of some fair queen was not the last straw which broke the Achaians' patience, and determined them to set out on the expedition which they must long before have planned? While they were fighting for trade, they may well have believed themselves to be fighting to revenge an insult."[23]

Leaf, a banker, classicist, and psychical researcher, was the foremost Homerist in Great Britain at the turn of the twentieth century. His re-creation of Achaean state expansionism in the ancient world must have looked prescient in war-torn Europe, but it was a rival scholar, Victor Bérard, whose name Joyce likely first encountered in *Troy* and who was to have the more far-reaching impact on *Ulysses*.[24] Evidence of extended note-taking from both *Troy* and Bérard's two-volume *Les Phéniciens et l'Odyssée* survives at the University at Buffalo, with Bérard's work either a corroboration of or else the ultimate source of Joyce's theory about the Semitic origins of the *Odyssey*. The Frenchman's inventive etymologies for place names in the ancient world likely appealed to Joyce, but *Les Phéniciens* also supplied him with a wealth of finer points and distinctions relating to the *Odyssey* (and, intriguingly, certain of their modern equivalents in *Ulysses*). For example, Molly's preference for French novels, which is divulged in "Calypso"—"Get another of Paul de Kock's," she instructs her husband. "Nice name he has"—ranks among the novel's less remarked-on Homeric correspondences.[25] The detail derives from Bérard's observation that Ithacan emigrants in Homer's time fueled a vogue for all things Egyptian when they returned home to the Greek island. Perhaps Joyce was struck by this epic correlate for the figure of the Irish returned Yank; importantly, however, the substitution of French novels for Egyptian cultural trappings was Bérard's own. In *Les Phéniciens*, he makes an explicit comparison of ancient Ithacans to their early twentieth-century counterparts, the so-called *Australiens* or Australian-ized Greeks who, their fortunes made in Sydney and Melbourne, returned to the Ionian island:

> C'est à eux que Port Vathy doit sa propreté, ses maisons confortables, sa salle de lecture, où les Ithaciens d'aujourd'hui viennent lire surtout les romans français—au temps d'Ulysse, dans leurs *megara*, ils s'intéressaient aux contes d'Égypte.

> [It is to them that Vathy owes its cleanliness, its comfortable houses, its reading room, where the Ithacans of today come to read French novels mainly—in Ulysses's day, in their palaces, they took an interest in tales of Egypt.][26]

The conceit of providing contemporary equivalents for classical precursors or side notes was not, then, original to Joyce, even if he did trace the Homeric correspondences with a thoroughness and wit far surpassing the parallels that are scattered across *Les Phéniciens*. Years later, Joyce was to acknowledge his wider debt to Bérard in suitably epic terms, pairing the scholar with another French contemporary whose writing had proven germinal for *Ulysses*: "Dans le cheval de bois emprunté à Dujardin, j'ai logé les guerriers volés à Victor Bérard" (In the wooden horse borrowed from Dujardin, I put the warriors stolen from Victor Bérard).[27] The reference, of course, is to Édouard Dujardin's *Les lauriers sont coupés*, a relic of Joyce's first brief stint on the European mainland in 1902–3 and a formative influence on his development of the interior monologue.[28] Implicit in this providential encounter with a work is the degree to which, for Joyce, location could play into composition.

Over the years he spent conceptualizing and writing *Ulysses*, periodic upheaval and new settlement exposed him to a much wider, much richer variety of material than any single, pro-longed residency could have. Ever a quick study, he took what he needed and moved on—upping sticks before stagnation should set in. As the Joyce family moved across the Continent, whether as economic migrants to Rome in 1906 or to Third Republic France fourteen years later or as displaced persons fleeing Austria-Hungary for Switzerland, each act of social, economic, or political transplant brought Joyce into contact with a different subset of the print sphere and with different agents and actors ready to be rallied to his cause. With the relocation, first, to Zurich and subsequently to Paris, writing *Ulysses* became less a retreat to the privacy of the literary workshop than almost a

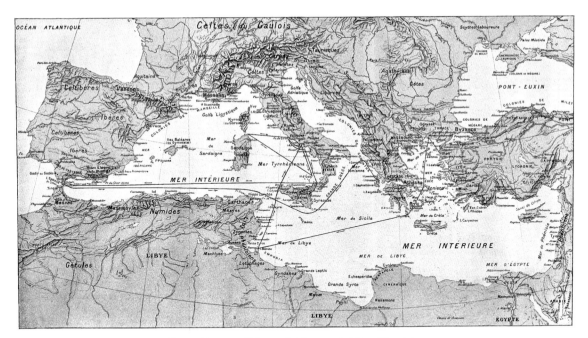

Fig. 4.6. Voyages of Ulysses, folding map in Victor Bérard, *Les Phéniciens et l'Odyssée*, 1902–3. Princeton University Library.

group undertaking—both interpersonally and intertextually—as mounting celebrity placed Joyce at the center of an ever-widening circle of fetchers and carriers, deputies and intermediaries who sourced books or read material on his behalf, chipped in money, typed up manuscripts, or interceded with publishers and the press, forming, in effect, the professional buffer between him and the world that would characterize the long years of "Work in Progress."

Fig. 5.1. Man Ray, photograph of James Joyce, 1922. The Morgan Library &
Museum, New York. Gift of Sean and Mary Kelly, 2018.

CATHERINE FLYNN

5. Joyce in Paris, 1920–1922

In April 1922, two months after the publication of *Ulysses*, at a Paris café that Verlaine and Mallarmé had frequented in the nineteenth century and that would become a central meeting place for Surrealists and Existentialists, the American artist and novelist Djuna Barnes wrote of meeting James Joyce: "Sitting in the cafe of the Deux Magots, that faces the little church of Saint Germain-des-Prés, I saw approaching, out of the fog and damp, a tall man, with head slightly lifted and slightly turned, giving to the wind an orderly distemper of red and black hair, which descended sharply into a scant wedge on an out-thrust chin."[1]

Barnes gives us an image of an embattled but defiant figure. Meeting the author of the novel that had provoked obscenity trials, Barnes portrays Joyce as a kind of martyr: "At the moment of seeing him, a remark made to me by a mystic flashed through my mind 'A man who has been more crucified on his sensibilities than any writer of our age,' and I said to myself—'this is a strange way to recognize a man I never laid my eyes on.'" Barnes herself thus remarks on the fanciful nature of her assessment. Joyce indeed identified this as a general tendency: "'Nobody,' said Joyce, 'seems to be inclined to present me to the world in my unadorned prosaicness.'"[2] His biographer Richard Ellmann notes that, at the time, "Journalists indulged their fancy freely, and mentioned his daily swim in the Seine, the mirrors with which he surrounded himself while he worked, the black gloves he wore when he went to bed. These rumors he at once resented and enjoyed."[3] Noticing Barnes's fascination with his waistcoat—"the most delightful waistcoat it has ever been my happiness to see. Purple with alternate doe and dog heads"—he smiled and remarked,

"'Made by the hand of my grandmother for the first hunt of the season' and there was another silence in which he arranged and lit a cigar."[4] Inheritance, apart from this heirloom and a couple portraits, had not featured in Joyce's life.[5] On the Parisian Left Bank, in some degree of material comfort, he playfully constructs a new self. Paris was, for Joyce, a uniquely supportive environment and perhaps the only city in the world where *Ulysses* could come to fruition and find publication.

Who was Joyce when he moved to Paris in July 1920? By that time, he had lived away from Ireland for almost sixteen years. Sylvia Beach, the owner of the bookstore Shakespeare and Company, noticed the persistence of an Irish "timbre" in his voice.[6] The Joyces had passed the First World War in the neutral city of Zurich. Ten years in the Austro-Hungarian city of Trieste meant that Joyce and his children, as well as his partner, Nora Barnacle, spoke the local dialect, Triestino, at home. By 1920, he had seen the publication of a number of works: a book of poetry, *Chamber Music* (1907); of short stories, *Dubliners* (1914); a novel, *A Portrait of the Artist as a Young Man* (1916); and a play, *Exiles* (1918). Excerpts of *Ulysses* had been appearing in serialized form since 1918 in the American journal *Little Review* and had featured in the *Egoist*, a London literary review, in 1919. Joyce thus had a reputation among literati, but it was in Paris that he would become famous.

Joyce had spent four months in Paris as a young man. In *James Joyce and the Matter of Paris*, I argue that he was drawn to the city as the contemporary center of literary innovation. By the age of twenty, he was already versed in the groundbreaking literature of the *poètes maudits* and the scandalous works of Émile Zola.[7] The young Joyce struggled and starved in Paris, yet the scattered writings he produced there formed the basis for his later works.

The aesthetic essay that Joyce would attribute to Stephen Dedalus in *Portrait*, the poems that would become part of *Chamber Music*, the epiphanies that would be reworked in *Ulysses* all grappled in different ways with the aesthetic challenge Joyce encountered in Paris: to reconceive of the role of art in a world structured by consumer capitalism.

This first period in Paris is anticipated by Stephen Dedalus as he is poised for exile at the end of *Portrait*, and it is the subject of his reminiscences in *Ulysses*. One of his most evocative memories of Paris in *Ulysses* is of an Irish expatriate: "Son of the wild goose, Kevin Egan of Paris."[8] Joyce based Egan closely on Joseph Theobald Casey of the Irish Republican Brotherhood, who left for Paris after being cleared of involvement in the IRB attempt to dynamite him out of Clerkenwell Prison, where he was being detained for his role in the Manchester Rescue of September 1867. Joyce befriended Casey and his son Patrice, and in *Ulysses*, he depicts Egan as a lost man, "unsought by any save by me.... Loveless, landless, wifeless."[9] His teeth green from absinthe, Egan lives east of Montmartre on rue de la Goutte-d'Or ("of the drop of gold"), while his former wife lives happily with "two buck lodgers" on the rue Gît-le-Coeur ("here lies the heart"),[10] a ten-minute walk from Les Deux Magots.

Joyce's decision to return to the French capital in 1920 was largely based on economic concerns. In Trieste, after the war, he was beset by material difficulties. Prices had increased almost tenfold since 1914. "I live in a flat with eleven other people and have had great difficulty in securing time and peace enough to write those two chapters," he wrote to Ezra Pound, who had been spending time in Paris and suggested it as an affordable alternative.[11] Although Joyce had been considering London and Dublin, the favorable postwar French exchange rate

Fig. 5.2. Wyndham Lewis, portrait of Harriet Shaw Weaver, 1925. Pencil on paper. The Poetry Collection of the University Libraries, University at Buffalo, The State University of New York.

attracted him. Even then, Joyce wrote to his patron Harriet Shaw Weaver that he had come to Paris for only "three months to write the last adventure Circe in peace (?) and also the first episode of the close. . . . I am very tired of it and so is everybody else."[12] Soon after his move, Weaver gifted him a further two thousand pounds, announcing that she wanted to free his "best and most powerful and productive years" from material worries.[13]

This relative comfort was an ironic contrast to the four impoverished months Joyce spent in Paris from November 1902 to April 1903. During that period, he wrote almost daily to his family of his financial worries. His ostensible project of studying medicine abandoned due to a lack of funds, he walked the streets of Paris hungrily, composing short works that proved to be seminal to his later writings. Returning to Paris in 1920, Joyce would stay until the German invasion in 1939. His early, lonely starvation was replaced by familial feasting at venues such as the Left Bank restaurant Michaud's, as witnessed by Ernest Hemingway.[14] This curative excess accompanied the burgeoning of *Ulysses*; in the French capital, the book grew more capacious, ambitious, and assured.

There were many reasons why *Ulysses* flourished in Paris. As Joyce wrote to his brother Stanislaus soon after he arrived, "Odyssey very much in the air here. Anatole France is writing *Le Cyclope*, G. Fauré the musician an opera *Penelope*. Giraudoux has written Elpenor (Paddy Dignam). Guillaume Apollinaire *Les Mamelles de Tirésias*.'"[15] Ellmann remarks, "It was a new and heady feeling to discover he was a leader in a movement."[16] Yet this movement existed independently of Joyce; in postwar Paris, Homer's epic of homecoming and recovery after the long Trojan war spoke to writers, musicians, and poets. In these *années folles*, the ten years after the war, the city attracted writers and artists of many nationalities. This bustling scene featured Pablo Picasso, Marc Chagall, and the American expatriates called the Lost Generation by Gertrude Stein, including Ernest Hemingway, F. Scott Fitzgerald, Djuna Barnes, and Jean Rhys, as well as frequent visitors such as T. S. Eliot and Wyndham Lewis, and, disenchanted with imperial London, Pound himself.

If these and other significant figures mingled in the Left Bank, Joyce avoided most of them. "Joyce has few friends," Barnes notes.[17] Stein, who held one of the most important salons in Paris, responded monosyllabically to Joyce's remark on how odd it was not to have met, since they lived in the same quartier.[18] Yet her intense competitiveness is described by Hemingway: "If you brought up Joyce twice, you would not be invited back. . . . You could always mention a general, though, that the general you were talking to had beaten. The general you were talking to would praise the beaten general greatly and go happily into detail on how he had beaten him."[19] Joyce's encounter with Marcel Proust, too, was fraught, as reported variously; one version depicted Joyce trembling with rage at Proust's love of aristocracy.[20] These giants of modernism lived in close proximity to one another, in relations of silent and productive rivalry.

Joyce wrote to Frank Budgen of his own awkwardness: "It seems to me I have made a bad impression here. I am too preoccupied (Bloomesque word) to rectify it."[21] However, he enjoyed a Left Bank literary network that was less public than the salons and far more important, providing him with everything he needed. Pound contacted Ludmila Bloch-Savitsky to translate *Portrait*, for which she arranged a contract with Éditions de la Sirène. She also lent her flat; the Joyces had been staying in cramped quarters at the Hotel Lenox on the rue de l'Université and enjoyed three and a half months in her apartment in the sixteenth district (although Joyce called it a "matchbox").[22] Her friend André Spire, a poet, organized an "afternoon supper" for Joyce and invited various literary friends, including Adrienne Monnier, owner of the bookstore La Maison des Amis des Livres, who brought her partner, Sylvia Beach, despite Beach's reservations about attending the party of someone she didn't know personally. From their first encounter, Beach showed a tactful understanding of Joyce. He, alone, did not drink at the afternoon meal, going so far as to turn his glass upside down as a signal to Spire; in

Fig. 5.3. John Rodker, James Joyce, Sylvia Beach, and Cyprian
Beach in the Shakespeare and Company bookshop, 1921. Special
Collections Research Center, Morris Library, Southern Illinois
University Carbondale.

response, Pound lined up every wine bottle in front of him, to the great amusement of the other guests. Away from the main conversation, Joyce confided in Beach that he had resolved not to drink before eight in the evening.[23] Her support became essential to him. If Joyce told Lewis that Paris was "'the last of the human cities' guarding its intimacy in spite of its size,"[24] it was largely because of Beach and her bookstore. All of the apartments in which he stayed during this period were within a ten-kilometer radius of the shop. He visited it daily to borrow books, cash checks, hear Beach's accounts of literary Paris, and talk with her about progress on *Ulysses*.

The unusual conjunction in Shakespeare and Company of an English-speaking supporter and the Parisian literary scene was crucial to the publication and reception of *Ulysses*. France was perhaps the *only* place at the time in which it could be published. An obscenity trial began in New York in February 1921 following a complaint, lodged by the secretary of the New York Society for the Suppression of Vice, regarding an excerpt of the "Nausicaa" episode in the July–August 1920 issue of the *Little Review*. The journal was found guilty, its editors were fined, and *Ulysses* was effectively banned in the United States. Despite having published *Portrait* and *Dubliners*,

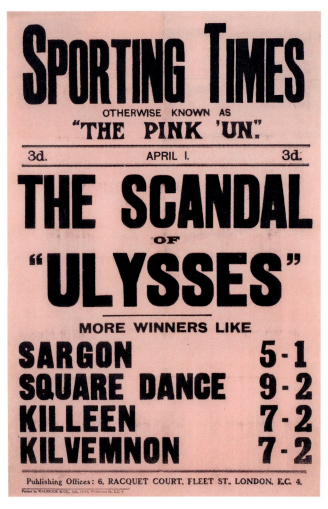

SPORTING TIMES

OTHERWISE KNOWN AS
"THE PINK 'UN."

3d.   APRIL 1.   3d.

THE SCANDAL
OF
"ULYSSES"

MORE WINNERS LIKE

SARGON	5 - 1
SQUARE DANCE	9 - 2
KILLEEN	7 - 2
KILVEMNON	7 - 2

Publishing Offices: 6, RACQUET COURT, FLEET ST., LONDON, E.C. 4.
Printed by WALBROOK & CO., Ltd., 13-19, Whitefriars St., E.C. 4

Fig. 5.4. *Sporting Times* poster, 1 April 1922. The Poetry Collection of the University Libraries, University at Buffalo, The State University of New York.

the New York publisher B. W. Huebsch requested revisions, which Joyce refused to make, causing Huebsch to refuse to publish it. It was immediately following that disappointment that Beach offered to publish *Ulysses*. An article in the international *Chicago Tribune* subsequently reported, "it is said that [*Ulysses*'s] present publication may mean that Miss Beach will not be allowed to return to America."[25] Weaver abandoned her plan to publish it in England because of English publishers' fear of prosecution.[26] English reviewers expressed distaste far more extreme than Virginia Woolf's; she had refused to publish *Ulysses* with Hogarth Press, describing it in her diary as "the book of a self-taught working man . . . egotistic, insistent, raw, striking, & ultimately nauseating."[27] An article by "Aramis" in the *Sporting Times*, titled "The Scandal of *Ulysses*," protests that Joyce "has ruled out all the elementary decencies of life and dwells appreciatively on things that sniggering louts of schoolboys guffaw about."[28] The poet and critic Edmund Gosse wrote in a letter to Louis Gillet, "Mr. Joyce is unable to publish or sell his books in England, on account of their obscenity. He therefore issues a 'private' edition in Paris, and charges a huge price for each copy. He is a sort of Marquis de Sade, but does not write so well."[29]

Gosse was correct both about the luxury edition and about Paris as a literary scene accustomed to obscene material. France was considered an epicenter of obscenity in the sixteenth and seventeenth centuries. Many of the greatest artistic works of the nineteenth century tested public mores. Two of the greatest triggered obscenity trials: Baudelaire's *Les fleurs du mal* and Gustave Flaubert's *Madame Bovary*. Émile Zola's writing was internationally famous for its frank depiction of sexuality. Beach chose as the printer for *Ulysses* Maurice

Fig. 5.5. Sylvia Beach and James Joyce in the Shakespeare and Company bookshop, ca. 1926. The Poetry Collection of the University Libraries, University at Buffalo, The State University of New York.

Darantiere, the son of the printer of Joris-Karl Huysmans's scandalous Decadent novel, *À rebours*, which was referred to by anglophone readers as the "Yellow Book" and used to undermine Oscar Wilde's reputation in his prosecution for gross indecency.

Robert Spoo describes the strategy of the deluxe edition as a means to evade censorship. In the nineteenth century, handsomely designed limited editions pitched to wealthy and sophisticated readers were considered to be released from the standards of decency necessary for the ordinary reader.[30] This strategy was followed with *Ulysses*:

Beach proposed a thousand copies of the first edition, which went on sale through advance subscription. One hundred copies would be printed on handmade Holland paper, signed by the author, and made available for purchase at 350 francs. A further 150 copies, on expensive *vergé d'Arches* paper, would sell for 250 francs. The remaining 750 copies, which were the first to be printed and were on more affordable linen paper, would sell for 150 francs. Ellmann notes, "Joyce was to receive the astonishing royalty of 66% of the net profits."[31]

The intensity of Beach's support for Joyce is made clear in her letter to the wealthy Irish-American

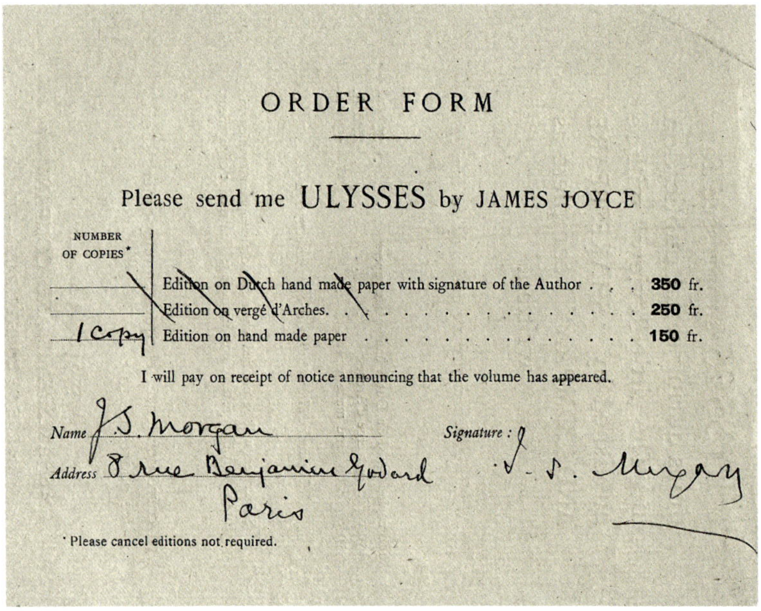

ORDER FORM

Please send me ULYSSES by JAMES JOYCE

NUMBER
OF COPIES*

_____ | Edition on Dutch hand made paper with signature of the Author . . **350** fr.

_____ | Edition on vergé d'Arches . . . . **250** fr.

1 copy | Edition on hand made paper . . . . **150** fr.

I will pay on receipt of notice announcing that the volume has appeared.

Name *J. S. Morgan*   Signature :

Address *8 rue Benjamin Godard*
          Paris

* Please cancel editions not required.

Fig. 5.6. Junius Spencer Morgan,
order form for the first edition
of *Ulysses*, ca. 1922. The Poetry
Collection of the University Libraries,
University at Buffalo, The State
University of New York.

lawyer John Quinn: "I give [Joyce] everything I can spare but as you may imagine my shop has not been in existence long enough to support a family of four people as well as myself. . . . It is up to all of us who want the most important book of today to appear to come to the help of its author."[32] Quinn was buying in installments from Joyce the manuscript of *Ulysses* in fair copy and refused to give him any other money. Beach's extraordinary generosity was closely tied to her sense of involvement in an artistic venture that elevated Shakespeare and Company. Prior to 1921, few American writers had visited the bookstore, but it gained fame through its association with Joyce's book. She wrote to her mother, "*Ulysses* means thousands of dollars in publicity for me"; "*Ulysses* is going to make my place famous"; "Already the publicity is beginning and swarms of people visit the shop on hearing the news. I'm getting out a bulletin . . . and if all goes well I hope to make money out of it, not only for Joyce but for me. Aren't you excited?"[33] She later declared that she sold more copies of Joyce's books than of any other writer.[34]

A crucial event in the advance publicity for *Ulysses* was a lecture on 7 December 1921, in French, at Monnier's bookstore by Valery Larbaud, one of the most important and well-regarded literary figures in France at the time. Joyce met this "godfather" of Shakespeare and Company on Christmas Eve 1920, four days after he had completed the first draft of "Circe."[35] Larbaud declared, "The *Circe* episode alone would make the reputation of a French writer for life."[36] It was, indeed, in terms of the French heritage of literary obscenity that he recognized Joyce's achievement, declaring that the book was as "great and comprehensive and human as Rabelais."[37] He included a warning in the lecture program: "Certain pages have an uncommon boldness of expression that might quite legitimately be shocking."

Two hundred and fifty people attended the lecture at La Maison des Amis des Livres. Admission fees were charged and given to Joyce. Larbaud had commissioned translations of excerpts from "Sirens" and "Penelope" and hired an actor to read original passages from "Sirens." His lecture helped

Maurice Darantiere
maistre imprimeur
a Dijon

2.249

dix huit a v r i l 1921

Miss Sylvia B e a c h
P a r i s (VI°)
rue Dupuytren, 8

D e v i s d'impression pour un volume in-4° couronne (format
des Cahiers de la Maison des Amis des Livres)

Prix de la feuille de seize pages comprenant composition, mise
en pages, mise en train, tirage et façonnage:
fr..... 274, 40 pour mille exemplaires, composition en romain
didot de neuf.

le manuscrit de Ulysses comprenant environ 500 pages dactylogra-
phiées fournirait environ 37 feuilles de 16 pages: 592 pages.
Avec le romain elzévir de dix dont nous vous remettons aussi un
spécimen, on arriverait à 720 pages. Mieux vaut s'en tenir au
didot romain de neuf.

La justification du tirage est   hollande.... 100 ex.
                                  vergé d'Arches.... 150 ex.
                                  pur fil.... 750 ex.

37 feilles à fr. 274, 40............. 10.152, 80
papiers texte....................... 16.823, 16 +
couverture, environ..................   400 -
placards, environ....................   500 -

les corrections d'auteur pourront être exécutées sur le manuscrit avant la mise en composition. Les corrections ultérieures
seront facturées (celles d'auteur seulement) fr. 4, 75 l'heure.

Maurice Darantiere

Maurice D a r a n t i e r e

Fig. 5.7. Maurice Darantiere to Sylvia Beach, 18 April 1921. Typed letter signed. The Poetry Collection of the University Libraries, University at Buffalo, The State University of New York.

Parisian literati to see the significance of *Ulysses* and, perhaps more importantly at this early moment, to understand how to make sense of its unprecedentedly difficult prose. Using the Homeric schema that Joyce had given him as an entry point,[38] Larbaud announced, "We begin to discover and to anticipate symbols, a design, a plan, in what appeared to us at first a brilliant but confused mass of notations, phrases, data, profound thoughts, fantasticalities, splendid images, absurdities, comic or dramatic situations."[39] His lecture was subsequently pub-

lished in the influential and prestigious literary magazine *Nouvelle Revue Française*.

Beach observed, "Such generosity and unselfishness toward a fellow writer as Larbaud showed to Joyce is indeed rare."[40] Joyce wrote to his father that "it cannot be denied that the greater part of my reputation is due to the generous admiration of French writers here."[41] Larbaud's lecture did not just promote the novel; it acted as a galvanizing writing deadline. It also had a deeper motivating effect on Joyce, which was further augmented by the loan the

Fig. 5.8. Déjeuner "Ulysse," Hôtel Léopold, Les Vaux de Cernay, 27 June 1929. The Poetry Collection of the University Libraries, University at Buffalo, The State University of New York.

wealthy but retiring Larbaud had made of his plush apartment in the fifth district from June to October 1921. "Is it possible that I am worth something? Who would have said so after my last experience in Trieste?" Joyce wrote to his friend Alessandro Francini Bruni.[42]

It was within this context of support, license, and rivalry that Joyce effected the massive and rapid development of the manuscript of *Ulysses*. Critics often point to the end of serialization in the *Little Review*, which granted Joyce freedom from deadlines and word limits, as the reason for the remarkable expansion of the manuscript in Paris. Yet in the French capital, Joyce wrote *more* quickly and in groundbreaking ways. In a little over a year, he realized "Circe" and wrote "Eumaeus," "Ithaca," and "Penelope," the four most stylistically adventurous and intellectually demanding episodes of the novel. While Joyce referred to preexisting notes, the episodes developed in unexpected ways as he repeatedly rewrote them. He worked such long hours that he suffered attacks of exhaustion and iritis. Following a break of five weeks and a regimen of cocaine for the pain in his eyes, he wrote to Weaver on 7 August, "I write and revise and correct with one or two eyes about twelve hours a day I should say, stopping for intervals of five minutes or so when I can't see any more. My brain reels after it."[43] By September 1920, he referred to "the enormous bulk and the more than enormous complexity of my damned monster-novel."[44]

In "Circe," *Ulysses* becomes self-reflexive. As Bloom and Stephen experience the red-light district of "Nighttown," events from the fourteen preceding episodes appear again in hallucinatory form. Having returned to the city that earlier posed with such power the question of the nature of art in the world of exchange, Joyce replays his novel in the most intense locus of capitalism, refracting its encounters through the lens of commercial profit. In Bella Cohen's brothel, Stephen tells the women about the Heaven and Hell Club in Montmartre. Paris features not just in the episode's events, however, but also in its form. In 1903, Joyce bought Édouard Dujardin's novel *Les lauriers sont coupés*, whose "monologue intérieur" provided the basic form for the initial style of *Ulysses*, and in the teeming Paris of 1920, Joyce mingled elements of other French texts to heady effect in "Circe": the hallucinatory play-script of Flaubert's *La tentation de saint Antoine*; the urban visionary texts of Gérard de Nerval and Arthur Rimbaud; the manic performance of mass production in Apollinaire's *Les mamelles de Tirésias*. Bloom's dialogue with the soap, his visions of redemption and abjection, and his birthing of multiple profitable children are inspired by these works.

Critics have discussed the centrality of Flaubert's farcical encyclopedia *Bouvard et Pécuchet* in the late episodes.[45] Flaubert's parody of the Enlightenment desire for objective truth finds elaboration in the periphrastic clichés of "Eumaeus"; his satire of its drive toward total knowledge finds new articulation in the ponderous

Fig. 5.9. Alfred Jarry, *Véritable portrait de Monsieur Ubu*. Woodcut in Jarry's *Ubu roi: Drame en cinq actes en prose*, 1896. The Morgan Library & Museum, New York. Gift of Robert J. and Linda Klieger Stillman, 2017.

scientism of "Ithaca." In these later episodes, Joyce also draws on other French writers, notably the nineteenth-century absurdist Alfred Jarry, around whom a scandal arose in 1921 and whose lover, Léon-Paul Fargue, was a regular at Shakespeare and Company. Jarry's obscene neologisms can be traced in Molly Bloom's thoughts in "Penelope."

"Penelope" functions as a grand retort to Joyce's writings, during his first period in the city, on materialistic transactions on the Parisian boulevard.

Epiphany 33, one of his earliest prose poems, is the first of many Joycean scenes in which a male figure reflects on an erotically appealing woman. "Penelope," however, is centered on the perspective of a woman who has consciously been the recipient of many versions of the male gaze and who actively courts male desire. This deep history of Molly's monologue underlies Joyce's somewhat cryptic comments regarding the real-life inspiration for Molly: "Joyce used to tease [two younger American friends] by saying that Molly Bloom was sitting at another table in the restaurant, and they would try to guess which woman she was, always without success. This game he continued for years."[46] Molly is an amalgam of many people; in this story she is everywhere and nowhere in Paris. Her Parisian provenance also appears in the origins of the famous last words of the episode: the repetition of "yes" in various tones by Joyce's Paris friend Lillian Wallace, and the affirmative final word proposed by Jacques Benoist-Méchin in his French translation, "*je veux oui.*"[47]

Alongside his composition of the later episodes, Joyce amended the earlier ones, augmenting the Homeric references and adding new material. His expansion of the Odyssean parallels was undoubtedly a response to the Parisian interest in Homer's epic; the additional new material was also prompted by French texts. Inspired by Jarry's parody of the mass-market author Pierre Loti, Joyce expanded the passage in "Calypso" in which Bloom reads "Matcham's Masterstroke" in the outhouse; while the 1918 *Little Review* version is brief and discreet, the final version in *Ulysses* is boldly explicit, as Joyce notoriously intermingles in one sentence Bloom's reading and defecation, echoing Jarry's "Mort de Latente Obscure," which alternates descriptions of the bishop's bowel movement with lines he reads in Loti's "Tante Claire nous quitte."[48]

Joyce wrote between one-fifth and one-third of *Ulysses* on proofs, having received the first galleys from Darantiere on 10 June. Beach described the intensity of this process: "Every proof was covered with additional text . . . adorned with Joycean rockets and myriads of stars guiding the printers to words and phrases and lists of names all around the margins."[49] Her support continued despite the costs involved: "The printing had begun on our beautiful handmade paper, the printers would receive a telegram with several extra lines to insert. . . . [I] would never have dreamed of controlling its great author—so 'gave him his head.'"[50]

Only the deadline of his fortieth birthday brought a halt to Joyce's labor. On 2 February 1922, two copies of *Ulysses* arrived on the 7:00 a.m. train from Dijon. Joyce presented one to Beach, who displayed it in Shakespeare and Company: "Everyone crowded in from nine o'clock until closing time to see it."[51] Displayed in the window, the book continued to cause scenes. Beach saw the writer and Catholic convert Paul Claudel "stop at her shop window, glance at the *Ulysses* display, cross himself and hurry on past"; he later returned a signed copy with the comment that it was "devilish."[52] Other French writers were unappreciative. Paul Valéry was indifferent; André Gide described it as "a sham masterpiece."[53] Yet *Ulysses* was now launched. On 6 October, after he had finished the "Penelope" episode, Joyce wrote "Trieste – Zurich – Paris" as the last words of the book. A list of the cities of its composition, it is also an account of its widening area of impact, one that Paris helped extend to the world.

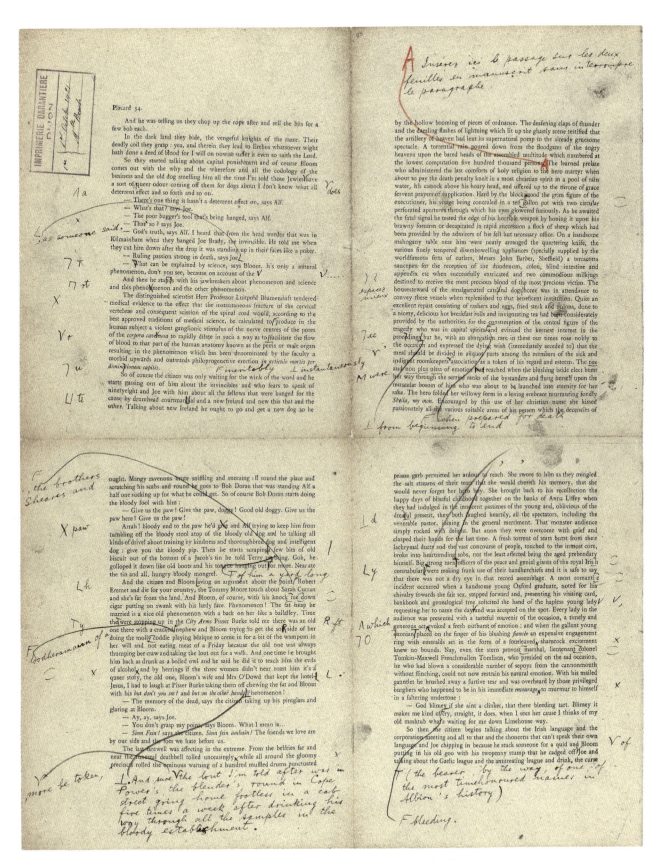

Fig. 5.10. James Joyce, "Cyclops" placard, 1 October 1921. Houghton Library, Harvard University. © The Estate of James Joyce.

Stately, plump Buck Mulligan came from the stairhead, bearing a bowl of lather on which a mirror and a razor lay crossed. A yellow dressinggown, ungirdled, was sustained gently behind him by the mild morning air. He held the bowl aloft and intoned:

— Introibo ad altare Dei.

Halted, he peered down the dark winding stairs, and called out coarsely:

— Come up, Kinch! Come up, you fearful jesuit!

MARIA DIBATTISTA

6. Revisioning *Ulysses*

"Stately, plump"—so with all due pomp *Ulysses* strolled into the modern world, bidding, through the portentous personage of Buck (Malachi) Mulligan, the world to make way. The world, wavering between astonishment and outrage, was unsure whether it was ready, or even right, to do so. Early installments published in the American avant-garde magazine *Little Review* piqued the curiosity of readers—but also aroused the zeal of censors. Agents of the U.S. Post Office, alerted to the apparent licentiousness of "Lestrygonians," "Scylla and Charybdis," and "Cyclops," seized and burned the issues in which they appeared. The "Sirens" episode was suppressed on

Fig. 6.1. James Joyce, *Ulysses*, "Telemachus" episode, page 1, Zurich [September–October 1917]. Autograph manuscript. The Rosenbach, Philadelphia (EL4 J89ul 922 MS). © The Estate of James Joyce.

different grounds. It was confiscated by British war censors who suspected the strangely worded text of being a nefarious piece of coded espionage.[1] Harriet Shaw Weaver's *Egoist*, the short-lived (1914–19) but influential literary magazine that pledged not to "recognize any taboos," managed to publish three installments before it had to abandon further serialization, owing to the difficulty in finding typists willing to transcribe Joyce's often undecipherable hand or printers to set typescripts studded with arrows and inserts that mystified as much as scandalized them.[2] Weaver still hoped to publish the novel under an English imprint, but the publishing houses she approached, including Virginia and Leonard Woolf's newly established Hogarth Press, declined.

At this critical juncture Sylvia Beach extended a now legendary invitation: "Would you let Shakespeare and Company have the honor of bringing out

Fig. 6.2. James Joyce and Sylvia Beach in the doorway of Shakespeare and Company, 1921. The Poetry Collection of the University Libraries, University at Buffalo, The State University of New York.

your *Ulysses*?"[3] Thanks largely to her timely intervention and entrepreneurial stamina, *Ulysses* was published, as Joyce was determined it would be, on his birthday, 2 February 1922. The first edition, error-filled but resplendent in its blue cover, sold out in little over a month. Subsequent editions, including the Egoist Press edition published in October that year in England, would continue to be plagued by errors, piracy—Samuel Roth, who illicitly trafficked in both high modernist (Aldous Huxley and André Gide) and pornographic literature, was the most successful and persistent offender[4]—and periodic confiscations both in the United States and in England.[5] Campaigns against *Ulysses* only began to relent with Judge Woolsey's 1933 ruling that "whilst in many places the effect of *Ulysses* on the reader undoubtedly is somewhat emetic, nowhere does it tend to be an aphrodisiac"[6] and therefore could be admitted into the United States. Bennett Cerf, the cofounder of Random

House who had connived to have the book brought to trial, received the news of the decision by phone. Within minutes, typesetters were at work setting text from Roth's 1929 edition, a pirated and corrupt version of Shakespeare and Company's ninth printing.[7] Although *Ulysses* would not be legally available in Britain until 1936, Woolsey's finding effectively granted *Ulysses* right of way through what T. S. Eliot called "the vast panorama of futility and anarchy that is contemporary history."

It was, however, no straight path that led Joyce to "the mythic method" that, by "manipulating a continuous parallel between antiquity and contemporaneity," had made, so Eliot proclaimed, "the modern world possible for art."[8] It took nearly twenty thousand hours[9] spread over eight years and three cities—"Trieste – Zurich – Paris, 1914–1921"—to realize that possibility. The composure of the novel's opening thus strikes a pose that camouflages its erratic genesis. The seed of the novel was implanted by an accident dating to 1904 that was as fateful, if not as personally consequential, as Joyce's meeting with Nora Barnacle. It appears that Mr Leopold Bloom, in whom the ghost of Odysseus is reputed to walk, had a real-life antecedent in a Mr J Hunter, who may or may not have been a Jew, may or may not have been a cuckold, but who apparently did rescue the young Joyce, as Bloom will rescue Stephen Dedalus, one night as he lay sprawled drunk in a Dublin gutter.[10] Two years after the incident, Joyce wrote his brother Stanislaus that he had a new story in mind for *Dubliners*. It was to be called "Ulysses" and was to "deal with Mr Hunter."[11]

But the project seemed stalled, if not stillborn, for "Ulysses," as Joyce confessed the following year, "never got any forrader than the title."[12] Perhaps Joyce could not bring himself to write of a modern Ulysses, a hero he had venerated since childhood, in

Fig. 6.3. Marie Monnier-Bécat, Shakespeare and Company signboard. Enamel on metal. Special Collections, Princeton University Library.

the same style of "scrupulous meanness" he adopted in dissecting the "moral history" of contemporary Dubliners.[13] Although Joyce, a fervid Ibsenite, briefly considered recasting "Ulysses" as "a Dublin 'Peer Gynt,'"[14] the idea of reincarnating Ulysses on the streets of Dublin lay dormant until 1914. Only then did the narrative that Joyce first envisioned, then abandoned as a short narrative and later revived as a possible sequel to *A Portrait of the Artist as a Young Man*,[15] assume the character and trajectory of a prose epic of modern life.

Both the character and trajectory would alter many times before the novel was published. Chapters serialized in the *Little Review* and the

Egoist were substantially revised for book publication. Even after heavily edited typescripts had been sent to Darantiere, the French printer who knew no English, Joyce continued to make extensive edits in his often-undecipherable hand. Michael Groden notes that "for some pages there are as many as thirteen different stages of development, beginning with the manuscript from which the typescript was prepared and ending with the published text."[16] He goes on to remark that roughly one-third of the novel was revised and amplified in the *placards*—single large sheets on which are printed eight unnumbered pages—and final page proofs.[17]

Nor were these edits and additions strictly of the kind that refine the "sense" of material verging on the inchoate. Joyce's art, like Shakespeare's, was "the art of surfeit";[18] plumpness more than clarity was a prime objective of his obsessive editing. Yet *Ulysses* also stands as a monument to Joyce's art of rule, of ordering as well as provisioning the literary domain he claimed as his own. The presumption of artistic sovereignty is implied in Stephen's mirthless conjecture "that Ireland must be important because it belongs to me."[19] But what is an aspirational, dubious, and quickly abandoned claim for Stephen is, for Joyce, a statement of accomplished fact: reality provides the details, he the novelistic world where they assume significance and value. To that end, nothing was too mundane (a bar of lemon soap), too abject (a piece of snot), too absurd (an ad for Plumtree's Potted Meat among obituary notices), or too lewd (Bloom's masturbating, Molly's sexual fantasies) to be denied a place—or a meaning—in his fiction. Late-stage typescripts and proof pages whose margins are overrun with arrows and inserted phrases show how relentlessly Joyce worked to find room for

what Wyndham Lewis, impressed but bewailing such Rabelaisian extravagance, called "this stupendous outpouring of *matter*, or *stuff*."[20]

Lewis looked upon this torrent of indiscriminate matter as "the very nightmare" of Joyce's naturalistic, not mythic, method and wished, "on the spot, to be transported to some more abstract region for a time."[21] The two methods were indissociable, however: Joyce the mythographer worked in tandem with Joyce the fact-checker. "Local colour. Work in all you know. Make them accomplices"[22] is the first artistic principle Stephen propounds in "Scylla and Charybdis." Joyce was faithful to this naturalist credo, sedulously verifying the names and circumstantial details pertaining to those real-life people, places, and events he wrote into his novel. This appeal to his Aunt Josephine for information exemplifies how meticulously Joyce observed the strictures of verisimilitude:

> I want that information about the Star of the Sea Church, has it ivy on its seafront, are there trees in Leahy's terrace at the side or near, if so, what, are there steps leading to the beach? I also want all the information you can give, tittle tattle, fact etc about Hollis Street maternity hospital. Two chapters of my book remain unfinished till I have these so I shall feel very grateful if you will sacrifice a few hours of your time for me and write me a long letter with details.[23]

No chapter was considered complete without the tittle tattle that speaks of the things and habits, the sights and sounds, often unremarked until someone gets them wrong, that assure us that the world of the novel is not only real but *actual*.

For the author who ventured that God was manifest in a "shout in the street,"[24] such humdrum information was the *prima materia* of creation. Joyce

Fig. 6.4. James Joyce, caricature of Leopold Bloom, ca. 1923. Pencil drawing on paper. McCormick Library of Special Collections, Northwestern University Libraries. © The Estate of James Joyce.

composed *Ulysses* with an eye for accuracy that would satisfy not only the town gossip but also the municipal engineer. Frank Budgen, Joyce's artistic whetstone during his years in Zurich, recounts how Joyce "wrote the 'Wandering Rocks' with a map of Dublin before him on which were traced in red ink the paths of the Earl of Dudley and Father Conmee. He calculated to a minute the time necessary for his characters to cover a given distance of the city."[25] Joyce made equally precise notations of the data he mined from civic records (*Thom's Official Directory of the United Kingdom of Great Britain and Ireland* was a particularly fertile source) and winnowed from newspapers, not easy to get in wartime Zurich, issued on or just before 16 June 1904, most notably the *Evening Telegraph*, in whose newsroom the "Aeolus" episode is set, and the *Freeman's Journal*, for which Bloom canvasses and whose racing column reported Throwaway as the winner of the Ascot Gold Cup race, a fact Joyce transposed into the novel as a runaway motif coursing around Bloom, the novel's designated "dark horse."[26]

Ulysses is not just cluttered with the mundane particulars writers less alert to their signifying power might throw away. It is also plumped up with arcane, sometimes maddeningly abstruse cultural references. Joyce logged the geographical coordinates of Odysseus's Mediterranean wanderings according to the navigational charts mapped in Victor Bérard's *Les Phéniciens et l'Odyssée*, a work that fired Joyce's imagination with its intriguing thesis that the *Odyssey* was of Semitic origin. He ransacked W. H. Roscher's *Ausführliches Lexikon der griechischen und römischen Mythologie*, his most significant borrowing, as Phillip Herring remarks, being "the post-Homeric theory of the unfaithful Penelope."[27] He jotted down the Elizabethan slang sported by the worldlings in Thomas Otway's plays (blub lips, fubsy, feage [which he then annotates as "whip, shake as one would a horse"]) along with the tropes found in a seventeenth-century French translation of Aristotle's *Rhetoric* (e.g., "antithesis in clauses to sustain length / of equal limbs + parisose").[28] Antithesis was to become the rhetorical basis for his mythical method, which also made comparisons, mainly invidious, though sometimes favorable, even ennobling, between classical and contemporary characters and manners.

More impressive than Joyce's amassing such material was what he managed to make of it. As Richard Ellmann remarked, "no one looking at the notesheets could have predicted how the fragments would coalesce."[29] In what might be called an "insider's look" into the making of *Ulysses*, Budgen likened Joyce's *omnium gatherum* "methods" to those of Rembrandt, an artist who

seemed to his neighbours to be a great harbourer of junk for junk's sake in the shape of odds and ends picked up in the market-place. Until, behold, the useless antique helmet, the strange unwearable eastern gown, the odd-shaped sword reappeared, flooded with light, in a picture, clothing and adorning a brace of his neighbours, true-to-life portraits yet

Fig. 6.5. James Joyce, schema of *Ulysses* made for George Antheil, 1924 or early 1925. Typescript. The Morgan Library & Museum, New York. Gift of Sean and Mary Kelly, 2018. © The Estate of James Joyce.

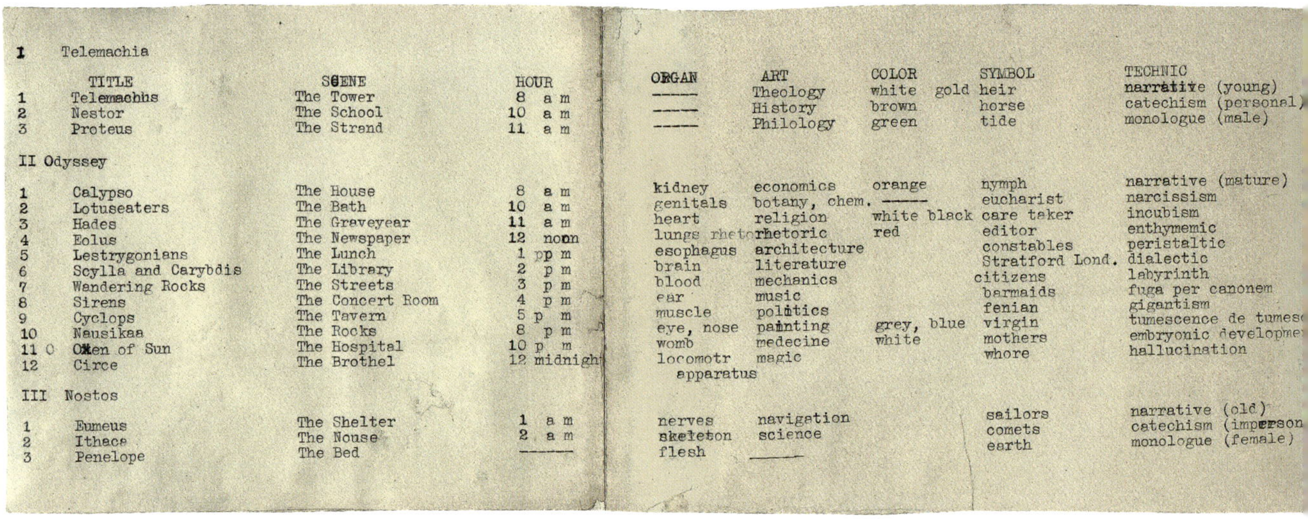

with all the significance of religious symbols. And in Joyce's case the word that fell from the lips of a car-driver or convive would be noted on the waistcoat pocket block, receive its shape and setting and be heard again with a new intonation in the mouth of one of the personages of his invention—wandering Jew, troglodyte or bartender, but for sure a phantom portrait of one of his neighbours.[30]

Budgen, a painter himself, appreciates Joyce's ecological ingenuity in recycling, as it were, the random but evocative life details the ordinary person would ignore or discard as so much cultural junk.

In light of these compositional vagaries, that comma interposed between stately and plump is no mere flourish; it presages even as it establishes a precarious balance between the stateliness of the novel's epic structure and the richly variegated material substance, ineluctably plump, of modern life. As *Ulysses* progresses, a danger emerges, soon maturing into active threat, that the plumpness meant to reinforce might obscure, even topple, the

	TITLE	SCENE	HOUR	ORGAN	ART	COLOR	SYMBOL	TECHNIC
I	**Telemachia**							
1	Telemachus	The Tower	8 a m	----	Theology	white gold	heir	narrative (young)
2	Nestor	The School	10 a m	----	History	brown	horse	catechism (personal)
3	Proteus	The Strand	11 a m	----	Philology	green	tide	monologue (male)
II	**Odyssey**							
1	Calypso	The House	8 a m	kidney	economics	orange	nymph	narrative (mature)
2	Lotuseaters	The Bath	10 a m	genitals	botany, chem.	----	eucharist	narcissism
3	Hades	The Graveyear	11 a m	heart	religion	white black	care taker	incubism
4	Eolus	The Newspaper	12 noon	lungs	rhetoric	red	editor	enthymemic
5	Lestrygonians	The Lunch	1 p m	esophagus	architecture		constables	peristaltic
6	Scylla and Carybdis	The Library	2 p m	brain	literature		Stratford Lond.	dialectic
7	Wandering Rocks	The Streets	3 p m	blood	mechanics		citizens	labyrinth
8	Sirens	The Concert Room	4 p m	ear	music		barmaids	fuga per canonem
9	Cyclops	The Tavern	5 p m	muscle	politics		fenian	gigantism
10	Nausikaa	The Rocks	8 p m	eye, nose	painting	grey, blue	virgin	tumescence de tumes
11 O	Oxen of Sun	The Hospital	10 p m	womb	medecine	white	mothers	embryonic developm
12	Circe	The Brothel	12 midnight	locomotr apparatus	magic		whore	hallucination
III	**Nostos**							
1	Eumeus	The Shelter	1 a m	nerves	navigation		sailors	narrative (old)
2	Ithaca	The House	2 a m	skeleton	science		comets	catechism (imperson
3	Penelope	The Bed	----	flesh	----		earth	monologue (female)

structure of mythic correspondences that gives the novel its formal stability, thus compromising the code by which to read the "signatures of all things."[31] By 1920, a year of major headway (completed drafts of "Nausicaa" and "Oxen of the Sun," beginning and finishing the phantasmagoric "Circe"),[32] the amount of stuff crammed into the novel had grown to such unwieldy proportions that Joyce himself spoke of *Ulysses* as "my damned monster-novel." But unlike Henry James, who imparted a stately form to the loose baggy monsters of nineteenth-century, especially Russian, fiction by the most disciplined acts of selection, discrimination, and inference, Joyce solidified his epic design by indulging, rather than restraining, his avidity for narrative "stuff." He delineated his design in a schema, "a sort of summary—key—skeleton—scheme," that he sent to Carlo Linati. *Ulysses*, Joyce explained, was

the epic of two races (Israel-Ireland) and at the same time the cycle of the human body as well as a little

story of a day (life). . . . It is also a kind of encyclopaedia. My intention is not only to render the myth *sub specie temporis nostri* [in the light of our own times] but also to allow each adventure (that is, every hour, every organ, every art being interconnected and interrelated in the somatic scheme of the whole) to condition and even to create its own technique. Each adventure is so to speak one person although it is composed of persons—as Aquinas relates of the heavenly hosts.[33]

Be not discouraged, Joyce seems to be urging, by the stupendous flood of mundane matter, the tide of recondite allusions. Though it may often appear a Dadaist extravaganza, the world of *Ulysses* is fundamentally an orderly one: its characters and their mythic shadows, the ads, bits and pieces of popular song and local idioms littering the narrative like so many disarticulated parts of a decomposing cultural body, the proliferation of increasingly idiosyncratic narrative styles as one moves deeper into the noisy Dublin night, are in fact intercon-

RESPONDENCES
phen- Telemachus-Hamlet : Buck Malligen -Antinous : Milkwomen -Mentor
ay Nestor: Pisistratus. Sargent : Helen : Mrs. O'Shea
teus Primal Matter: Kevin Egen - Nenelaus: Megapenthus : The Cockle-

ypso -The Nymph. Dlugacz: The Recal: Zion: Ithaca.
useaters: Cabhorses. Communicants: Soldiers, Eunnuchs, Bather, Watchers
ier, Grand and Royal Canals, Liffey- The 4 Rivers: Cunningham Sisyphus
wford - Eolus: Incest - journalism: Floating Island - press.
iphates - Hunger-: The Decoy : Food: Lestrygonians: Teeth
Rock - Aristotle, Dogma, Stratford: The whirlpool: Plato, Mysticism
chorus- Liffey: European bank - Viceroy : Asiatic bank- Conmee: Symple-
ens -barmaids: Isle -bar
an I Stake cigar challenge apotheosis
eacia Star of the Sea : Gerty -Nausikaa
oital- Trimacria: Lampetie, Phaethusa- Nurses: Helios- Horne: OXen -
ble -Bella:

eus -Skin the Goat: Sailor- Ulysses Pseudangelos: Melanthius- Corly
ymachus- Boylan: Suitors- scruples: Bow- reason
elope- Earth: Web- Movement

x

picker

of Cricket
: Father Coffrey - Cerberus : Caretaker -Hades Daniel O'Connell -
(Hercules : Dignam- Elpenos : Parnell: Agamemnon : Menton: Ajax

London : Ulysses : Socrates. Jesus- Shakespeare
-gades : Groups of citizens

Fertility : Crime -Fraud

nected, interrelated, parts of a grandiloquent, all-encompassing design. *Ulysses* may be a monster, but a special kind of monster, one whose form, like that of the heavenly hosts, unites the many and manifold, fuses the separate adventures, each a narrative "person" with a distinct style of "speaking," into a somatic whole.

These persons are often up to no good, which explains why Joyce's mythic method is more disposed to satirize than consecrate the unhallowed ground of modern life. The cheerful iconoclasm of the novel's bravura opening, jauntily counterpointing Mulligan's mock-intonation of the liturgical formula summoning congregants to Mass and his slangy taunt, "Come up Kinch, come up you fearful Jesuit," beckoning Stephen to an irredentist narrative in which he has little faith, is never chastened, much less renounced. That Mulligan's jocular insolence is a necessary incitement to Joycean storytelling is evident in late manuscript drafts of *Portrait*, in which Mulligan enters Joyce's imagination in the guise of a young buck named Doherty:

> But the echo of his laughter had been the remembrance of Doherty, standing on the steps of his house the night before saying:
> —And on Sunday I consume the particle. Christine, *semel in die*. The mockery of it all . . .[34]

In Doherty's joke-prescription for the ailing spirit, a daily dose of the holy particle—"Christine" refers to the Communion host and *semel in die* may sound liturgical, but it is medical Latin for once a day—Joyce is jesting his way toward a new mode of narrative, not yet mythic, yet charged with myth's power to forge sometimes unholy alliances between the spirited past and the dispirited present, spiritual essences and material bodies.

This new mode of storytelling first assumes the authority of a method in the penultimate diary entries of *Portrait* when Stephen, refusing the imposture of his friend Cranly's "grand manner," devises, in accordance with his mood, a "subtle and suave" way of representing the nature and origin of Cranly's character: "Cranly's despair of soul: the child of exhausted loins." He is exhilarated by his own formulation, sensing he has discovered a new, unencumbered way of reading reality: "Thought this in bed last night but was too lazy and free to add it. Free, yes. The exhausted loins are those of Elisabeth and Zachary. Then he is the precursor. Item: he eats chiefly belly bacon and dried figs. Read locusts and wild honey."[35]

No such helpful glosses are offered the reader of *Ulysses*. (Joyce objected to Eliot's gloss to *The Waste Land*.) Its author is a freer artist than his younger fictional surrogate, who, working out the mechanics as well as principles of the mythic method, wants to make sure of his findings: Cranly is John the Baptist, the precursor; I am the messiah, the son of the divine artificer deputed to forge the uncreated conscience of my race.

What the mythic method requires, however, is a certain coldness in manner to work its transfiguring magic. Stephen accepts—indeed, emotionally welcomes—this necessity when, in the penultimate entry, he relates how, feeling "sorry and mean" after his awkward encounter with his Dublin Beatrice, he quickly "turned off that valve at once and opened the spiritual-heroic refrigerating apparatus, invented and patented in all countries by Dante Alighieri."[36] What Dante invented and patented was not an apparatus but a literary mode, *il dolce stil novo*, the sweet new style. Stephen embraces the newness but abjures the sweetness in favor of the cool detachment of Dante's—and his own—sublimations. His "refrigerating apparatus" threatens to chill all the warm impulses of life in *Ulysses*, initially through the "cool" Mulligan, whose inaugural gesture is to mock the heat of creation—which Stephen in *Portrait*, invoking Shelley, had likened to "a fading coal"[37]—as an electric current that can galvanize dead matter, producing, in mockery of the "genuine Christine,"[38] Frankenstein's hideously proportioned, heteroclite monster-body. The potential for monstrosity, for uncontrolled growth and mis-shapen form, is activated once Stephen's "soulfree and fancy free" experiments with the mythic method become the property of the author of *Ulysses*. Once this transfer is effected, Joyce has more need than ever for the interior monologue, a device for channeling fragments of thought and fugitive feelings that can disrupt, though they cannot retard, the narrative momentum toward parody, inflated rhetoric ("Aeolus" and "Cyclops"), and monstrous spectacle ("Circe," the episode teeming with deranged forms, unholy rites, ghastly hallucinations, and dream monsters).

It takes the geniality of Leopold Bloom to inject a warmth into a novel in danger of succumbing to mockery's life-chilling cleverness. "Calypso," which restarts the novel, introduces Bloom as the hero and protector of warm, full-blooded life who "curiously, kindly" watches and feeds "the lithe black form" of the household cat. The Bloomian ethos of curiosity and kindness justifies as it fulfills Joyce's conception of Bloom as above all a good man. The rest of the day will reveal him in the more complicated moods and situations that show him to be "a complete man as well,"[39] deserving of Homer's epithet for Odysseus, *polytropos* [πολύτροπος]. Joyce primarily relied on the Butcher and Lang translation (1879), which translates *polytropos* as "so ready at need." Not quite the modern idiom, if not as

antiquated as Stephen's brandishing "the lancet of my art,"[40] the phrase gets at something morally distinctive in Joyce's conception of Bloom as a man ready at need—with a kind word (to the agitated Mrs Breen), with succor (securing insurance for the newly widowed Mrs Dignam), with advice (for Stephen, if he will heed it), and in one mock-glorious moment, with a valiant retort to a bigoted Citizen bloated with drink and the toxins of "force, hatred, history, all that."[41] The novel itself may itself be said to be composed by an author ready at need, ever resourceful in fulfilling the imaginative imperatives of Joyce's epic vision.

These needs became more exigent, the demands more exorbitant as Joyce's conception matured and the chapter-adventures took on the troublesome individuality of the narrative "persons" Joyce declared them to be. The first nine chapters were composed in what Joyce retrospectively would identify as the novel's "initial style," but starting in 1919 Joyce began devising new techniques to reflect the "character" not so much of his protagonists but of the Odyssean adventures enacted *sub specie temporis nostri*. The decisive swerve occurs in "Wandering Rocks," the only navigational peril Homer's Odysseus studiously avoids (twice!), but which Joyce confronts head on. The episode no longer foregrounds Bloom or Stephen but circum-ambulates, as it were, around eighteen narrative atolls on which various Dubliners are temporarily marooned, isolated from neighboring isles by a series of asterisks. This episode does track two headstrong navigators making their way *through* the rocks—Father Conmee and the viceregal cavalcade, the one blithely dispensing the religious nostrums and the other parading the temporal power that have kept Ireland in spiritual and political subjec-tion. Moving "forrard" is the prerogative of ecclesiastical or imperial power, while meandering Dubliners move somewhat blindly and often disconsolately through the maze of city streets. The labyrinth is the chapter's governing symbol, a reminder that concealed at the center of the city's Dedalian maze of thoroughfares and byways abides a monster.

From this point on, that monster, born of and nurtured by the overblown rhetoric and rabid ideologies ravaging modern life, begins to mutate and proliferate wildly, displacing character and event as the center of narrative. In the "last stage" of composition, between 1920 and 1922, Joyce, in addition to devising new styles for the remaining eight episodes, also revised the early and middle chapters drafted in the initial style, retroactively distending and exaggerating their innate features, an effective way to render novelistic persons, whether people or adventures, grotesquely oversized (one measure of monstrosity). Thus, for example, the 1918 *Little Review* version of "Aeolus" is recast to reveal Aeolus in his contemporary avatar, the bombastic windbag. This personation, the work of a waggish compositor, is effected by incorporating thirty more tropes to burnish the art of the chapter—rhetoric—and by inserting attention-grabbing, often preeningly clever headlines above blocks of narrative, thus mimicking the format and bold-cap typography of "A GREAT DAILY ORGAN"[42] delivering the news in stentorian tones.[43]

Stephen's mordant image for Irish art as "the cracked lookingglass of a servant" anticipates this splintering of the novel's surface with striations of style. This fractured veneer is directly refracted in the split narrative of "Nausicaa," whose first half reflects the "namby-pamby jammy marmalady drawersy (*alto là!*) style"[44] of a proletarian heroine who hangs a "grocer's christmas almanac" with its

"picture of halcyon days"[45] in the privy she disinfects every fortnight with chlorate of lime. Her narrative, reeking with the pungent sensations produced by the "effects of incense mariolatry, masturbation, stewed cockles, painter's palette, chit chat, circumlocutions, etc. etc.,"[46] achieves its mock-pathetic climax in a series of exclamatory, if sweetly soft, "O!"s. That is half the story. Upon Gerty's departure, wistfully marked by an ellipsis, the narrative abandons her "*alto là!*" style and reverts to the chagrined, even ungallant musings of Bloom's internal monologue (the novel's initial style). This sudden correction of narrative manner suggests that it is not so much Gerty showing her knickers as the sensationalist jammy marmalady verbiage Joyce sets flowing in, around, and through her that constitutes the supreme and shaming act of exhibitionist display.

This promotion of stylistic virtuosity at the expense, or rather as the *essence*, of narrative did not go unremarked, even by the most sympathetic readers. "Sirens" is the first episode to raise the alarm—Pound was among the first to sound it[47]—that the novel was wandering dangerously off course. Joyce insisted on the stately outlines of a conception that could survive any apparent discordance: "Sirens," he averred, was structured as "eight regular parts of a *fuga per canonem*," although he confessed that this regularity resembled and reflected "the progress of some sandblast."[48] Joyce never blinked at the devastation he wrought, even when his most remarkable literary innovations were marked for demolition. He valued, for instance, the interior monologue for its sturdiness "as a bridge over which to march my eighteen episodes," but "once I have got my troops across," he remarked, "the opposing forces can, for all I care, blow the bridge sky-high."[49] Joyce's refrigerating apparatus was ever "ready at need" to cool the creative heat

Nausicaa IIII Henri Matisse

Fig. 6.6. Henri Matisse, preparatory drawing for an illustration of
the "Nausicaa" episode in the Limited Editions Club *Ulysses*, 1935.
Red chalk on paper. The Pierre and Tana Matisse Foundation.

Fig. 6.7. Ottocaro Weiss, photograph of James Joyce playing a guitar, 1915. The Poetry Collection of the University Libraries, University at Buffalo, The State University of New York.

generated by his own incendiary imagination. He accepted that every artistic advance through the waste land of contemporary history necessitated the partial, or sometimes the complete, obliteration of entire modes and traditions of artistic expression: "Each successive episode, dealing with some province of artistic culture (rhetoric or music or dialectic), leaves behind it a burnt up field," he wrote to Harriet Shaw Weaver. "Since I wrote the 'Sirens' I find it impossible to listen to music of any kind."[50] The sense of devastation, but also of exhilarating invention, reaches an apotheosis in the dazzling pyrotechnics of "Circe," a performance so convulsive that Joyce eventually complains to Sylvia Beach that "Circe herself is punishing me for having written it."[51]

No matter if the goddesses, or muses, might take their revenge on Joyce for sandblasting through their established provinces of artistic culture: rhetoric, music, painting, magic. Joyce never desisted in his radical assaults on tradition, since only by such means could he clear space for a new apprehension of reality. The heavily scored manuscript pages, typescripts, and proof sheets of the novel, with their profusion of editorial signs and scrawled insertions, can thus be read as directions charting a path "forrader" to what the modern novel could become. Hugh Kenner, one of Joyce's most astute interpreters, first called attention to the Aristotelian "dagger definition" that may help us grasp the logic and grandeur of Joyce's epic-monstrous

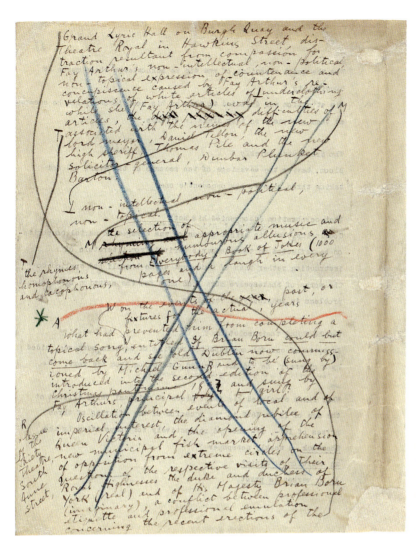

Fig. 6.8. James Joyce, one page of the "Ithaca" episode, 1921. Autograph manuscript. Morgan Library & Museum, New York. Gift of Rowland Burdon-Muller, 1950. © The Estate of James Joyce.

conception: "For what each thing is when fully developed, we call its nature, whether we are speaking of a man, a horse, or a family. Besides, the final cause and end of a thing is the best, and to be self-sufficing is the end and the best."[52]

Joyce's "monster-novel" was, then, no *lusus naturae*, but a wondrous creation born of Joyce's imaginative struggle to develop the full nature of a distinctly modern "thing"—the stately, plump story of a day whose minute, multitudinous, and evanescent particulars are transformed into the stuff of myth. The final cause and end of Joyce's epic labor of imagining, then revising, how that story should be told was a novel well stocked with all the provisions Joyce's art could devise, a novel that would be self-sufficing, that is, the best of its kind.

Fig. 7.1. Berenice Abbott, photograph of James Joyce, 1928. The Morgan Library & Museum, New York. Gift of Sean and Mary Kelly, 2018.

JOSEPH M. HASSETT

7. *Ulysses* and Free Speech
Looking Back to Move Forward

The publication of James Joyce's *Ulysses* in Paris in 1922 was preceded and followed by governmental efforts to ban it on the basis of laws against obscenity. The litigation that overcame those efforts at censorship established the principle that, as Louis Menand put it, "the artist must have absolute freedom to work with the world he or she has stumbled across, the world as it is."[1] This underlying principle was gradually extended to apply broadly to political speech in all its many forms.

As we celebrate the centenary of the publication of *Ulysses*, continuing threats to criminalize speech remind us that it is important to examine the *Ulysses* litigation to identify the ideas and acts of courage that prevailed and will likely be needed again. There is much truth to Menand's comment that Joyce's persistence was largely responsible for his novel's triumph over censorship. Even so, gifted,

courageous, and far-sighted publishers, creative lawyers, and wise and independent judges were needed as well.

Margaret Anderson, founder and editor of the *Little Review* and the first person to publish any of Joyce's pioneering novel, was warned that doing so would likely result in obscenity charges against her.[2] Captivated by the prose of the opening episodes, Anderson told her colleague and lover Jane Heap, "This is the most beautiful thing we'll ever have.... We'll print it if it's the last effort of our lives."[3] Her comment was eerily prophetic. The effort would exhaust Anderson and Heap and drive them from publishing.

Joyce's prose chimed with the Indianapolis-born Anderson's notions of life as a performance and of the role of art in enhancing the performance—ideas she embraced when she plunged into

Fig. 7.2. Berenice Abbott, photograph of Margaret Anderson, ca. 1928. The Metropolitan Museum of Art, New York. Gift of Laura May Isaacson, 1976.

Fig. 7.3. Berenice Abbott, photograph of Jane Heap, 1928. The Metropolitan Museum of Art, New York. Gift of Laura May Isaacson, 1976.

the exciting intellectual atmosphere of Chicago in 1908. Spurred by her need for inspiring conversation, Anderson founded the *Little Review* as an antidote to a materialistic society in which "we live too swiftly to have time to" appreciate the "glorious performance of life."[4] Anderson's first issue declared that the magazine would find life-enhancing art in books because books "register the ideas of an age; that is perhaps their chief claim to immortality." The spirit of the magazine is reflected in Anderson's assertion that "art is a challenge to life."[5]

Anderson's performance as editor caught the attention of Ezra Pound, one of the singular voices in modern poetry and an energetic promoter of

modernist writers. At about the time that Anderson and Heap moved the *Little Review* to New York, in early 1917, Pound opened a dialogue with Anderson that led to Joyce's sending episodes of *Ulysses* to Pound, who forwarded them to Anderson. Staring down possible prosecution and other sanctions under both state and federal law (which prohibited the mailing of obscene material), Anderson promptly announced to her readers in January 1918 that "we are about to publish a prose masterpiece." The first episode appeared in the March 1918 issue.

Despite the Post Office's interference with the delivery of issues containing three episodes,[6] which may have been prompted by zealous scrutiny of the magazine for subversive influence,[7] Anderson and Heap pressed ahead without criminal prosecution until the July–August 1920 issue, which contained the last section of the episode called "Nausicaa,"[8] the name of the princess who helps Odysseus when he is washed up on the shore of Phaeacia as he struggles to return to Ithaca. In a 3 September 1920 letter to John Quinn, a New York lawyer who had been providing financial support and advice to the *Little Review* and was seeking to negotiate a contract on Joyce's behalf for American publication of *Ulysses* in a limited edition, Joyce situated "Nausicaa" as the thirteenth of eighteen contemplated episodes that would mirror Homer's *Odyssey*.[9]

The "Nausicaa" episode unfolds on Dublin Bay's Sandymount strand, where Gerty MacDowell is sitting on a rock while a Benediction ceremony is being conducted in the adjacent Star of the Sea church. In the final part of the episode, Gerty notices Leopold Bloom staring at her. As the reader hears Gerty's perception of the Benediction, Gerty leans back to allow the increasingly excited Bloom to see her "nainsook knickers, four and eleven on account of being white," while swinging her foot in time with the Tantum Ergo hymn in a crescendo that peaks when a rocket from the fireworks at a nearby bazaar "sprang and bang shot blind blank and O! then the Roman candle burst and it was like a sigh of O! and everyone cried O! O! and it gushed out of it a stream of rain gold hair threads and they shed and ah! they were all greeny dewy stars falling with golden, O so lovely! O so soft, sweet soft!"

The fact that Bloom experiences an orgasm as the rocket bursts into beautiful display becomes apparent from several musings in the Bloomian interior monologue that now takes control of the narrative:

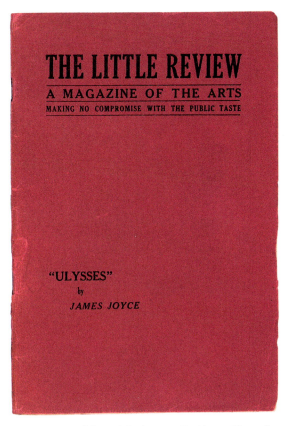

Fig. 7.4. Cover of the *Little Review*, 1918. The Morgan Library & Museum, New York. Gift of Annette de la Renta in memory of Carter Burden, 2005.

Mr. Bloom with careful hand recomposed his shirt.
Did she know what I? Course.
Lord, I am wet.
For this relief much thanks.[10]

As Vladimir Nabokov would later point out, the newness of this passage emphasizes the difference between cliché—words that were once original and vivid but have become hackneyed—and live lyrical language. "What Joyce does here," he writes, "is to cause some of that dead and rotten stuff to reveal here and there its live source, its primary freshness." He instances the "description of the church service as it passes transparently through Gerty's consciousness," noting that it "has real beauty and a luminous pathetic charm," as does "the tenderness of the twilight." "Of course," he concludes, "the description of the fireworks . . . is really tender and beautiful: it is the freshness of poetry still with us before it becomes a cliché."[11]

In 1920, John Sumner saw it differently. He was the successor to Anthony Comstock as secretary of the New York Society for the Suppression of Vice, an unusual organization invested by the New York legislature with authority to enforce the state's obscenity laws. He brought criminal charges based on the "Nausicaa" episode. Anderson and Heap, who insisted that literature could not be obscene,[12] reflexively turned to John Quinn for representation. The defense would have to contend with the fact that American courts followed an 1868 English decision, *Regina v. Hicklin*, which defined a work as obscene if any part of it tended to induce "thoughts of a most impure and libidinous character" in "those whose minds are open to such immoral influences."[13] Despite this forbidding climate, Judge Learned Hand, one of the most distinguished American judges of the first half of the twentieth century, had invited lawyers to challenge the *Hicklin* rule in an opinion issued in 1913 when, as a federal district judge in New York, he was presiding over the prosecution of publisher Mitchell Kennerley. While recognizing that precedent in the United States Court of Appeals for the Second Circuit required that he follow *Hicklin*, Hand's opinion focused on the harm to society of judge-made law that barred literature simply because some part of it sounded an erotic chord. He characterized *Hicklin* as reflective of "mid-Victorian morals" and questioned "whether in the end men will regard that as obscene which is honestly relevant to the adequate expression of innocent ideas, and whether they will not believe that truth and beauty are too precious to society at large to be mutilated in the interests of those most likely to pervert them to base uses."[14]

Hand's opinion was an open invitation to lawyers to use the ideas of beauty and truth to alter the law of obscenity so that, as Hand suggested, "shame . . . [would not] for long prevent us from adequate portrayal of some of the most serious and beautiful sides of human nature." Moreover, an argument that defended Joyce's prose in terms compatible with Hand's approach was articulated for Quinn in a long letter from William Butler Yeats's father, John Butler Yeats. In language that paralleled Anderson's idea of literature as a stimulus to a more deeply experienced life, the elder Yeats insisted, "The whole movement against Joyce and his terrible veracity, naked and unashamed, has its origin in the desire of people to live comfortably, and, that they may live comfortably, to live superficially." Joyce's genius, he wrote, "which loves the truth because it is genius, will not have it so."[15]

Quinn was the wrong choice to pursue this opportunity to reshape the law of obscenity. For one thing, he regarded the serialization of *Ulysses* as an obstacle to his effort to sell the novel as a whole, and he thus welcomed the silencing of the *Little Review*. Rather than challenging Sumner, Quinn urged Joyce, via Pound, to withdraw serialization rights from the *Little Review*[16] and tried to negotiate a deal in which serialization would cease in return for dismissal of the charges. The idea went nowhere. Joyce told Quinn that he thought withdrawal of the book would be "a sign of weakness,"[17] and he explained to his patron Harriet Shaw Weaver that withdrawal would suggest that he was passing

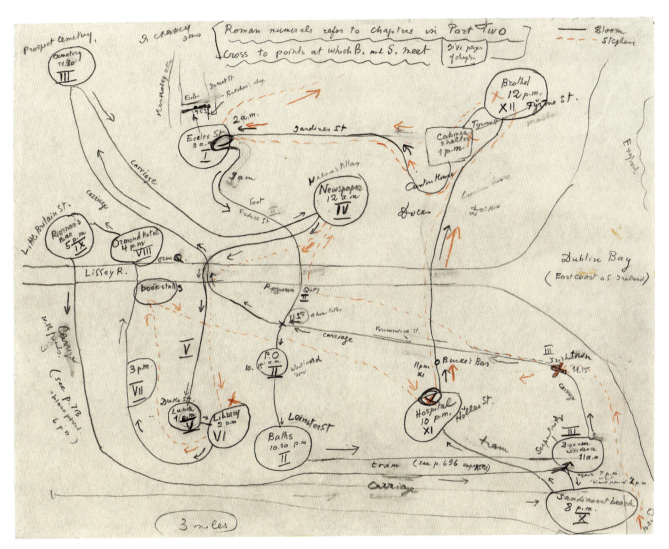

Fig. 7.5. Vladimir Nabokov, map of Leopold Bloom's and
Stephen Dedalus's travels through Dublin, ca. 1948–58. Graphite
and colored pencil on paper. The Henry W. and Albert A. Berg
Collection, New York Public Library, Astor, Lenox,
and Tilden Foundations.

sentence on his own writing and blaming the editors of the *Little Review* for publishing it, thereby prejudicing their position in court.[18]

Quinn's unsuitability was aggravated by misogyny compounded by prejudice against Anderson's and Heap's lesbianism. Quinn's vicious 16 October 1920 letter to Pound ranted against the "female urinal" from which the *Little Review* was published and accused his clients of having the "perverted courage of the bugger and the Lesbian." Moreover, Quinn was reluctant to be publicly identified as a "free smut, free sex advocate," a fate against which he warned Pound.[19]

Quinn's argument at a preliminary hearing on 21 October 1920 before New York City magistrate J. E. Corrigan did Joyce a double disservice, asserting that language that bore no resemblance to the text for which Anderson and Heap were being prosecuted was disgusting rather than sexually exciting. Specifically, Quinn urged the court that a writer induces disgust by saying that a woman is not beautiful: "She sweats, she stinks, she is flatulent. Her flesh is discolored, her breath is bad. She makes ugly noises when she eats and discharges other natural functions."[20] Of course, this imaginary text was not contained in the *Little Review*, and Quinn neglected to point out the merit of what was contained in the magazine. Quinn's further argument that Joyce's text was unintelligible was untrue and ineffective. The passage "where the man went off in his pants," Corrigan ruled, was unmistakable in meaning and "smutty, filthy within the meaning of the statute."[21] Corrigan ordered a trial on the merits before three judges in the Court of Special Sessions.

The defense Quinn presented at the February 1921 trial was even more tawdry and cynical. Whereas Anderson and Heap wanted a defense based on Anderson's belief that *Ulysses* was "the

prose masterpiece of my generation,"[22] the essence of Quinn's case, as reported in the 22 February 1921 *New York Tribune*, was that average readers would not be harmed by Joyce's prose "because if they read the magazine, which was improbable, they would be either unable to comprehend Joyce's style, or would be bored and disgusted."[23] Quinn followed up with what he told Joyce was the "good point" that the anger manifested in the prosecutor's argument was "my best exhibit" because it showed that *Ulysses* made people angry rather than "driv[ing] them into the arms of some siren."[24] Confusing the effect of being the prosecutor in an obscenity trial of *Ulysses* with the effect of reading the book, Quinn deprived the occasion of the seriousness it deserved.

Anderson and Heap were fined fifty dollars each, and it was stipulated that no further installments of *Ulysses* would be published in the *Little Review*.[25] Without consulting Joyce or even advising him of the result, Quinn did not file an appeal, even though there was a strong basis for one.[26] The author of *Ulysses* learned that one of its episodes had been found obscene only by reading the *New York Tribune*'s 23 February 1921 editorial comment on the trial,[27] which had found its way by chance to Sylvia Beach, proprietor of the now legendary Paris bookstore Shakespeare and Company.[28] The expatriate bookseller had been captivated by *Ulysses* when she read the episodes published in the *Little Review*, and she was thrilled to meet Joyce at a social event in Paris to which Pound brought him after convincing him to move to the French capital.[29] On a subsequent visit to Beach's bookstore, Joyce learned from a newspaper clipping that Quinn's defense of his masterpiece was essentially that it was disgusting and incomprehensible. Contemplating reports of the trial, Joyce wrote to Harriet Shaw Weaver that the offense was less grotesque than the

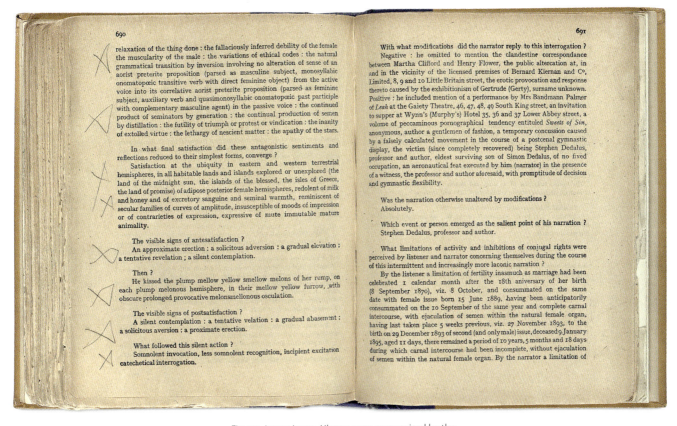

Fig. 7.6. James Joyce, *Ulysses*, 1930, copy seized by the
government and annotated by the prosecution in the case
United States v. One Book Called "Ulysses." Rare Book &
Manuscript Library, Columbia University.

defense.[30] After hearing Joyce lament that the New York conviction meant that his novel would never be published, Beach made an astonishing offer to publish the novel in France under the imprint of her bookstore.[31] Joyce accepted, and *Ulysses* was rushed into print in time for his fortieth birthday on 2 February 1922. Beach sold copies over the counter and by mail. Various efforts to evade customs authorities in England and the United States were sometimes successful and sometimes met by seizure and destruction of the books.[32]

In the summer of 1931, two impulses converged that would ultimately end the novel's exile: Joyce's concern that unauthorized editions of *Ulysses* would deprive him of the American market,[33] and the interest of two New Yorkers, lawyer Morris Ernst and publisher Bennett Cerf, in waging a legal battle to permit American publication of *Ulysses*.

Ernst's fight to legalize *Ulysses* took advantage of a provision of the Tariff Act of 1930 that required the government to commence a legal proceeding against a book seized by customs authorities and authorized the would-be importer to intervene in the proceeding to contest the legality of the seizure.[34] Energetically taking the battle to the enemy, Ernst and Cerf had Joyce mail a copy of *Ulysses* to Cerf's firm, Random House, and made sure that it was seized.[35] Ernst's role as defender of *Ulysses* benefited from the government's concurrence in his effort to steer assignment of the ensuing case to Judge John Munro Woolsey, whose role would be especially important because the parties stipulated that he would, in effect, be judge and jury, deciding questions of both law and fact.

The defense was also aided by the critical approbation the novel had received following its 1922 publication by Sylvia Beach. Joyce contributed to this helpful aura of high-mindedness by

adding additional parallels between *Ulysses* and the *Odyssey*,[36] providing a detailed elaboration of the Homeric correspondences (and other stylistic features) to the distinguished French novelist, translator, and critic Valery Larbaud, and helping arrange a lecture and article by Larbaud.[37] While publication of the complete novel facilitated the comparison with Homer, it also meant that Ernst was burdened by the concluding Molly Bloom monologue, a highly sexual reverie that Joyce himself called "probably more obscene than any preceding episode."[38] Even as he made efforts to inoculate his text against suppression, Joyce did not hesitate to spit in the censor's eye, adding, for example, additional graphic detail to the "Nausicaa" episode, such as that, as Gerty leaned back, Bloom's "hands and face were working and a tremour went over her."[39]

Ernst's brief laid the groundwork for a change in legal doctrine by emphasizing Learned Hand's suggestion in *Kennerley* that the standard for obscenity should vary with the mores of the time.[40] To fortify the judges who would have to deal with the eroticism and earthiness of Joyce's prose, Ernst forcefully urged the importance of truth in literature. Notably, he argued that Macaulay's praise of Milton's willingness to speak out in favor of divorce and regicide "applied with equal force to Joyce." His quote from Macaulay's essay on Milton set a high bar for Joyce to scale: "There is no more hazardous enterprise than that of bearing the torch of truth into those dark and infected recesses in which no light has ever shone. But it was the choice and pleasure of Milton to picture the noisome vapours and to brave the terrible explosion."[41] Ernst maintained that Joyce was equal to the challenge: "It may be that in *Ulysses* Joyce has seen fit to cast light into some of the murky chambers of the human mind. It is only by such exposure that we can hope to banish darkness and taint. Joyce's penetration and courage deserve praise, not condemnation."[42]

Ernst's powerful argument found a receptive audience in Judge Woolsey, who broke new ground by deciding a legal question on the basis of an analysis of literary technique. Without explicitly using the term "stream of consciousness," Woolsey focused on Joyce's "honest effort to show exactly how the minds of his characters operate."[43] Failing "to be honest in developing the technique which he has adopted in 'Ulysses,'" he opined, ". . . would be psychologically misleading" and "artistically inexcusable." Woolsey's analysis brought him to the precise point John Butler Yeats had made in his 1920 letter to Quinn: the reason for the outcry against Joyce was his terrible veracity. As Woolsey wrote, "It is because Joyce has been loyal to his technique and has not funked its necessary implications, but has honestly attempted to tell fully what his characters think about, that he has been the subject of so many attacks and that his purpose has been so often misunderstood and misrepresented."

Woolsey's appreciation of the truth and beauty of Joyce's novel enabled him to swallow the admittedly "strong draught" of Joyce's prose. His role as the finder of fact, including the ultimate fact of obscenity, enabled him to maneuver around the traditional *Hicklin* doctrine. Even the valiant Woolsey, however, paled at the prospect of offering himself as the barometer of whether *Ulysses* excited lustful thoughts. Instead, he reported the combined decision of himself and two friends. Woolsey's carefully hedged report avoided the question whether any of the three had been stimulated to lustful thoughts in the course of duty. Instead, the report was that "in its entirety" the "net effect" of *Ulysses* was not "to excite sexual impulses or lustful

Fig. 7.7. A souvenir edition of Judge Woolsey's decision, 1935. The Morgan Library & Museum, New York. Gift of Sean and Mary Kelly, 2018.

thoughts." Woolsey's favorable decision was vulnerable to the argument that, whatever the "net effect" of *Ulysses*, it contained specific passages that were obscene, and the book thus ran afoul of the statute under the traditional *Hicklin* rule. The government so argued in appealing to the Second Circuit Court of Appeals. The three-judge panel of the appellate court consisted of Learned Hand, who had been promoted to that court, his cousin Augustus Hand, and Martin Manton.

Writing for a majority consisting of himself and his cousin, Augustus Hand affirmed Woolsey's decision. His opinion begins by identifying Joyce "as a pioneer of the 'stream of consciousness' method of presenting fiction," which "attempts to depict the thoughts and lay bare the souls of a number of people . . . with a literalism that leaves nothing unsaid."[44] Hand's description of the text highlights its truth and beauty: "It seems," he wrote, "to be sincere, truthful, relevant to the subject, and executed with real art."

Then, in one of those touches that makes judging an art, Hand brought *Ulysses* within a line of precedents that permitted a greater range of sexual reference in scientific works by framing the "question before us" as "whether such a book of artistic merit *and scientific insight* should be regarded as 'obscene' within section 305(a) of the Tariff Act" (emphasis added). Characterizing his decision in *United States v. Dennett* as holding that "works of physiology, medicine, science and sex instruction are not within the statute, though to some extent and among some persons they may tend to promote lustful thoughts," Hand concluded: "We think the same immunity should apply to literature as to science, where the presentation, when viewed objectively, is sincere, and the erotic matter is not introduced to promote lust and does not furnish the dominant note of the publication." In finding that *Ulysses* was entitled to such immunity, Hand emphasized the book's "evident truthfulness."

Hand's recognition that society could no more thrive without truthful works of fiction than without truthful works of science transformed the law of obscenity. He held that "the proper test of whether a given book is obscene is its dominant effect" and that the opinion of literary critics is admissible on this central question. Observing that *Hicklin* "would exclude much of the great works of literature and involve an impracticability that

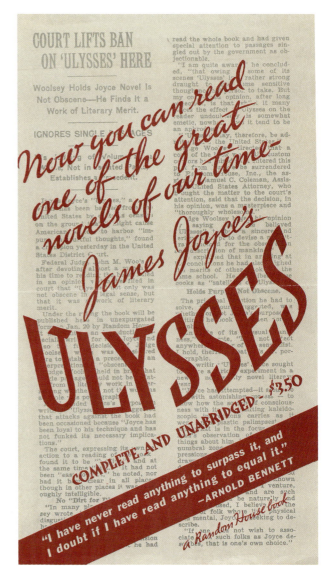

Fig. 7.8. Random House, *Now You Can Read One of the Great Novels of Our Time*, 1933. Rare Book & Manuscript Library, Columbia University.

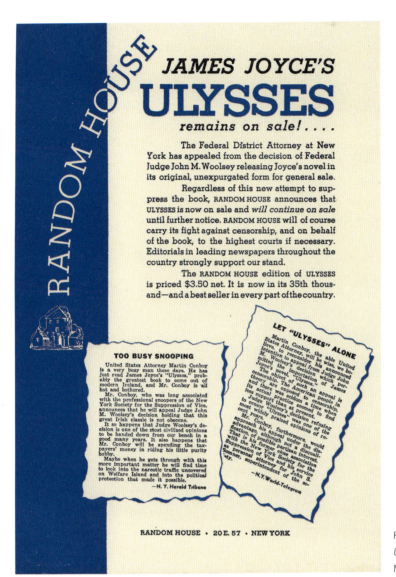

Fig. 7.9. Random House, *James Joyce's Ulysses Remains on Sale!*, 1934. Rare Book & Manuscript Library, Columbia University.

cannot be attributed to Congress," the Hands exercised their power as appellate judges to overrule the earlier Second Circuit decision that had adopted *Hicklin*. The government decided not to seek review by the Supreme Court.

When Joyce learned of Woolsey's decision in December 1933, he observed, "Thus one half of the English speaking world surrenders. The other half will follow."[45]

In fact, England did follow, but not without difficulty. Although T. S. Eliot, the Faber director who dealt with Joyce, was eager to publish a series of episodes in the *Criterion Miscellany*, he feared that publication of the entire book, as Joyce wanted, would result in prosecution.[46] Joyce responded to Eliot that he would not permit "any authorities in either of Bull's islands to dictate to me what and how I am to write."[47] Joyce's rationale for resisting expurgation was true to the principle that guided the favorable federal court decisions. As he explained to Sisley Huddleston, "To consent would be an admission that the expurgated parts are not indispensable. The whole point about them is that they cannot be omitted. Either they are put in gratuitously without reference to my general purpose; or they are an integral part of my book. If they are mere interpolations, my book is inartistic; and if they are strictly in their place, they cannot be left out."[48]

Joyce finally reached agreement with The Bodley Head for publication in 1936 of a deluxe edition of a thousand copies, which included Woolsey's decision. The British government obtained copies of the District Court and Court of Appeals decisions in the *Ulysses* case and relied on them in deciding not to prosecute The Bodley Head for publishing *Ulysses*.[49]

The ideas animating the *Ulysses* decisions found fuller expression in the United States Supreme Court's 1957 ruling in *Roth v. United States*, 354 U.S. 476 (1957), which effectively held that the test of obscenity articulated in the Second Circuit's decision in *Ulysses* was required as a matter of constitutional law. Justice Brennan's opinion for the Court made clear that the First Amendment's protection of freedom of speech and press extends to the arts, and that, accordingly, "portrayal of sex, e.g., in art, literature and scientific works is not itself sufficient reason to deny material the constitutional protection of freedom of speech and press." Citing the Second Circuit's *Ulysses* opinion as reflecting the

constitutionally required standard for determining obscenity, Brennan held that the "'Hicklin test,' must be rejected as unconstitutionally restrictive of the freedoms of speech and press." Seven years later, in *Jacobellis v. Ohio*, 378 U.S. 184 (1964), Justice Brennan, writing for a plurality, glossed his opinion in *Roth* by saying that it recognized "that obscenity is excluded from the constitutional protection only because it is 'utterly without redeeming social importance,' and that . . . [it] follows that material dealing with sex in a manner that advocates ideas . . . or that has literary or scientific or artistic value or any other form of social importance, may not be branded as obscenity and denied the constitutional protection." In short, so long as a book has an iota of literary value, it cannot be obscene. This formulation approximates Anderson and Heap's position that literature cannot be obscene.

Justice Brennan's opinion in *Roth* rested on the general proposition that the constitutional safeguard of the First Amendment "was fashioned to assure unfettered interchange of ideas for the bringing about of political and social changes desired by the people."[50] Brennan later quoted that very language in *New York Times Co. v. Sullivan*, 376 U.S. 254, 269 (1964), to protect newspapers from defamation suits for criticizing public officials unless the statement was knowingly or recklessly false. The same concept underlies Brennan's opinions protecting expressive flag-burning: *Texas v. Johnson*, 491 U.S. 397, 414 (1989), and *United States v. Eichman*, 496 U.S. 310 (1990).

These foundational principles are under constant challenge, not only by attacks on literature under obscenity laws but also by efforts to make it easier for public officials to silence critics[51] and by ominous threats to prosecute advocates of racial equality for such crimes as treason, sedition, and hate speech. For example, former president Trump has asserted that painting the words "Black Lives Matter" on Fifth Avenue would be "a symbol of hate" and thus a hate crime, that a demand for racial equity would constitute treason and sedition, and that it should be a crime to protest America's failure to live up to its ideals by burning a flag.[52]

In a frightening era in which acts of love and support for minorities can be met with hatred from defenders of the status quo, and even characterized as crimes, one of the most significant passages from *Ulysses* is Leopold Bloom's reaction to anti-Semitic and xenophobic taunting. Despite a vile verbal onslaught, Bloom responds magnificently:

Force, hatred, history, all that. That's not life for men and women, insult and hatred. And everybody knows that it's the very opposite of that that is really life.

–What? says Alf.

–Love, says Bloom. I mean the opposite of hatred.[53]

As we celebrate the courage and intelligence of those who brought *Ulysses* to the reading public, it is long past time to establish irrevocably that it is no crime to assert that minority lives matter—and to moot that question entirely by making real the promise of the Declaration of Independence that all are created equal.

DERICK DREHER

8. The Rosenbach Manuscript

On 16 January 1924, Philadelphia dealer Dr. A. S. W. Rosenbach took his seat at the Anderson Galleries for the second session of the sale of the legendary library of New York lawyer John Quinn. It was no surprise to see the "Napoleon of the auction rooms" at the sale, which featured in excess of twelve thousand lots of modern literature over the course of five sessions. Back in November 1923, Rosenbach had paid over $72,000 for manuscripts by Joseph Conrad, garnering headlines, if not resales—he wanted to keep them for his personal collection. Rosenbach ended up leaving the

saleroom on this particular day with the manuscript for James Joyce's novel *Ulysses*.

In hindsight, any price would have been a bargain for such a treasure, but Rosenbach was the only bidder and paid just $1,975. The manuscript of *Ulysses* has been in Philadelphia ever since and is unquestionably the most celebrated item in the collection of The Rosenbach, the museum and library founded by the dealer and his brother Philip.

What exactly was the object offered, why was it for sale, and why did Rosenbach acquire it? The entry in the catalogue is terse, perhaps of necessity for such a sprawling sale, and provides few answers. It simply lists the "ORIGINAL AUTOGRAPH MANUSCRIPT OF 'ULYSSES', written on over 1200 pages," and describes the slipcases in which the various chapters were stored. No price range was provided, though apparently the low estimate for

Fig. 8.1. Frank Budgen, sketch of James Joyce, ca. 1919, detail. Charcoal on wove paper, matted and framed with an explanatory note from the artist. The Rosenbach, Philadelphia (2004.0156).

what the catalogue asserts to be "THE COMPLETE MANUSCRIPT of this remarkable work, one of the most extraordinary produced in modern times and hailed by critics as epoch-making in modern literature," was $2,000. The remainder of the entry quotes T. S. Eliot's praise for the book, or more precisely, his rejection of another critic's negative review. The introduction to the larger section on Joyce also praises the author's industry, noting that his "modern Odyssey contains nearly 300,000 words (many of which are peculiar)."[1]

To be fair, Joyce's reputation was not yet established the way it is now, nor was *Ulysses* accepted as the greatest English-language novel of the twentieth century, as the Modern Library termed it in 1998. At the time of the sale, the novel was best known for what it was *not*: it could not be legally bought and sold in the United States. Portions of the "Nausicaa" chapter of the unfinished novel were featured in the July–August 1920 issue of a literary periodical called the *Little Review*, drawing the attention of the New York Society for the Suppression of Vice. The editors, Margaret Anderson and Jane Heap, were arrested in October 1920 and charged with publishing obscenities, only to be defended at their subsequent trial by none other than John Quinn. His argument—essentially that the book was too difficult to understand to be titillating—did not sway the court, and *Ulysses* was banned for sale in the United States, a decision only overturned in 1934.

Perhaps the notoriety of *Ulysses* was part of the lure for Rosenbach, who enjoyed collecting (and selling) unusual items. Even with a gift for marketing himself, he also sought out subject matter that made it easier to get publicity, ultimately driving sales. On the other hand, the proprietor of Anderson Galleries, Mitchell Kennerley, had presented

Rosenbach with a copy of *Ulysses* immediately after its 1922 publication, making Rosenbach one of the first people in the United States to own the book.

Or again, it may have been a whim. Whatever the proximate reason for the purchase, Rosenbach decided to keep the manuscript for his personal collection. Perhaps Joyce's offer to Quinn to buy it back helped convince the dealer; Quinn warned the author that Rosenbach would ask a much higher price. In the ensuing correspondence, Rosenbach misspelled *Ulysses*, prompting Joyce to pen a limerick lampooning him in a May 1924 letter to Harriet Shaw Weaver:

> Rosy Brook he bought a book
> Though he didn't know how to spell it.
> Such is the lure of literature
> To the lad who can buy it and sell it.[2]

The *Ulysses* manuscript was one of 29 Joyce lots in this particular sale that were described in just five pages of text. Joyce's manuscript for *Exiles* was also offered, as were his autograph corrections for *A Portrait of the Artist as a Young Man* and *Dubliners*—together with printed editions of these and other works. It was an impressive group, though also nothing like the 230 lots of Joseph Conrad (including all of the author's manuscripts) offered in the first sale, which were lovingly described over the course of fifty pages. Quinn had amassed the largest and most important collection of modern literature in private hands, and now it was all for sale.

In the foreword to the catalogue, Quinn wrote, "I have been asked to state what determined me to sell my library and also to write about the books and manuscripts. I am willing to comply with the first request." He goes on to describe being faced with needing to purchase a much larger house or to place

Fig. 8.2. John Quinn Sale at the Anderson Galleries, New York, with
Dr. A. S. W. Rosenbach and A. Edward Newton among others in
attendance, 1924. The Rosenbach, Philadelphia (2006.2451).

much of his library in storage for years at a time. Not willing to take either step, he opted to sell everything instead. Quinn did not disclose that he was terminally ill, but surely his awareness of his grim outlook helped shape his decision. At the time, he also owned the largest private collection of modern European art, and he sold it, too. He died in July 1924.

As was the case with so many of the books and manuscripts Quinn collected, he approached Joyce directly to purchase the *Ulysses* manuscript, making an unsolicited offer on 26 June 1919.[3] It was not their first deal; Quinn had already purchased the corrected proof sheets of *Portrait* and the manuscript

of *Exiles* in March 1917, and soon after he offered to buy any other manuscripts Joyce had available.

At the time of Quinn's offer, *Ulysses* was not yet finished. Joyce ignored Quinn initially, perhaps because there was no pressing need: the heiress Edith Rockefeller McCormick was providing Joyce with a stipend that covered his basic expenses. In October 1919, however, McCormick ended this arrangement. Joyce quickly sent her the manuscript in hopes she would resume her support, or at least purchase the manuscript. She declined, so on 14 October, Joyce cabled Quinn to request "MAXI-MUM ADVANCE MANUSCRIPT ULYSSES."[4] It took several months to finalize the arrangements, but by

Fig. 8.3. Envelope containing episodes 1–9 of the *Ulysses* manuscript sent to John Quinn by James Joyce, postmarked Paris, 12 July 1920. The Rosenbach, Philadelphia (EL4 J89ul 922 MS Supplement). © The Estate of James Joyce.

February 1920, the deal was done. On 24 June 1920, Joyce mailed Quinn a large envelope containing episodes 10 through 14.[5] A month later, now in Paris, Joyce mailed Quinn the manuscript for episodes 1 through 9. That later envelope arrived first, a source of some consternation for Joyce until the second one also arrived. The address panels for both envelopes survive at The Rosenbach.

It becomes clear from their correspondence that Quinn and Joyce both viewed the *Ulysses* manuscript as an object that would eventually be sold. To this end, Quinn seems to have impressed on Joyce that the physical appearance of the manuscript would affect the eventual resale value. This was not the first time Joyce had thought about its potential market value. In a January 1918 letter to Ezra Pound, he expressed his concerns about the cost of having such a long manuscript typed,[6] but just as quickly concluded he might bring in the necessary funds by

selling it. In 1920, Joyce suggested that Quinn might have a typescript made from the manuscript, which was by then in New York, in order to share the text with potential publishers. Quinn termed this suggestion impractical in a letter he sent Ezra Pound shortly thereafter, believing the manuscript to be illegible. Pound concurred: "Re/Joyce . . . . He beats me. How the hell anybody could have supposed *that* mess of a manuscript could be anything but a curiosity destined for you [*sic*] collection!!!!"[7]

Joyce had begun writing out the manuscript on loose sheets of paper in August 1917. He had been working on *Ulysses* since 1914, but his notes and drafts up to this point were intended for his own consumption and generally written in composition books. What he began creating now was a full draft of the book for a typist. It was necessary because of the agreement Joyce had just signed to publish excerpts in the *Little Review*, the first of which appeared in March 1918. The French typists struggled with his handwriting and vocabulary alike. By 1920, Sylvia Beach, the eventual publisher of the first edition of *Ulysses* at her Paris press, Shakespeare and Company, resigned herself to copying out the manuscript in a more legible hand. In 1921, as work continued on the novel, Joyce resumed using composition notebooks, and this is the way the final two episodes are preserved. Quinn was already in possession of the other episodes of the manuscript and Joyce was likely no longer concerned with its physical appearance.

It is challenging to describe what the Rosenbach manuscript of *Ulysses*, in its totality, actually is. It may be easiest to begin by explaining what it is not. In several important respects, it is not what it was described to be in the sale catalogue for Quinn's library. First, the claim that the manuscript is "over 1200 pages" is incorrect. It consists of 698 loose sheets

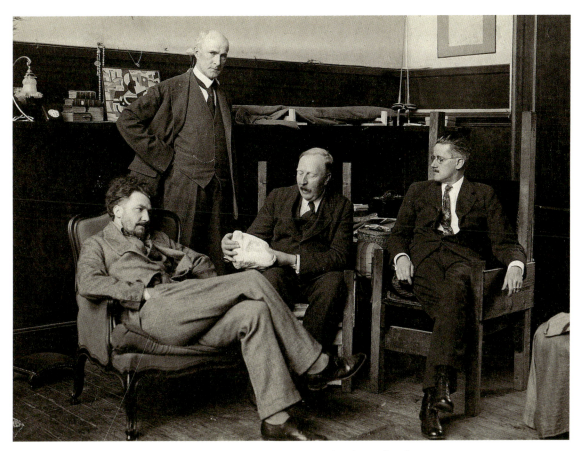

Fig. 8.4. Ezra Pound, John Quinn, Ford Madox Ford, and James Joyce at Pound's Paris apartment, 1923. The Poetry Collection of the University Libraries, University at Buffalo, The State University of New York.

and two composition books containing 60 and 20 leaves, respectively. Second, it is not "the complete manuscript." For reasons that are not entirely clear and may just have been an error, the last few pages of the final episode—the famous final sentence in its entirety—were never sent to Quinn. Quinn later inquired about the missing pages but Joyce told him that he had added the sentence on the proofs. That was not true; these pages remained among Joyce's papers and were later acquired by the Poetry Collection at the University at Buffalo. (For more information about this collection, see chapter 9.) Third, the manuscript is not entirely "in the author's hand."

Sixteen pages of the "Wandering Rocks" episode were written not by Joyce but by his friend Frank Budgen. Joyce suffered from a chronic eye condition and opted to dictate this section of the novel to Budgen during a particularly difficult outbreak. Joyce added a note at the end of the section explaining that it "was written by my friend Francis Budgen at my dictation from notes during my illness January–February 1919." Joyce went so far as to sign the note, an indication that the materiality and authenticity of the manuscript were important to him.

There is another interesting point about Budgen's assistance. At one point while taking a

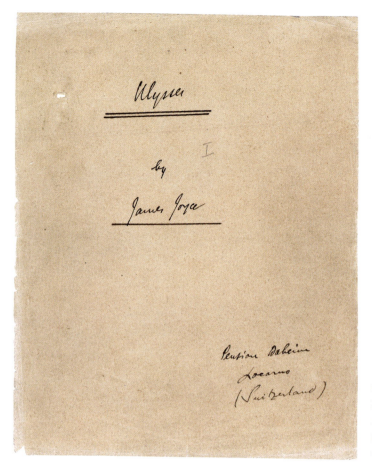

Fig. 8.5. James Joyce, *Ulysses*, title page, Zurich [September–October 1917]. Autograph manuscript. The Rosenbach, Philadelphia (EL4 J89ul 922 MS). © The Estate of James Joyce.

break from dictation, he made a portrait drawing of Joyce. It appears to be drawn on a sheet of paper from precisely the same pile Budgen had been using to write out the text. How appropriate that Budgen's literal portrait of the artist comes from the same stock of paper on which Joyce used words to compose a literary self-portrait.

Dictation was, in any case, not Joyce's usual working method. When Quinn asked him what his practice was, Joyce replied, "I cannot dictate to a stenographer or type. I write all with my hand. When the fair copy is ready I send it to a typist."[8] Joyce uses the words "fair copy" in a very traditional way, implying them to mean a clean draft of a finished text, written out by the author immediately in advance of typing and publication.

Determining whether the Rosenbach manuscript of *Ulysses* should in fact be viewed as a fair copy is the biggest single question surrounding it. Is it the actual draft on which the novel is based, or a fair copy in Joyce's hand, made expressly for Quinn (and the eventual resale), or even something different altogether? Given the many differences between the manuscript and the published text of *Ulysses*, it is tempting to think of it as an advanced draft—neither the first expression of the author's thoughts nor a simple copy of something completely finished. Without specifically trying to answer the fair copy question, Vicki Mahaffey writes that the manuscript "is both a relic and a window into the lives of its author and its owner. It is a monument to success and a record of struggle. It allows us to follow the movement of Joyce's mind and hand—man and *manus*—for a limited period in the composition of *Ulysses*. It gives ample evidence of the difference a single penstroke can make to the meaning of a word or phrase."[9]

The differences between the manuscript and the published text are most pronounced in episodes 5 through 9, 11, 13, and 14. The published text of these chapters is believed not to have been prepared from the Rosenbach manuscript but from a separate, later draft that does not now survive. These are sometimes termed the "collateral" episodes, meaning they are not the primary line of transmission. Still, they are the most complete record available of the creation of the episodes, representing the point at which Joyce first wove the various strands of earlier drafts and notes into a continuous narrative.

Examining each of the eighteen episodes in the manuscript allows additional conclusions to be drawn. As a practical matter, this task first became easy to undertake when The Rosenbach published a complete facsimile of the manuscript in 1975. This was followed by the James Joyce Archive beginning in 1977, which sought to publish facsimiles of all other known Joyce manuscripts and typescripts. Now comparisons between various versions could be made easily. In 1986, Hans Walter Gabler edited a new version of *Ulysses* that took advantage of this fact, correcting thousands of prior errors in the process. Of course, his corrections were not without controversy, igniting what came to be known as the "Joyce wars" in the academic world. The Rosenbach manuscript was ground zero for these literary skirmishes.

It is fair to say that there is still no authoritative version of the text, and there likely never will be. Joyce edited while copying, and once his copying was complete, he edited more. He sent postcards requesting changes to his typist in the earliest days

and corrected the printed page proofs in the final days. Seen in the context of Joyce's near-endless editing, the manuscript should not be viewed as a fair copy but as an advanced draft, except for the most faithful chapters.

Nonetheless, the appearance of "Telemachus," the first episode of *Ulysses*, reveals why many people came to view the Rosenbach manuscript as a fair copy. From the opening line to the end of the first page, there is not a single correction or edit. Indeed, the page looks almost as if drafted to inform the typesetters how the final printed version was meant to look (the page is also sadly browned from years of overexposure to light during the last century). The "clean" text continues throughout the episode, with just a handful of insertions or deletions over thirty pages of manuscript. Another hallmark of Joyce's manuscripts is also evident on these pages: the ever-increasing indent on the left margin, which some have attributed to the author's poor eyesight but may just have been a mannerism.

The four episodes that follow ("Nestor," "Proteus," "Calypso," and "Lotus Eaters") are very similar to "Telemachus" in their relatively neat appearance, with few corrections of any kind. So, too, with the sixth through ninth episodes ("Hades," "Aeolus," "Lestrygonians," and "Scylla and Charybdis"). While these episodes are written in a much looser hand, as if Joyce had been rushing through them (this is particularly true of portions of "Hades" and "Scylla and Charybdis"), they do not leave the impression of an author setting forth his earliest and most tentative thoughts so much as an author preparing a new draft of something he had already completed, for the purpose of publication or sale. Joyce had both in mind. Until recently, however, earlier drafts were not available for any of these chapters except "Proteus," for which an early notebook is preserved in the Buffalo collection. In 2002, the National Library of Ireland was able to acquire a substantial trove of early drafts for *Ulysses* that included partial drafts of "Proteus" and seven other episodes. The drafts are strikingly different from the manuscript in their appearance, from the format (larger paper taken from notebooks, often quadrille-lined) to the extraordinary number of changes and corrections.

These nine episodes constitute the first part of the novel. Joyce wrote "End of First Part of 'Ulysses'" on the last page of "Scylla and Charybdis," adding his address in Zurich and "New Year's Eve 1918" and, of course, signing the page. This first part of *Ulysses* also comprised, as noted above, the second group of manuscripts mailed to Quinn. It is hard to view these first nine chapters of the manuscript as anything other than fair copy. At the same time, one cannot ignore the fact that the printed text shows frequent deviations even from these pages. They do not constitute the finished version, faithfully and "merely" recopied. They are more properly an advanced draft that formed the basis for a later iteration (sometimes several later iterations) and eventually found their way into print.

Episodes 10 through 16 of the Rosenbach manuscript include more frequent deletions, insertions, or entire sentences moved around. Because of the many changes, these episodes have an appearance more consistent with the way most people tend to envision a "true" manuscript: a handwritten record that is a direct antecedent of the final published text, and one that reflects the author's struggles along the way. However, as noted above, only three of these episodes are actually the direct sources for the published chapters, with episodes 11, 13, and 14 evincing considerable differences suggesting that Joyce's publishers relied on the typescript of a later version of those chapters. Paradoxically, episodes 13 and 14 are the "cleanest" chapters in this group, showing far fewer changes than the others.

The last two episodes of the novel, "Ithaca" and "Penelope," are a fascinating part of the Rosenbach manuscript. Joyce wrote them into composition notebooks over the course of 1921. The first thirty-two pages of "Ithaca" are written on the recto pages of a quadrille notebook with a plain blue cover. Joyce edited these pages heavily, sometimes using a red pencil and sometimes drawing arrows across to the verso page, where he then wrote out longer corrections. The episode consists of a call-and-response-style spoof of the catechism, with dozens of mostly brief questions followed by often extensive answers. The final question in this notebook, "Where?" is to be followed by a period, a full stop. Joyce drew one in ink, but evidently unsure his French typist would recognize it as such, he wrote in pencil right after it: "La réponse à la dernière demande est un point" (the answer to the last question is a period).[10]

Joyce wrote a new section that was to be inserted into the middle of the "Ithaca" episode in a separate, shorter quadrille notebook with a green paper cover. It is odd that Joyce began a new notebook, given that he had only used about half of the blue notebook for the first section. He filled the twenty pages of the second notebook with twenty-one pages of text (writing page 21 on the verso of the penultimate page). As before, this smaller notebook is filled with corrections in colored pencil and ink.

For the final, "Penelope" episode of the manuscript, the reader must return to the blue notebook in which "Ithaca" began: one flips the book over and starts from the "back," where Joyce has written "Penelope" at the top. One can only conclude that Joyce had already begun to write "Penelope" before he decided to add a large section to "Ithaca." Perhaps he perceived the blue notebook

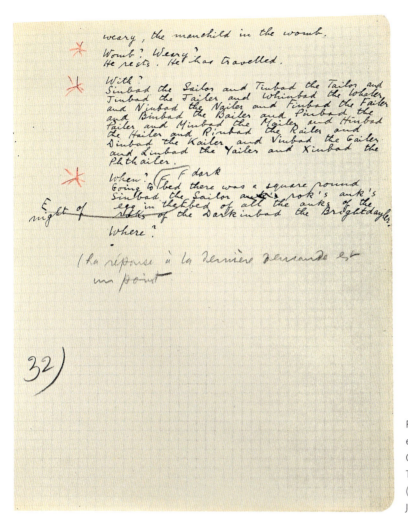

weary, the manchild in the womb.

Womb? Weary?
He rests. He has travelled.

With?
Sinbad the Sailor and Tinbad the Tailor and Jinbad the Jailer and Whinbad the Whaler and Ninbad the Nailer and Finbad the Failer and Binbad the Bailer and Pinbad the Pailer and Minbad the Mailer and Hinbad the Hailer and Rinbad the Railer and Dinbad the Kailer and Vinbad the Bailer and Linbad the Yailer and Xinbad the Phthailer.

When? Going to bed there was a square round Sinbad the Sailor and rok's auk's egg in the bed of all the auks of the rocs of the Darkinbad the Brightdayler.

Where?

(La réponse à la dernière demande est un point

32)

Fig. 8.6. James Joyce, *Ulysses*, "Ithaca" episode, page 32, Paris [August–October 1921]. Autograph manuscript. The Rosenbach, Philadelphia (EL4 .J89ul 922 MS). © The Estate of James Joyce.

no longer had room, although there are fifty-nine blank leaves separating the two chapters. This is perhaps the single best example of Joyce's "additive" style: he simply could not stop adding as he edited, even when he had literally no room to continue. Perhaps this also explains why the last several pages of "Penelope" are not found in either notebook but rather on loose sheets of paper that eventually found their way to a different home.

The Rosenbach manuscript is in part a fair copy. It is in part a "proper" manuscript anticipating the author's final text. It is also in part an advanced draft, a "collateral" text that evinces significant changes to the published version, whether its pages are "clean" or not. It is an enigmatic object, to be sure, but also, as Michael Barsanti has written, "nevertheless the only complete handwritten, hand-made draft of *Ulysses*. It documents the moment at which Joyce's private vision turned outward to face the world."[11]

Fig. 9.1. Joyce family portraits in Librairie La Hune's *Exposition en hommage à James Joyce*, Paris, 1949. The Poetry Collection of the University Libraries, University at Buffalo, The State University of New York.

JAMES MAYNARD

9. The Origins of the University at Buffalo James Joyce Collection

The Poetry Collection of the University Libraries, University at Buffalo, The State University of New York is the home of the UB James Joyce Collection, the world's largest and most comprehensive collection of manuscripts and works by and related to the renowned Irish author. In total, it comprises tens of thousands of pages of the author's working papers, notebooks, manuscripts, photographs, correspondence, portraits, publishing records, important memorabilia, and ephemera, as well as Joyce's Paris library.[1] Supplementing the archive is a complete set of first editions, including most issues and states of every book published by Joyce, translations, a large number of his magazine appearances, and virtually all significant criticism. Together, these materials span the entire course of Joyce's artistic life and provide unmatched glimpses into his writing process and literary relationships.

The James Joyce Collection came to the Poetry Collection in six primary installments from four different sources. The first arrived in the fall of 1950—nine years after Joyce's death—and consisted of the majority of the items that were part of the Librairie La Hune's 1949 *Exposition en hommage à James Joyce* titled "James Joyce: Sa vie, son œuvre, son rayonnement."[2] Organized by several friends of Joyce's family, including Maria Jolas, Lucie Léon, and Bernard Gheerbrant, the founder of La Hune as a bookstore and gallery space on the Boulevard Saint-Germain in Paris, and on view from 15 October through 10 December, the exhibition included the family's collection of Joyceana, which, after traveling to London in June 1950 to be displayed for a month at the Institute of Contemporary Arts, was then to be sold to help provide financial support to Nora and Giorgio Joyce.

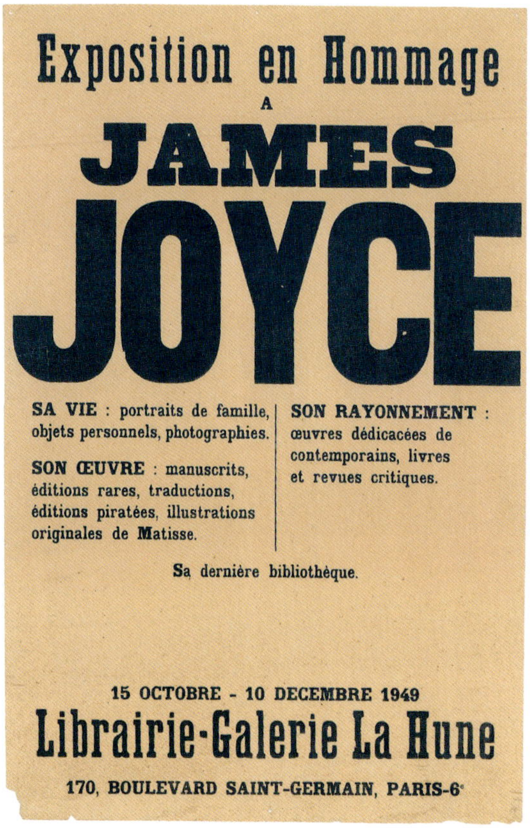

Fig. 9.2. Poster advertising Librairie La Hune's *Exposition en hommage à James Joyce*, Paris, 1949. The Poetry Collection of the University Libraries, University at Buffalo, The State University of New York.

Fig. 9.3. Bloomsday map in Librairie La Hune's *Exposition en hommage à James Joyce*, Paris, 1949. The Poetry Collection of the University Libraries, University at Buffalo, The State University of New York.

Fortunately for what was then the private University of Buffalo, English professor Oscar A. Silverman, later Charles Abbott's successor as director of the University Libraries and namesake of today's Silverman Library, was in Paris on sabbatical in the fall of 1949 and visited the exhibition several times, including once with Lucie Léon, the widow of Paul Léon.[3] Upon his return to Buffalo, Silverman helped set into motion a series of events that resulted in Charles Abbott's receiving a letter from Gheerbrant dated 7 June 1950 offering the items in the La Hune exhibition for sale.[4] Gheerbrant wrote to say that the family was asking $10,000 for the collection and that he hoped to avoid dispersing it. Recognizing the enormous opportunity at hand to add to the holdings of what was then known as the Lockwood Memorial Library, Silverman and Abbott acted swiftly to marshal university support, and that same day Abbott sent a cablegram to Gheerbrant offering a $100 option, drawn up by the dean of the law school, to purchase the entire collection pending his review of a complete list of its contents.

Gheerbrant accepted this proposal in a cablegram indicating that the option was good until 20 June. After having had the chance to review additional documentation, Abbott both cabled and wrote on 15 June to agree to the family's price, although he still had questions about exactly what was included in the purchase. These concerns were quickly addressed by Gheerbrant, and on 21 June Abbott sent him a check for $5,000, with the other half to be paid once the entire collection arrived. The funding for this acquisition came by virtue of a gift from Margaretta F. Wickser made in memory of her husband, Philip J. Wickser, a Buffalo arts patron, book collector, and lawyer who was president of the American Bar Association.[5] Concerning

the acquisition, Abbott wrote to Gheerbrant on 10 July that "we are delighted that the Joyce collection is to become a part of our holdings in the field of modern literature. I can assure you (and the Joyce family) that we shall give it the best of care and will cherish it as one of our most precious possessions."

The Joyce family collection of nearly six hundred items from "James Joyce: Sa vie, son œuvre, son rayonnement" arrived in September 1950 and comprised a substantial body of holograph manuscripts featuring twenty-two loose sheets of Joyce's early "epiphanies"; the earliest extant notes for *Exiles*; notebooks and draft copybooks for *Ulysses* (including various manuscripts for six episodes: "Proteus," "Sirens," "Cyclops," "Nausicaa," "Oxen of the Sun," and "Circe"); a notebook with fair copies of poems from *Pomes Penyeach*; sixty-nine of the seventy notebooks known to exist for *Finnegans Wake*; and additional notebooks written while Joyce was living in Zurich, Trieste, and Paris, as well as various other notes and manuscripts. Also included were many letters to Joyce by such associates as Richard Aldington, Margaret Anderson, Sylvia Beach, Samuel Beckett, Nancy Cunard, T. S. Eliot, Ford Madox Ford, Ernest Hemingway, Valery Larbaud, Ezra Pound, John Quinn, and W. B. Yeats, as well as Joyce's father and brother; three of his canes (two of them monogrammed), a pair of eyeglasses, two British passports issued in 1924 and 1935, French identity and ration cards from 1939, the Joyce family crest and coat of arms, and other personal effects; Joyce's collection of newspaper and other clippings; and various editions of the author's published works. Not everything listed in the La Hune exhibition catalogue came to Buffalo. For instance, when informed that Joyce's death mask had been loaned to the exhibition by Carola Giedion-Welcker, Charles Abbott wrote to her to ask if she would consider adding it to the collection.

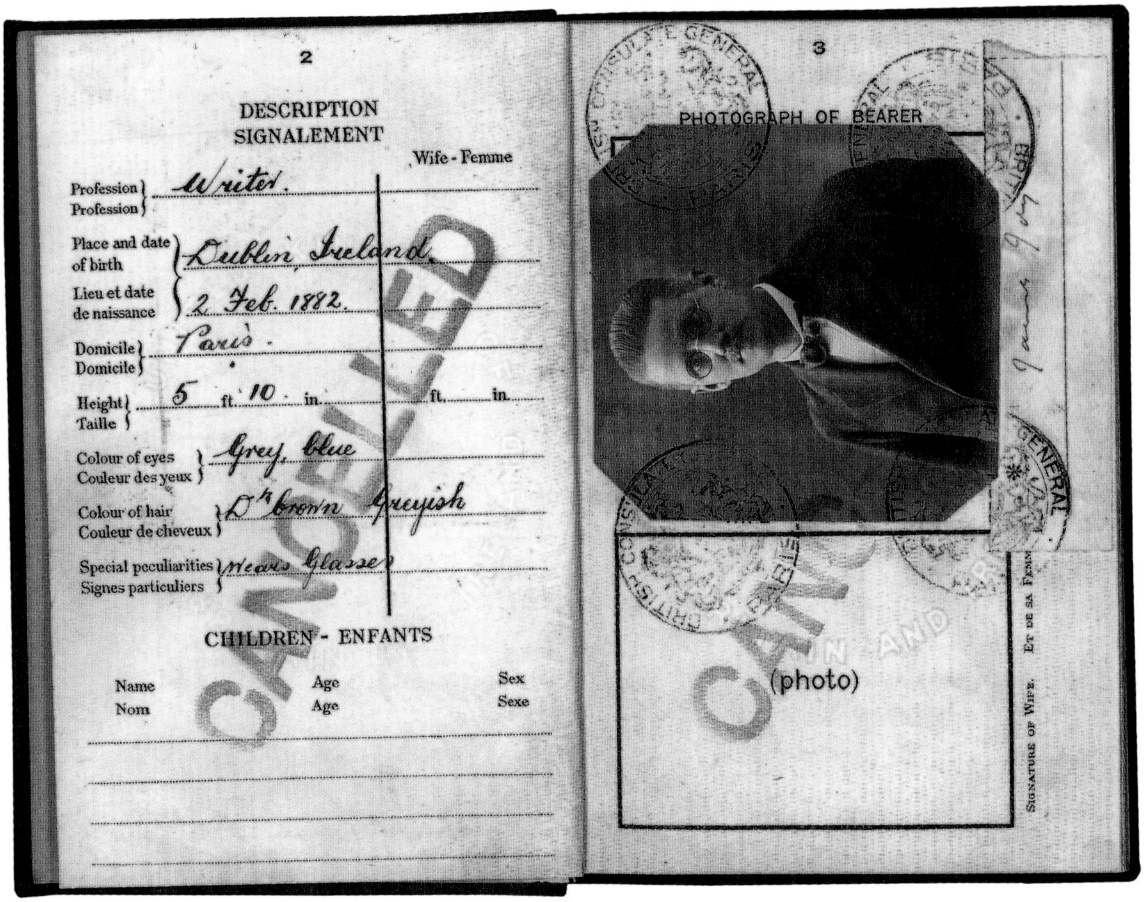

Fig. 9.4. James Joyce's passport, 1924. The Poetry Collection of the University Libraries, University at Buffalo, The State University of New York. © The Estate of James Joyce.

There was also a significant collection of family photographs and portraits as well as the surviving contents of Joyce's Paris library, containing more than 468 books, many of them signed and inscribed to Joyce by his contemporaries, and periodicals.[6] Among the portraits are paintings and sketches of Joyce; his wife, Nora; his father, John Stanislaus; his mother, Mary Jane Murray; his daughter, Lucia; his paternal grandparents and great-grandparents; Livia Veneziani Schmitz, who was the wife of Ettore Schmitz (Italo Svevo) and served as a model of sorts for Anna Livia Plurabelle; and Harriet Shaw Weaver by such artists as John Comerford, Patrick Tuohy, Frank Budgen, Tullio Silvestri, Umberto Veruda, and Wyndham Lewis.[7]

That all of these materials even survived to make it to the exhibition at La Hune and eventually to Buffalo is a remarkable story in itself. When the Joyces left their apartment at 34 rue des Vignes at the end of 1939 in advance of the Nazi occupation of Paris, eventually making their way to Zurich, they left their belongings behind. At that time many of Joyce's affairs were taken care of by his friend and secretary Paul Léon, and as the story goes, it was Léon who twice crossed the streets of occupied Paris with a handyman and a pushcart to rescue materials from Joyce's apartment, having bribed the concierge, and who later bought back additional items when they were auctioned off by the owner of the apartment as reimbursement for unpaid rent.[8] Although the belongings were safeguarded by Paul and Lucie Léon and eventually returned to Nora Joyce after the war, Paul himself was arrested by the Nazis on 21 August 1941. In 1942 he was transferred to Auschwitz, where he was murdered. Consequently, it is no exaggeration to say, along with Sam Slote and Luca Crispi, respectively, that "were it not for Léon and his dedication to Joyce there would be no

Fig. 9.5. B. W. Huebsch. The Poetry Collection of the University Libraries, University at Buffalo, The State University of New York.

collection of Joyce material at Buffalo," and "the breadth and scope of the Joyce scholarship that has followed, whether textual or bibliographical, would not have been possible."[9]

Two more installments were donated in May 1951 and December 1959 by B. W. Huebsch, whose New York publishing company of the same name published the first edition of Joyce's *A Portrait of the Artist as a Young Man* and the first American editions of *Dubliners*, *Exiles*, and *Chamber Music* before merging with the Viking Press in 1925. These included several letters between Joyce and Huebsch, a few page proofs for *Portrait* and errata lists made by Joyce based on Huebsch's first edition of the novel, and additional errata lists prepared by Joyce for *Dubliners* and *Finnegans Wake*.

Another large and significant consignment came in 1959 with the purchase of Joyce materials from Sylvia Beach, the legendary proprietor of the famous modernist bookstore Shakespeare and Company and publisher of the first edition of *Ulysses*, thanks to Constance and Walter Stafford's hands-on negotiations as well as their financial commitment. In 1958 Oscar Silverman learned from Jackson Matthews, a poet, scholar, and translator of Paul Valéry who was one of Beach's friends, that her Joyce collection might be available.[10] After initiating contact with her that fall, Silverman flew to Paris on 30 November along with his friends Constance and Walter Stafford, who were interested in supporting an acquisition of Beach's materials. Walter Stafford, who received his medical degree from UB in 1944, taught neurology and served as associate dean of academic affairs in the university's medical school. At the time, Beach was busy organizing the exhibition *Les années vingt: Les écrivains américains à Paris et leurs amis, 1920–1930* that ran from 11 March through 25 April 1959 at the Centre Culturel Américain in Paris. Of their conversation and the role played by the Staffords, Silverman writes, "Miss Beach had insisted on the transatlantic telephone the previous week that she had no time to discuss the matter of disposing of her collection with us. Nevertheless, through the charm of the young woman, Mrs. Stafford, who, with her husband, was to present the collection to the University, Miss Beach agreed at least that she would make no disposition of her materials without giving us first chance."[11] On 6 December Silverman made a formal offer of $55,510 to Beach for her Joyce collection. Eventually an agreement was reached, and a few months later Beach traveled to Buffalo, where on 7 June 1959 she was presented by the University with an honorary doctorate in recognition of her courage and foresight in publishing *Ulysses* in 1922. Silverman and the Staffords returned to France later that summer to help pack up her collection in August; afterward, the Staffords flew back to the States, while Silverman, at Beach's request, accompanied the materials by boat on the Cunard Line's *Queen Elizabeth*. More Beach materials arrived after her death in 1962, again through the support of the Staffords and the generosity of Mrs. Spencer Kittinger and the Friends of the Lockwood Memorial Library, following the publication of Peter Spielberg's descriptive catalogue of the Joyce Collection.[12]

The Beach portion of the UB James Joyce Collection provides a fascinating record of how *Ulysses* was produced. It encompasses copies of the Linati and Beach schemas; holograph manuscripts for *Ulysses*, including drafts of the episodes "Cyclops," "Oxen of the Sun," and "Eumaeus" as well as an addition to "Circe" and five loose sheets that are a later fair-copy manuscript of the final sentence of "Penelope" (continuing the manuscript of *Ulysses* that A. S. W. Rosenbach obtained from John Quinn in 1924); typescripts for all but the first episode of *Ulysses*; drafts for the design of the novel's front matter, many in Joyce's hand, and proofs of the cover; 157 letters from Imprimerie Darantiere, the French publishing firm in Dijon that printed *Ulysses*; 279 items of correspondence from Joyce to Beach; copies and drafts of Joyce's outgoing correspondence; numerous drafts of the subscription forms used to sell *Ulysses*, along with seventy-five completed forms from such notable figures as W. B. Yeats, William Carlos Williams, Peggy Guggenheim, Hart Crane, and Samuel Roth; Beach's accounting diaries; and the pen Joyce used to sign the first one hundred copies of *Ulysses*. No proper version of the material history of

Fig. 9.6. Sylvia Beach's apartment in Paris. The Poetry Collection of
the University Libraries, University at Buffalo,
The State University of New York.

modernism would be complete without these records and documents. Also included is one of the world's great association copies: copy number 2 of the first edition of *Ulysses*, signed and inscribed by Joyce "To Sylvia Beach in token of gratitude James Joyce Paris 13 February 1922," bound by Beach in blue Morocco (to approximate the color of the French paper wrappers) along with Joyce's poem of appreciation and homage, "Who is Sylvia," written after William Shakespeare's lines beginning "Who is Silvia" in *The Two Gentlemen of Verona*. The circumstances of this gift and of her many extraordinary experiences with Joyce and other writers are

engagingly told in her memoir, *Shakespeare and Company*, which was published the same year her collection arrived in Buffalo.[13]

Far from focusing only on *Ulysses*, the Beach collection also features the only known holograph of Joyce's 1904 essay "A Portrait of the Artist" along with notes on the plot and characters of *Stephen Hero*, written in his sister Mabel's copybook and gifted to Beach in January 1928; several holograph and typescript versions of Joyce's occasional verses, such as "P.J.T.," his limerick parody of the painter Patrick Tuohy; typescripts, galley and page proofs, and errata for *Finnegans*

Fig. 9.7. Oscar A. Silverman in Paris. The Poetry Collection of the University Libraries, University at Buffalo, The State University of New York.

Wake; holograph and typescript drafts of Joyce's lecture "Daniele Defoe" and a scribal copy of his essay "The Day of the Rabblement"; copies of the recordings of Joyce reading from *Ulysses* ("Aeolus") and *Finnegans Wake* ("Anna Livia Plurabelle"); and other miscellaneous manuscripts. Additionally, there are photographs, many of them signed and dated by Joyce, and editions of Joyce's publications inscribed to Beach. Some of Beach's Joyce material had previously been shown as part of the La Hune exhibition and later in *Les années vingt*. Accompanying it all are Beach's own carefully prepared notes and dates documenting, as best she could, the circumstances in which she received everything. In this regard, she was not only Joyce's friend, agent, and publisher but also one of his first archivists. Indeed, over the years Beach kept such Joyce-related items as a leather wristwatch strap that had once belonged to the writer; a radiograph of his teeth; different menus, including one from the 7 June 1929 "Déjeuner *Ulysse*" organized by Beach and her partner, Adrienne Monnier, to celebrate the first French translation of the novel; the label from a bottle of Clos Saint Patrice/Châteauneuf-du-Pape; and two Irish lace handkerchiefs she received from Lucia Joyce.

Finally, nearly two decades after she had first helped prepare the exhibition of Joyce family items at the Librairie La Hune, Maria Jolas provided the sixth and final installment to the UB James Joyce Collection in 1968. This acquisition consisted of 1927–28 galley proofs (known in French as *placards*) from the serialized publication of *Finnegans Wake* as "Work in Progress" in *transition*, the experimental literary journal that Maria and her husband, Eugene Jolas, established in Paris and distributed through Sylvia Beach's Shakespeare and Company. These six galley proofs, all heavily revised by Joyce, are from *transition* issues 4, 5, 11, 12, and 13. In truth, though, the Poetry Collection continues to add to the UB James Joyce Collection whenever possible through the purchase of new editions of Joyce's writings, scholarly publications related to Joyce, and the acquisition of archival and other materials.

Today, the Poetry Collection and the University Libraries continue to explore how to share this renowned collection with a wider and more inclusive audience, with the goal of creating a UB James Joyce Museum. In addition to a permanent exhibition space, we are also seeking to guarantee the Joyce Collection's future growth through a preservation and acquisitions endowment, a James Joyce curator, and programming and exhibition funds.

In this pursuit our aim is nothing less than to invite the entire world to experience the literary life and works of Ireland's James Joyce while ensuring the continuation of the UB James Joyce Collection as an international destination for research and discovery. And it is for this reason, too, that we are honored and pleased to provide major contributions from the UB James Joyce Collection to The Morgan Library & Museum's exhibition *One Hundred Years of James Joyce's "Ulysses."*

Fig. 10.1. Reto Guntli, photograph of Sean and Mary Kelly.
Courtesy of Sean Kelly, New York.

10. Sean Kelly

COLM TÓIBÍN: Sean, can you tell me where and when you came across or first read *Ulysses*?

SEAN KELLY: I know that I first encountered it when I left home. So, my guess is that I was between about thirteen and fifteen. I was living on the streets in London. I remember that I had heard about this book which was supposed to be impossible to read and very difficult. I don't know why, but if you set me a challenge, I like to rise to it.

One of the things that I didn't know before I picked it up was that it was set on my birthday. But I found that out very quickly, then I started to make these other mental connections to it.

CT: Could you give us an idea what your other reading was at that time?

SK: I was reading a lot of the classics in European and American literature. Dostoevsky. Salinger. I didn't take to Proust too well. But I was especially attracted to the classics. With hindsight I realize I was trying to educate myself because I wasn't getting a formal education, and this was my way of trying to compensate for that.

CT: What was the experience of reading *Ulysses* for you?

SK: I mean, just absolutely mindboggling, to be honest. I can remember that around that time I was also reading a lot of very current '60s, hippie-ish literature. Things like Richard Brautigan's *Trout Fishing in America*, which I still love to this day as well as everything else he wrote—and Carlos Castaneda and many other writers at that time. But

Ulysses just really blew me out of the water. I've never read it formally. I've never read it with a guide, and I've never taken a seminar on it. I would love to do that, and I've often said to you that when you're teaching it, I would love to sit in the back of the room and do it properly.

The classics felt very much as if they belonged to the nineteenth century, and the Richard Brautigans of this world felt like they belonged to the moment. But *Ulysses* felt like it belonged out of time. Right down to the way that it was written or constructed, I found the whole thing so extraordinarily rich. It felt absolutely like the most groundbreaking piece of literature I had ever picked up. I was just amazed by it.

Over the years my repeated readings of it have rewarded me so much and made me understand a lot about the human condition. I can go back to it ten, twenty, thirty, forty, fifty years later and have such a different reading experience because, obviously, I've changed and my experience and knowledge have changed, but the book stands up and has remained consistent. It's like a fulcrum for everything that moves me. I always find it rewarding, always shocking and astounding.

CT: I think that happens to readers of the book where a passage or an episode that seemed inaccessible or difficult or just didn't speak to them at a certain time then comes to the fore on a rereading. I think that can happen, for example, with "Wandering Rocks" or "Oxen of the Sun"—"Wandering Rocks" being the episode where the scenes are spliced as though it's a sort of film edit, and "Oxen of the Sun" being the one where the history of English prose in parody is used in the hospital as the woman is having the baby. I now find those two sections absolutely fascinate me as did "Cyclops"

once upon a time or "Penelope," Molly Bloom's soliloquy. I was just wondering if you'd give us some idea of how rereading actually changes the whole way you think about a book, particularly this book.

SK: I always feel for me it's more like absorption rather than analysis. I think the thing that interested me about it then was that everybody was so appalled and shocked by it, and I didn't find it shocking at all. I just thought that such events were part of our day, part of our life, like going to the bathroom, or making love, or having a tender moment, or a fight. I found them very contemporary, not shocking at all. I've visited Dublin and gone to Sweny's chemist, to the tower in Sandycove, but I'm not a junkie like that. I don't need that kind of fix. I feel like I can step into that book and it feels utterly contemporary, even when obviously a lot of it is not. You wouldn't go to a newspaper's offices and place an advert, et cetera, but I belonged to the world where you could, so I find it absolutely absorbing and contemporary as an experience.

CT: Sean, could you give us an account of your own life between the time you read the book and the time that you began to collect Joyce material? What happened to you in those years?

SK: Well, I ran away from home when I was thirteen and I was living on my own. I was living rough. I met my wife Mary just before I was sixteen. I hadn't had any formal education from the age of thirteen onwards. Mary went to Bath Technical College, one of the places at that time where you could focus on specific academic goals.

I also enrolled there but I was still living rough and, frankly, it was a good place to hang out. I went on the student union and became the social secretary, the guy who booked the bands and took care of the social side of the college. That was very helpful because (a) it gave me somewhere to live, the office, where I used to sleep on top of the filing cabinets because I didn't have anywhere else to go—and (b) it put me in contact with musicians and artists. I got very involved with rock and roll at that time, which was, in an earlier era, a bit like running away and going to the circus, but I ran away and got involved with bands. So, for a long time I was involved with a lot of creative people who were making music.

Mary got her A levels and took a gap year, sometime around 1972 or 1973. We stayed in Bath. She then got a place in Cardiff to study pharmacy, the University of Wales Institute of Science and Technology (UWIST). I went to Cardiff with her, got an apartment, and set up somewhere for us to live. I applied to art school—although I didn't have any formal education. At that time, you could get in on the basis of a portfolio, so I put together a portfolio, applied to Cardiff College of Art, and got offered a place.

CT: What was in the portfolio?

SK: It wasn't very traditional. I wasn't making life drawings or anything like that, but I was always making things. I put in what interested me, conceptually oriented work rather than representational, a lot of collaged drawings, appropriated material reworked. I got offered a place, but they resisted taking me because I didn't have a traditional education. During the interview they said, "Why are you here and why are you applying?" I told them and they asked, "What will you do if you don't get in?" I replied, "I'll apply next year. So, you might as well let me in this year, because my girlfriend/wife is here and I'll just keep applying because I'm going to stay here and I want to come." I think in the end I was so cheeky that I wore them down.

They did give me a place: I started in 1974, did my BA, and graduated in 1978. In 1976 Mary's Aunt Flossy died and left us £500 with the suggestion, "Why don't you buy yourself a sofa?"—which seemed to me terribly sensible and completely not what I wanted to do. So, I suggested to Mary, "Why don't we take the £500 and go to America for four months?"

So, we went to America for four months on the basis of Aunt Flossy's gift. We flew Freddie Laker then took Greyhound buses all over the country, which was incredibly formative for me because I realized how much I loved being here, especially New York. My sister Lynne had come a couple of years earlier and was living in Chicago, where she was working for a fashion store called Ultimo. She knew all the artists and collectors in Chicago. We got to meet them and it was just mind-blowing. It opened my eyes to not only the artists, the Hairy Who and the realist artists who were there, but also the collectors.

I returned to college in the fall of 1976 just absolutely astonished at the breadth, depth, and wealth of the visual arts experience in America. It was like somebody peeled the layers off my eyes, and I knew that I would return.

After I graduated in 1978, I worked as an artist, teacher, and lecturer until about 1980 or 1981. Mary had finished college. At that point I needed a job, I was finding being in the studio very tough. My studio was in the docks in Cardiff. I needed to go somewhere else, do something else. At that time, I was approached by the Welsh Arts Council to take on the position of exhibitions officer at the Glynn Vivian Art Gallery in Swansea.

Fig. 10.2. Glynn Vivian Art Gallery, Swansea. Courtesy of Glynn Vivian Art Gallery.

I jumped into it and ran it for four years, then I moved back to Bath. I approached South West Arts with an idea for the Bath Festival. The festival was the second-most important festival after Edinburgh but had no visual arts component.

So, I wrote a program, went to them, and said, "Look, I think it would be really exciting to do this. Are you interested?" South West Arts put up £7,000, which was my entire budget, including my salary. I set up what became known as ArtSite and it became very successful. I was spending about £1 million pounds a year by the time I left. After five years of doing it—it was very tough, very intense—I realized that I was effectively raising all the money and spending it. I could see that under Margaret Thatcher public subsidy was going to be withdrawn or diminished. My deal with the Festival was, "If you're not going to give me the money, then you can't tell me how to spend it if I raise it." As long as I didn't go into debt, I had artistic control.

I had a fantastic five years, but I didn't want to end up running the same thing for a long period of time. So, I told them I was going to leave, and I did. Through a contact of Edward Lucie-Smith, the writer and critic, I got a job in America. I moved there to work for a gallery in 1989 just as the market totally collapsed.

CT: Talk to me about the beginnings of collecting Joyce material, as to what state was the market in or how easy was it to find things. How did you go about that?

SK: I tend to follow my instincts. I love books. I'm profoundly influenced by my environment; it was very, very difficult when I was homeless not to have things. My books and my record collection were always incredibly important to me and went everywhere I went. Even when we sold everything to come to America the books came along with us.

I was always acquiring things and visiting book dealers wherever I went to ferret stuff out. We went to see friends in Santa Barbara, and I remember on that trip that we went to one of the better-known book dealers in L.A. and bought a few things that are now in the Morgan collection—not very expensive things, but it was a lot of money for me at that point. I suppose I was really putting together— well, I wouldn't call it a collection. I was putting together books on *Ulysses*, association material, interpretive biographical material on Joyce.

While we were in Santa Barbara, Mary and I visited the dealer Ralph Sipper. As I was leaving, I asked him if he had anything on Joyce. He said, "Not very much," but he had just done a show that had some of the literary classics in it, and he added, "I do have a first edition." My first instinct was to say, "I could never afford that." I think it was priced at $20,000 or thereabouts. He replied, "I could give you a discount on it," but I was dubious and said something like, "I'm sure I still couldn't afford it." He offered it to me for $12,000, it was coming up to my fortieth birthday, I said to Mary, "I'd really like to buy this for my birthday," and asked him if I could pay $1,000 a month on my credit card. Ralph was very nice and allowed me to pay it off over a year. That is one of my *Ulysses* first editions now in the Morgan, one of the 750 copies on handmade paper. Then I had the bug for the more rare, esoteric material, but that was the first major thing I bought.

CT: And what happened next? Do you visit the bookstores in the various places in America where such material is available? Or did you become more organized?

SK: I got very organized. When I find my way to something, then I get serious about it. I started to do my research and found my way to other dealers like Rick Gekoski and Glenn Horowitz and I began to visit the book fairs. Being a dealer in a different

Fig. 10.3. Augustus John, crayon portrait of James Joyce, collotype frontispiece in *Collected Poems of James Joyce*, 1936. One of three lettered copies *hors de commerce*. The Morgan Library & Museum, New York. Gift of Sean and Mary Kelly, 2018.

area, not books but art, my concern was that I didn't want people to know who I am or what I'm doing. So, I tried to be a little bit under the radar, I would never go in and tell people who I was or leave a card or anything of that sort. I always wanted to be very private. But I did get very, very serious about it, and that's when I really started buying better things and expanding a little outside the *Ulysses* department. I found people whom I liked or trusted. I talked to Rick about it a lot and I'd ask for his opinions and suggestions where else I could get advice.

CT: Sean, I was wondering if it's possible to connect that early reading of the book, a novel that really does make it new in so many ways, and what you've been doing as a gallerist. You are at the cutting edge of what's going on in visual art, and I wonder if you could connect your interest in this book and your way of approaching contemporary art.

SK: I think I'm somebody who has kind of good street sense. I never approach these things analytically, but I think that one thing leads you to another. So, Joyce—inevitably Joyce, if one reads about Joyce, you start to get immersed in the classics. So, Joyce takes you to Pound, and Eliot.

I do the same thing with visual arts. The people I really felt connected to or admired were all the outsiders. They weren't the people who were making the most money. It wasn't Picasso. When I got involved with Joyce, I discovered that he lived the life of a real artist. He lived in penury. He lived off his friends and patrons. He lived from hand to mouth, and gave up a lot for his art.

I never had any idea of being in the art world in the way that I am now. Thirty years ago, it was a very different world. Now the amount of money in the art world is somewhat problematic and antithetical to the idealism I found in Joyce and Duchamp. They're my go-to guys. They're my touchstones. I set out on this experiment to see if I could be in the art world in as pure a way as possible and survive it and be in a world where there's a lot of money and not change my ideals or idealism, and actually work with artists because I wanted to work with them as artists, not because I could make a lot of money from it. Honestly, to this day, that's my guiding principle. I'm still trying to do it in a way the artists I admire would have understood or appreciated.

I don't naturally veer towards Picasso. I veer towards Duchamp. I don't naturally veer towards artists who are market darlings. I veer towards artists who I believe are instrumental in changing the language we use, who may perhaps not be as successful in their lifetimes. But it's my job to create an environment where I can support them and make them as successful as they can possibly be, and perhaps change our visual language, change the landscape.

Did Joyce take me to where I am now? Absolutely, no question—because without his example I would never have thought of all the things that I've been able to conjure up. I think he and Duchamp are these incredible paradigms, inspirational in literature and the arts. They're touchstones for me. They're like shamans.

CT: When I first saw the collection, it was in your house upstate where a space had been created, a beautiful library. And I thought, "How do you part with that?" Tell me about the impulse to remove that from your own house to a public institution.

SK: Well, the building itself, the house upstate, had been conceived around the Joyce material, to be honest. I certainly talked with the architect Toshiko Mori about it a lot. In many respects the library was kind of

Fig. 10.4. William Waldron, photograph of Sean and Mary Kelly's library, *Architectural Digest* (November 2011).

the intellectual heart of the building, of course the idea was that it would never leave. Actually, Rick was responsible for this because he and Belinda [Kitchin] came up one weekend to visit with us. We had a lovely weekend and drank far too many good bottles of red wine. Rick spent a couple of days upstairs going through all the material. I didn't ask him to, although I was very happy he did it of course. I remember very distinctly: he came downstairs and sat down looking a little bit shocked. I was somewhat concerned and wondered if he had found that something that wasn't

correct. In a very Rick way he said, "My God, Sean. That's got to be one of the best collections in private hands in the world. What are you going to do with it? You have such a responsibility."

I was totally shocked and really taken aback for a couple of reasons. One was that I had never ever thought of the Joyce material as being a collection. And I hadn't thought about my responsibility to the material, because of course it wasn't kept in perfect environmental conditions.

Rick and I started a conversation about what

Fig. 10.5. Marcel Duchamp, front cover of *transition* 26 (1937). The Morgan Library & Museum, New York. Gift of Sean and Mary Kelly, 2018.

else one could add to the materials that would make it more complete. When we started talking about it—the conversation went on for a number of months—it became apparent that there really wasn't anything more that I could add to it that was likely to come on the market at a price I could afford. In some ways it would never be complete.

I was quite shocked thinking about Rick's use of the word "collection." I had never thought of myself as a Joyce collector. It brought me up short and I had to think what that meant to me. I suppose that process took a year or so. By that point I was more conscious of a sense of the responsibility to the collection. In the end I concluded that the collection should go somewhere that it could have a broader audience and be looked after better than we could. We discussed the fact that the two major things that I collect are Joyce and Duchamp. So, I sat down with

Mary and the kids and said, "I would like one of these collections to remain intact and have our name attached to it and be in a public institution. Which one do you feel least attached to?"

Our children are in the art world, and they said, "We'd rather have the Duchamp." They feel more attached to Duchamp than they do to Joyce. We told them, "Okay, give the Joyce material to an institution we feel strongly about. And if we do that, then you can do what you want with the Duchamp material. It can be sold. It can be broken up. There's no restrictions on it."

After we agreed on that, Mary and I discussed where should it go—who we should we talk to. We both wanted to see if the Morgan would be interested, because we love it, it's a jewel, like the Frick. The Morgan and the Frick are two examples of institutions that are the perfect size and exemplify the perfect level of scholarship; the richness of the experience is so profound. At that point we approached Colin [Bailey] through Declan [Kiely], who was still at the Morgan at that time. It turned out that the Morgan was not strong in Joyce and would like to collect in that area, that was how it happened.

JOHN BIDWELL: Sean, when was the last time you read *Ulysses*?

SK: We used to go to the Caribbean every summer with the kids. I know that is probably the least likely place to read *Ulysses*, but it was my summer reading. I would reread it every summer. I read it for about seven or eight years every August. I suppose the last time I read it was probably about seven years ago.

JB: You've said that you never really thought of yourself as a collector. So, you had relationships with antiquarian booksellers like Rick, Ralph

Sipper, and Glenn Horowitz. Did you think about using a list, a catalogue, or a bibliography?

SK: Not really. I did get hold of the publications that Horowitz had done on Joyce when he was putting together collections for sale. I consulted those and talked to Rick about a list of gaps in our collection, as it were, but not really an institutional bibliography, no.

JB: And you have made it clear that you don't consider yourself a completist.

SK: No. That's not the aim for me. I think when one goes down these rabbit holes with somebody like Joyce or Duchamp, there are people deeply obsessed with the material who are often burrowed in defending their positions. I've never wanted to be like that. I didn't want it to be like collecting baseball cards: where you have to have every one. I'm not really wired like that. I've always collected things since I was a kid, like stamps or cards, but somehow I'd never quite filled the book, if you know what I mean. I'd always sort of lose interest. I liked the pursuit and the thrill of the chase more than filling out the book.

JB: Do you detect any connections between your Joyce collection and your Duchamp collection, either an artistic relationship or maybe just some kind of resonance?

SK: Profoundly. Although they didn't know each other well, they certainly knew of each other. I think they met on at least one occasion. There was a dinner they both attended. I don't think they are linked in an obvious way other than as sort of the czars of modernism. But in less specific ways I

Fig. 10.6. Constantin Brancusi, portrait of James Joyce, 1929. Pencil on paper. The Poetry Collection of the University Libraries, University at Buffalo, The State University of New York.

think the resonances between them are incredible and profound. Of course, Brancusi is the fulcrum around which much of this hinges because he made a frontispiece drawing of Joyce that depicts him as an abstraction [fig. 10.7]. Duchamp made his living in America as Brancusi's dealer for decades and sold all the great Brancusi works to the Arensbergs, etc.

So, there are connections. But I think the biggest connection is this shared ideal of modernist reimagining and restructuring of the world. Those connections are very rich and meaningful to me.

Fig. 10.7. Constantin Brancusi, abstract portrait of James Joyce in
Joyce's *Tales Told of Shem and Shaun*, 1929. The Morgan Library &
Museum, New York. Gift of Sean and Mary Kelly, 2018.

JAMES JOYCE

Advance Press Notices.

— Mr. EZRA POUND in — *Instigations* — His profoundest work... an impassioned meditation on life... He has done what Flaubert set out to do in Bouvard et Pécuchet, done it better, more succint.

— Mr. RICHARD ALDINGTON in — *The English Review* — A most remarkable book... Bloom is a rags and tatters Hamlet, a proletarian Lear... An astonishing psychological document... ULYSSES is more bitter, more sordid, more ferociously satirical than anything Mr. JOYCE has yet written... A tremendous libel on humanity which I, at least, am not clever enough to refute.

— THE OBSERVER — ... Whatever may be thought of the work, it is going to attract almost sensational attention.

— THE TIMES — ... ... of the utmost sincerity ... complete courage.

— Mrs. EVELYN SCOTT in — *The Dial* — A contemporary of the future... His technique has developed unique aspects that indicate a revolution of style for the future... This Irish artist is recreating a portion of the English language... He uses the stuff of the whole world to prove one man.

— THE NEW AGE — ... One of the most interesting literary symptoms in the whole literary world, and its publication is very nearly a public obligation.

— Mr. VALERY LARBAUD in — *La Nouvelle Revue Française* — Avec ULYSSES, l'Irlande fait une rentrée sensationnelle et triomphante dans la haute littérature européenne.

Fig. 11.1. Portrait of James Joyce in a Shakespeare and Company prospectus for *Ulysses*, 1921. The Morgan Library & Museum, New York. Gift of Sean and Mary Kelly, 2018.

RICK GEKOSKI

11. The Sean and Mary Kelly Collection

We speak of people who are "born" collectors, but until I first met my friend Sean Kelly I had never encountered a born James Joyce collector. I mean this both psychologically and astrologically. Of Irish heritage himself, Sean's first encounter with Joyce's masterpiece was life-changing and life-defining:

> I left home when I was thirteen, about the same time I first picked up *Ulysses* and read it. Joyce felt he must leave the stifling confines of Ireland to become the artist he needed to be. I had always known I would be an artist from an early age. I guess as a young person picking up the book for the first time the similarities and parallels were striking. It was a book I felt connected to, I could escape into and which enveloped me, it was a visceral world which enthralled and rewarded me, as it has continued to

do for over fifty years each time I return to it, which over the years has been often.

This precocious identification with Joyce seems predestined when you learn that Sean Kelly was born on 16 June: Bloomsday.

Since childhood, he has collected "things" in a way that he describes as "obsessive," a necessary quality in ambitious collecting. Some twenty years ago, after establishing himself first as a museum curator and latterly (since 1991) as one of the world's most distinguished gallerists, Sean bought a first edition of *Ulysses* for $12,000. It is still his favorite Joyce item. One wonders what took him so long. The answer is not lack of desire but lack of funds. He was building his business and reliant on the kindness of strangers: a generous dealer allowed him to pay off the book in twelve monthly installments. Soon, such

Fig. 11.2. Endpapers of *Marcel Duchamp, Man Ray: 50 Years of Alchemy, Essay by Chrissie Iles* (2004), one of the twenty-six copies in the limited edition, catalogue of an exhibition at the Sean Kelly Gallery, 28 January–4 March 2000. The Morgan Library & Museum, New York. Gift of Sean and Mary Kelly, 2021.

strangers became friends, and Sean played a more and more active role in their lives.

Joyce material may have stretched his resources, but from the point of view of a major art dealer, it was "hugely undervalued . . . but I shouldn't complain because the financial disparity between the markets is what allowed me to collect." Having begun, the momentum was inexorable. He began seriously to seek out and when possible to acquire rare material by Joyce, as well as various items for his other primary collection, focused on Marcel Duchamp: "these

giants of the twentieth century, who produced masterpieces, were deeply intellectual, but who had powerful senses of humour and set verbal and mental traps for their reader/viewer throughout their work and oeuvre. . . . I want to dive as deeply as possible and swim in their oceans, I want connoisseurship, I want to lose myself in their worlds."

Sean's reference to "connoisseurship," a term more usually associated with the art world, is unusual in the rare books context. For book collectors to become immersed in a writer's "world," they have to focus on *process*, on how a writer's books were conceived, printed and produced, marketed, sold, and distributed. And the writer: how did he become who he was, how did he live, what did he look and sound like? The pressing imperative? *Make it real.*

And that is a big ask in today's market. *Ulysses* was published a hundred years ago, since which time Joyce has been avidly collected. Even when contemporary collectors have the discrimination, the appetite, and the means, they will have to interrogate the available material critically, to separate what is merely stuff from things of intrinsic interest and resonance. Joyce now resides at Buffalo, Princeton, and Texas, the National Library of Ireland, and the British Library: the vast bulk of the letters are housed there, there is almost no proof material on the open market, and manuscripts are so uncommon that single pages of *Ulysses* can fetch more than a page from Audubon's *Birds* or the Gutenberg Bible.

Surprisingly, there are problems with the books too. At first, this seems counterintuitive: in his relatively short writing life, Joyce produced the four major books for which he is remembered (*Dubliners*, *A Portrait of the Artist as a Young Man*, *Ulysses*, and *Finnegans Wake*), only the first two of which are widely read. First editions of these books may be expensive but they are not *rare*, in the most accurate contemporary definition of the term: a rare book is one you cannot find for sale on the internet. Today, if you want to collect a major author or subject, you can. But, paradoxically, it won't be much fun if you're just ticking off the items. The real pleasure lies in doing more than this, and better. Sean puts this crisply: "I want to do my homework, have the best possible information available and find the best possible example of the piece I am looking for and

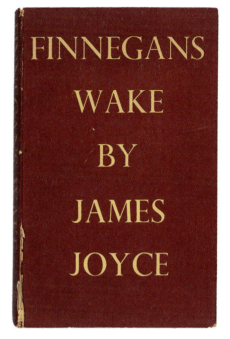

Fig. 11.3. Advance copy, James Joyce, *Finnegans Wake*, 1939. The Morgan Library & Museum, New York. Gift of Sean and Mary Kelly, 2018.

then be able to contextualize it qualitatively, historically and aesthetically to make the most informed evaluation/decision about the work. . . . Of course taste plays a part in it, but being dependent on scholarship really should elevate it above a consideration in which taste is a significant factor."

Associated with Sean's Joyce collection was a research library of hundreds of books about Joyce and his milieu. Good acquisitions are always based on good scholarship.

Much of the fun came with the scarce private press books, issued by a variety of small independent publishers who, while remembered in the rare book trade, are otherwise forgotten today: the Black Sun Press, the Corvinus Press, the Egoist Press, the Odyssey Press, the Servire Press, the St. Dominic's

A S WE THERE are where are we are we there from tomtittot to teetootomtotalitarian. Tea tea too oo. **Unde et ubi**

with his broad and hairy face, to Ireland a disgrace. Whom will comes over. Who to caps ever. And howelse do we hook our hike to find that pint of porter place? Am shot, says the bigguard.[1] **Sie**

[1] Rawmeash, quoshe with her girlic teangue. If old Herod was to go for me like he does Snuffler I'd do nine months for his beaver beard.

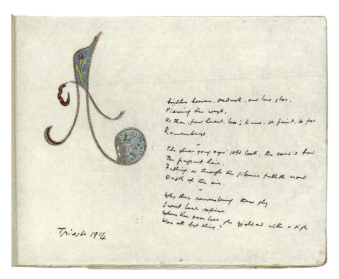

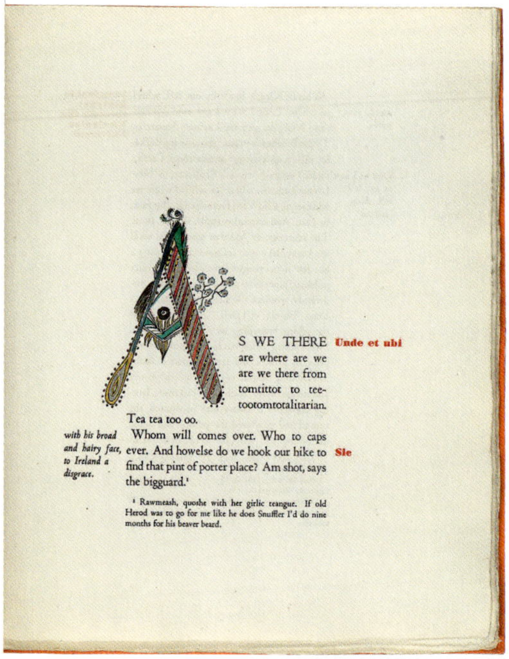

Fig. 11.4. Lucia Joyce, ornamental initial in James Joyce, *Pomes Penyeach,* 1932. The Morgan Library & Museum, New York. Gift of Sean and Mary Kelly, 2018.

Fig. 11.5. Lucia Joyce, ornamental initial in James Joyce, *Storiella as She is Syung,* 1937. The Morgan Library & Museum, New York. Gift of Sean and Mary Kelly, 2018.

Press, Transition Books, and others. In the early years, like all of the emerging figures of modernism, Joyce was entirely dependent on small presses and little magazines; it was only in 1924 that a major publisher issued a Joyce title, when Jonathan Cape acquired the rights to *Portrait*. From a collector's point of view, that's grand: loads of ephemeral works and limited editions, many of which were published in editions of twenty copies or less. I once sold a copy of *Work in Progress, Part 18* (1930) to an ecstatic collector who said he had been searching for it for thirty-eight years. No wonder: only five copies were printed to establish American copyright, and none were for sale.

As I write, there are more than twenty Joyce titles and variants that are *not* offered on the internet. And however hard and long you search, you *cannot* find everything. The first separately published Joyce item is *Et Tu Healy*, a poem lamenting the death of Parnell, written by the nine-year-old Joyce and printed as a broadside by his proud father. No single copy has survived, though Joyce's brother Stanislaus remembered copies strewn on the floor and trampled by the movers when the family moved house. Of Joyce's next three publications, two are also broadsides (*The Holy Office*, in 1905, and *Gas from a Burner*, in 1912), both self-published, extremely scarce, and commensurately expensive (figs. 11.6 and 3.3).

To a collector of Sean Kelly's percipience this scarcity of material was not dispiriting but enabling. He is no mere ticker-offer: yes, he wanted as many of

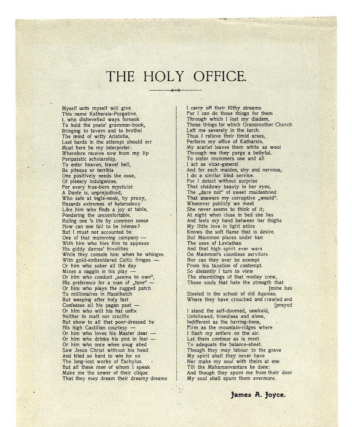

the books as he could find, but he wanted much more than that: books with particularly interesting associations, letters, manuscripts, photographs, recordings, and publishing ephemera. Of these, three items stand out.

First, there is the *Schema for Ulysses* (fig. 6.5), a modest manuscript that exists in only seven (differing) examples, some holograph and some typed. It lists the Homeric title for each of the eighteen chapters of *Ulysses* and indicates its structure: "Episode, Time, Scene, Color, Technique, Correspondences, Science/Art, Meaning, Organ, Symbols." In 1920/21 Joyce gave copies of this homely guide to a few friends (Sean's copy was given to the composer George Antheil), and it became, when printed by Stuart Gilbert in *James Joyce's Ulysses: A Study* (1930), the first point of entry into that difficult text. As so often with Joyce, his apparent explanation (he called it "a sort of summary-key-skeleton-scheme . . . to my damned monster-novel") causes as many problems as it solves. If you approach *Ulysses* largely through its parallels with the *Odyssey*, you miss most of what is genuinely moving, memorable, and funny about it.

Second, there is the 78 rpm record of Joyce reading from *Ulysses* in 1924. This was limited to twenty copies, signed by Joyce—many of which will, of course, have been lost or broken, others scratched and impossible to play. This disc provides the most wonderful opportunity to hear Joyce reading from his masterpiece, and the background scratchiness of all 78s adds to the sense of authenticity. It is a

Fig. 11.7. Recording of James Joyce reading from the "Aeolus" episode of *Ulysses*, 1924. The Morgan Library & Museum, New York. Gift of Sean and Mary Kelly, 2018.

perfect, definitive reading by the author, unshowy, musically enunciated, profoundly moving and memorable—preferable by far to hearing some actor using the text as if it were a script, and producing not a reading but a performance.

Third, there are the two stunning photographic portraits of Joyce, by Man Ray in 1922 and Berenice Abbott in 1928, with her notes on the back of the image (figs. 5.1 and 7.1). These bring one closer to the man, to that tilted-headed, quizzical look that characterized him, than the many, many words of his many, many biographers. It brings him into the room.

To amass such treasures you need a number of qualities, beyond obvious manic acquisitiveness and an adequately stocked purse. You need, foremost, an eye for what are the best, the most essential objects that help to tell the story of James Joyce, to fill it out, to humanize and add texture to it. You need, too, an interest in interrogating how it is that a work comes to be. Gallerists are of course fascinated by the stages from the inception of an artistic idea or image, to its first incarnations in drawing and sketches, to the finished product, which is the culmination of that process and most fully understood in relation to it. The Kelly Collection is thus rich in Joyce's contributions to little magazines, like the *Egoist*, in which his major works were first published in installments, which were themselves revised when it came to book publication. Even when Joyce's books arrived in their final form, though, there is much to notice in the process of their dissemination. Sylvia Beach may never have published a book before *Ulysses*, but she was adept at marketing it: thus we have her personally annotated *Prospectus for Ulysses*, in which she has crossed out the printed line "will be published in the Autumn of 1921," replacing it in ink with "IS NOW READY." Miss Beach's pique was justified: Joyce kept revising and revising the proofs

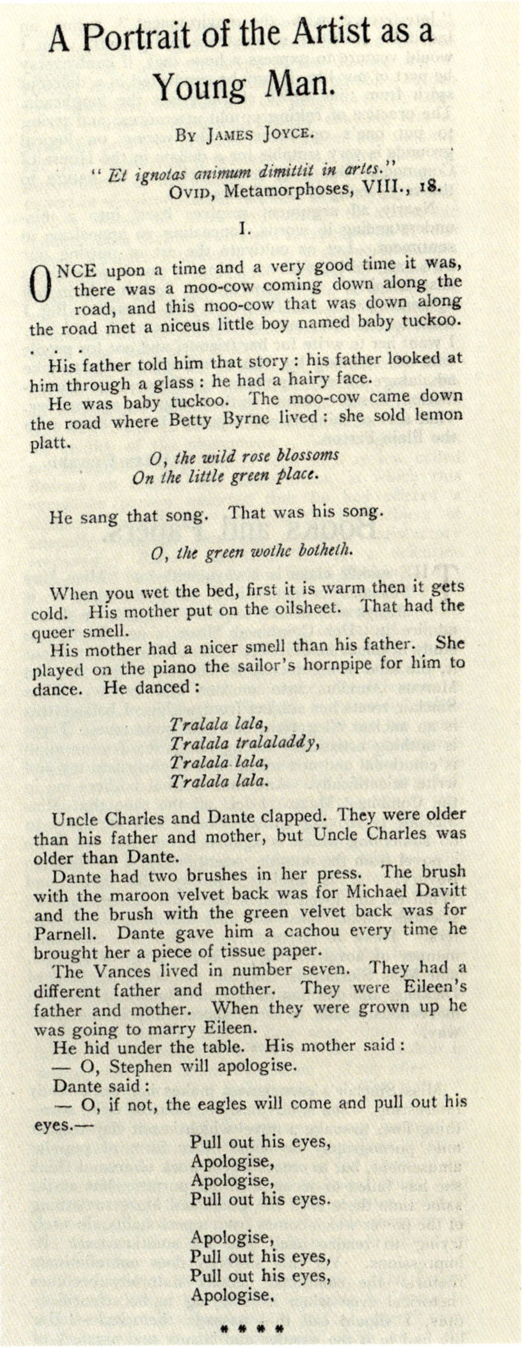

A Portrait of the Artist as a Young Man.

BY JAMES JOYCE.

" *Et ignotas animum dimittit in artes.*"
OVID, Metamorphoses, VIII., 18.

I.

ONCE upon a time and a very good time it was, there was a moo-cow coming down along the road, and this moo-cow that was down along the road met a niceus little boy named baby tuckoo. . . .

His father told him that story: his father looked at him through a glass: he had a hairy face.

He was baby tuckoo. The moo-cow came down the road where Betty Byrne lived: she sold lemon platt.

O, the wild rose blossoms
On the little green place.

He sang that song. That was his song.

O, the green wothe botheth.

When you wet the bed, first it is warm then it gets cold. His mother put on the oilsheet. That had the queer smell.

His mother had a nicer smell than his father. She played on the piano the sailor's hornpipe for him to dance. He danced:

Tralala lala,
Tralala tralaladdy,
Tralala lala,
Tralala lala.

Uncle Charles and Dante clapped. They were older than his father and mother, but Uncle Charles was older than Dante.

Dante had two brushes in her press. The brush with the maroon velvet back was for Michael Davitt and the brush with the green velvet back was for Parnell. Dante gave him a cachou every time he brought her a piece of tissue paper.

The Vances lived in number seven. They had a different father and mother. They were Eileen's father and mother. When they were grown up he was going to marry Eileen.

He hid under the table. His mother said:

— O, Stephen will apologise.

Dante said:

— O, if not, the eagles will come and pull out his eyes.—

Pull out his eyes,
Apologise,
Apologise,
Pull out his eyes.

Apologise,
Pull out his eyes,
Pull out his eyes,
Apologise.

* * * *

Fig. 11.8. James Joyce, "A Portrait of the Artist as a Young Man" in the *Egoist*, 1914–15. The Morgan Library & Museum, New York. Gift of Sean and Mary Kelly, 2018.

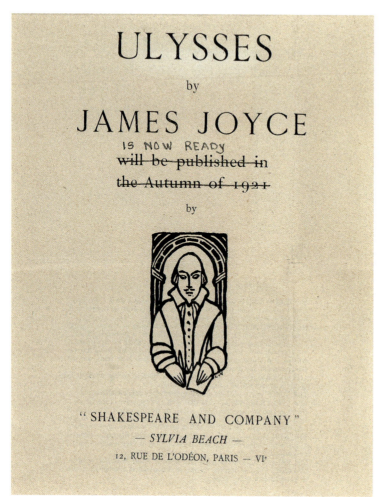

ULYSSES

by

JAMES JOYCE

IS NOW READY
~~will be published in~~
~~the Autumn of 1921~~

by

"SHAKESPEARE AND COMPANY"

— *SYLVIA BEACH* —

12, RUE DE L'ODÉON, PARIS — VIᵉ

Fig. 11.9. Shakespeare and Company prospectus for *Ulysses*, 1921, annotated by Sylvia Beach. The Morgan Library & Museum, New York. Gift of Sean and Mary Kelly, 2018.

of the book, and publication had to be delayed. If only her author were as efficient as she!

Sean has described the collection as "pretty comprehensive. . . . Of course one can always add more, but I don't think there are too many sizable omissions." He would have liked to have added a dust jacket to his copy of *Dubliners*, and perhaps acquired a few more letters, significant inscribed books, and ultra-rarities, which occur regularly but infrequently on the market. But even someone of

Sean's energy and acquisitiveness can't wait another thirty-eight years to add the odd, fugitive pamphlet.

Curiously enough, it was only quite late in the project that he thought of his Joyces as a coherent entity rather than the diverse outward manifestations of an inward passion: "until that point I hadn't really considered it to be a 'collection,' just a number of things." Once he recognized that what was on his shelves was not a bunch of Joyce stuff but a carefully curated, and important, *collection*—an insight he kindly attributes to a discussion with me—he ironically began to feel the burden of it. The material was too important to hoard on his shelves; it deserved a wider audience and a more secure long-term home. Sean, Mary, and their children, Lauren and Tom, agreed to look for a public institution in New York to which they might donate the collection: "The Morgan was our first choice and we were very happy when they were so positive about receiving the collection, and what a good fit it was with their existing modernist holdings, which included very little Joyce material of quality."

One day, not a surprise but still a shock, the material was no longer in that internal glass-fronted room beautifully shelved and perfectly displayed in the Kellys' wonderful house in the Hudson Valley. The collection had been over twenty years in the making, an act of loving homage to Sean Kelly's inspiration and hero. Surely, its loss must have hurt? "We are extremely happy that the collection has gone to the Morgan and will carry our family name attached to the gift in perpetuity. No regrets. Money is money, but the collection will remain at the Morgan forever, to be enjoyed by a large public audience." As a leading international art dealer, Sean is constantly acquiring wonderful things and then letting them go. But the Joyce Collection was not business, it was love: it had to go to exactly the right home. And it has.

I began by citing a parallel between the lives of James Joyce and Sean Kelly, so I hope I may be forgiven by ending with another. When young Stephen Dedalus prepares to leave Dublin at the end of *Portrait*, he announces portentously that he is going "to create in the smithy of my soul the uncreated conscience of my race." Well, it says he is a *young* man, and this sounds a trifle pompous. But what Stephen intended, his creator achieved: the heritage of Ireland (indeed of the world) was significantly altered by his genius.

At a more modest level—I hope he is not embarrassed by the comparison—Sean has always had in the forefront of his mind the desire to make a difference, to contribute to what he calls "heritage." His gallery, the magnificent house and extension in the Hudson Valley, the artists he has represented, and the collections he has amassed are part of a conscious effort to make, and then to leave behind, things of the highest quality, from which the public might profit and learn.

There is a sentiment in Joyce's play *Exiles* (1918) which is apposite to the gift of the Sean and Mary Kelly Collection: "While you have a thing it can be taken from you. . . . But when you give it, you have given it. No robber can take it from you. . . . It is yours then for ever when you have given it. It will be yours always."

Theirs forever, and ours too. What a wonderful gift that is.

NOTES

CHAPTER 1

1. James, *Letters*, 4: 6.
2. Joyce, *Ulysses*, 556.
3. Joyce, 80.
4. Joyce, 29.
5. Joyce, 81.
6. Joyce, 113.
7. Joyce, 66.
8. Joyce, 112.
9. Joyce, 508.
10. Joyce, 180.
11. Joyce, 181.
12. Joyce, 192.
13. Joyce, 196.
14. Joyce, 203.
15. Joyce, 204.
16. Joyce, 207.
17. Joyce, *Occasional, Critical, and Political Writing*, 118.
18. Joyce, *Ulysses*, 207.
19. Rubenstein in Latham, *Cambridge Companion to "Ulysses,"* 119.
20. Joyce, *Ulysses*, 202.
21. Potter, "Local Democracy."
22. Fairhall, "Colgan-Connolly."
23. Joyce, *Ulysses*, 390 and 391.
24. Fairhall, "Colgan-Connolly," 291.
25. Quoted in Fairhall, 292.
26. Quoted in Fairhall, 292.
27. Cronin, *Question of Modernity*, 64.
28. Joyce, *Dubliners*, 192.
29. Joyce, 200.
30. Joyce, 211.
31. Yeats, *Autobiographies*, 245.
32. Quoted in Ellmann, *James Joyce*, 643.
33. Ellmann, 22.
34. Joyce, *Ulysses*, 73.
35. Joyce, 102.
36. Joyce, 104.
37. Joyce, 186.
38. Joyce, 215 and 216.
39. Joyce, 225.

40. Joyce, 225.
41. Joyce, 226–27.
42. Joyce, 225.
43. Joyce, 225.
44. Joyce, 229.
45. Joyce, 540.
46. Joyce, 45.
47. Joyce, 636–37.
48. Joyce, 541–42.
49. Joyce, 541.
50. Quoted in Nolan, *James Joyce and Nationalism*, 58.
51. Levine in Attridge, *Cambridge Companion to James Joyce*, 141.
52. Joyce, *Ulysses*, 6.
53. Joyce, 17.
54. Joyce, *Portrait*, 159.
55. Deane in Attridge, *Cambridge Companion to James Joyce*, 38.
56. Killeen, *"Ulysses" Unbound*, 166.
57. Quoted in Nolan, *James Joyce and Nationalism*, 4.
58. Quoted in Nolan, 8.
59. Duffy in Latham, *Cambridge Companion to "Ulysses,"* 81.
60. Manganiello, *Joyce's Politics*, 166.
61. Joyce, *Dubliners*, 224.
62. Joyce, *Stephen Hero*, 103.
63. Quoted in Buckland, review of *Patrick Pearse*, 334.
64. Joyce, *Dubliners*, 224.
65. Yeats, *Collected Poems*, 180.
66. Joyce, *Critical Writings*, 167.
67. Joyce, *Ulysses*, 267–68.
68. Joyce, 271 and 272.
69. Joyce, 273.
70. Quoted in Nolan, *James Joyce and Nationalism*, 50.
71. Quoted in Nolan, 122.
72. Joyce, *Ulysses*, 251.
73. Quoted in Gifford and Seidman, *"Ulysses" Annotated*, 310.

74. Joyce, *Ulysses*, 239.
75. Joyce, 252.
76. Joyce, 254.
77. Joyce, 255.
78. Gifford and Seidman, *"Ulysses" Annotated*, 337.

CHAPTER 2

1. Barta, *Bely, Joyce and Döblin*, 47.
2. Bennett, "Review, *Outlook*, 1922," 221.
3. Joyce, *Ulysses*, 58.
4. Joyce, *Letters*, 2:186.
5. A selection of Dublin maps can be viewed at http://www.riverrun.org.uk/joycetools.html.
6. Budgen, *James Joyce*, 69.
7. Joyce, *Ulysses*, 582.
8. Gunn and Hart, *James Joyce's Dublin*, 32–34.
9. Joyce, *Ulysses*, 46.
10. Gunn and Hart, *James Joyce's Dublin*,15.
11. Joyce, *Portrait*, 55.
12. Joyce, *Ulysses*, 48.
13. Joyce, 119.
14. Joyce, 544.
15. Daly, *Dublin*.
16. Joyce, *Ulysses*, 77.
17. Joyce, 133.
18. McManus, *Dublin*, 22 and 31.
19. Cameron, "Notes," 457 and 462.
20. Cameron, 457.
21. Joyce, *Ulysses*, 360.
22. Brady, "Dublin," 10.
23. Jameson, "*Ulysses* in History," 144.
24. Jameson, 143.
25. Kiberd, *"Ulysses" and Us*, 159–61.
26. Igoe, *Real People of Joyce's "Ulysses,"* 293; Joyce, *Ulysses*, 240.
27. Mahaffey, *States of Desire*, 211.
28. Ellmann, *Four Dubliners*, 56.
29. Joyce, *Ulysses*, 3.
30. Joyce, 5 and 7.

31. Joyce, 5.

32. Joyce, 121.

33. Joyce, 125.

34. Joyce, 350.

35. Curtis, *To Hell or Monto*, 120.

36. Luddy, *Prostitution and Irish Society*, 40.

37. Flynn, *James Joyce*, 128–68.

38. Hutchins, *James Joyce's Dublin*, 99.

39. Joyce, *Ulysses*, 308.

40. Joyce, 643.

41. Joyce, 643–44.

42. Power, *From the Old Waterford House*, 63–64.

43. Laing, *Lonely City*, 1–8.

CHAPTER 3

1. The principal academic studies of Joyce and Trieste are Hartshorn, *James Joyce and Trieste*; Crivelli, *James Joyce: Itinerari Triestini*; McCourt, *Years of Bloom*. See also McCourt, "Joyce and Trieste."

2. Joyce, *Letters*, 2:114.

3. Joyce, *Ulysses*, 514.

4. Joyce, *Letters*, 1:215.

5. Joyce, *Finnegans Wake*, 301.

6. See McCourt, *Roll Away the Reel World*.

7. Stanislaus Joyce, "Triestine Book of Days," 12 October 1908. A copy of this unpublished document is kept at the McFarlin Library at the University of Tulsa.

8. Melchiori, *Joyce's Feast*, 109.

9. Quoted in Crise, *Epiphanies*, 20.

10. Svevo, *James Joyce*, no page given.

11. Joyce, *Finnegans Wake*, 228.

12. Joyce, *Letters*, 2:249.

13. Quoted in Gorman, *James Joyce*, 143.

14. See Catherine Flynn's discussion of Larbaud's central role in launching *Ulysses* in 1922 in her essay in this volume.

15. In his *Modernism in Trieste*, Salvatore Pappalardo provides a fascinating examination of how the idea of Europe features in the modernist literature of Joyce but also of Robert Musil, Italo Svevo, Theodor Däubler, and Srečko Kosovel, all of whom had a deep connection with the Adriatic city.

16. According to Svevo's niece Alma Oberti di Valnera, quoted in Moloney, *Friends in Exile*, 55.

17. Ellmann, *Consciousness of Joyce*, 118.

18. Budgen, *James Joyce*, 153.

19. Döblin, "*Ulysses* by Joyce," 514.

20. Joyce, *Selected Letters*, 268.

21. Joyce, *Finnegans Wake*, 228.

22. Eliot, *Daniel Deronda*, 3:258.

23. Karl Marx, quoted in Morris, *Trieste*, 30.

24. Joyce, *Ulysses*, 643.

25. Joyce, *Finnegans Wake*, 464.

26. Hubert Butler, undated nine-page manuscript entitled "James Joyce in Trieste," pp. 3–4, Crampton family papers, Bennettsbridge, Co. Kilkenny, papers in possession of the Crampton family. Cited in Tobin, "The Minority Voice," 67.

27. Joyce, *Finnegans Wake*, 423–24.

28. Joyce, 35.

29. James Joyce, "Ireland: Island of Saints and Sages," in Joyce, *Occasional, Critical and Political Writing*, 118.

30. Joyce, *Ulysses*, 277.

31. Joyce, *Finnegans Wake*, 129.

32. Scipio Slataper, *Il mio carso* (Florence: Libreria della Voce, 1912) quoted in Robinson, "Stranger in the House of Hapsburg," 325.

33. Joyce, *Giacomo Joyce*, 9.

34. For a discussion of Habsburg Trieste, see Robinson, "Stranger in the House of Habsburg."

35. Joyce, *Letters*, 2:167.

36. Joyce, *Ulysses*, 520.

37. Joyce, 532.

38. Joyce, 311.

39. Davison, *James Joyce*, 128.

40. Joyce, *Finnegans Wake*, 295, 365 and 349.

41. Joyce, *Ulysses*, 271–72.

42. Moravia, "Omaggio a Joyce," 12. The English translation is by Serenella Zanotti in *Reception of James Joyce in Europe*, 2:336.

CHAPTER 4

1. Stoppard, *Travesties*, 1.

2. Joyce, *Ulysses*, 644.

3. Joyce to Ezra Pound, 20 August 1917, in Joyce, *Selected Letters*, 227.

4. Joyce to Harriet Shaw Weaver, 30 June 1915, in Joyce, *Letters of James Joyce*, 1:82.

5. Joyce to Pound, 30 June 1915, New Haven, Beinecke Rare Book & Manuscript Library, Ezra Pound Papers, 1868–1976 (YCAL MSS 43), Series I, Box 26, Folder 1112.

6. Joyce quoted in Jolas, "My Friend James Joyce," 87–88.

7. Brändle, "Sich treffen, lernen, verweilen," 35–36.

8. For the passage's final form, see Joyce, *Ulysses*, 222.

9. About a third of the "Wandering Rocks" fair copy is in the hand of Frank Budgen. For more, see Derick Dreher's essay in this volume.

10. For the War Office proposal, see H.G. Wells to Pound, July 1915, in Pound, *Pound/Joyce*, 37.

11. Edmund Gosse to W.B. Yeats, n.d. [late August 1915], and Yeats to Gosse, 28 August [1915], quoted in R.F. Foster, "Yeats at War," 128. Pound's summary is Pound to Joyce, 6 September 1915, in Pound, *Pound/Joyce*, 42.

12. The insular metaphor is a commonplace, but see, for example, "Citizen Army of Switzerland," 509.

13. See Huber, *Fremdsein im Krieg*, 64.

14. Joyce to Stanislaus Joyce, 29 March 1932, in Joyce, *Letters*, 3:241.

15. Claud W. Sykes, "James Joyce and the English Players" (unpublished typescript), Carbondale, Morris Library, Southern Illinois University, Harley K. Croessmann Collection, Series 1: Herbert Gorman Papers, 1902–1939, Box 3, Folder 3, f. 2.

16. Ellmann, *James Joyce*, 422.

17. McCormick's copy is listed in McCormick, *Library*, item 298.

18. Budgen, *James Joyce*, 199.

19. Zabel, "Lyrics of James Joyce," 210.

20. Litz, "Author in *Ulysses*," 114.

21. Joyce quoted in Georges Borach, "Gespräche," 5; "Conversations," 325.

22. Joyce in Borach, "Gespräche," 5; "Conversations," 325.

23. Leaf, *Troy*, 328–29; Rose and O'Hanlon,

Lost Notebook, xxix. Joyce's note-taking from *Troy* is contained in this reconstructed notebook.

24. Leaf, *Troy*, viii and passim.
25. Joyce, *Ulysses*, 53.
26. Bérard, *Phéniciens*, 2:527.
27. Joyce to Louis Gillet, 20 November 1931, quoted in Francine Lenne, "James Joyce," 161.
28. For more on Joyce's turn-of-the-century experience of Paris, as well as his first exposure to Édouard Dujardin, see Catherine Flynn's essay in this volume.

CHAPTER 5

1. Barnes, "James Joyce."
2. Quoted in Ellmann, *James Joyce*, 522.
3. Ellmann, 512.
4. Barnes, "James Joyce."
5. "I got from him his portraits, a waistcoat, a good tenor voice, and an extravagant licentious disposition (out of which, however, the greater part of any talent I may have springs)." Joyce, *Selected Letters*, 361.
6. Fitch, *Sylvia Beach*, 63.
7. Flynn, *James Joyce*.
8. Joyce, *Ulysses*, 34.
9. Joyce, 36.
10. Joyce, 36.
11. Joyce to Pound, 5 June 1920, in Joyce, *Selected Letters*, 253.
12. Joyce to Weaver, 12 July 1920, in Joyce, *Selected Letters*, 265.
13. Weaver to Joyce, 25 August 1920, in Ellmann, *James Joyce*, 491.
14. Hemingway, *Moveable Feast*, 48.
15. Joyce to Stanislaus Joyce, 25 July 1920, in Joyce, *Letters*, 3:10.
16. Ellmann, *James Joyce*, 490.
17. Barnes, "James Joyce."
18. Ellmann, *James Joyce*, 592.
19. Hemingway, *Moveable Feast*, 60.
20. Flynn, *James Joyce*, 173.
21. Joyce to Budgen, 24 October 1920, in Joyce, *Selected Letters*, 273.
22. Michaelmas (29 September) 1920, in Joyce, *Selected Letters*, 271.
23. Fitch, *Sylvia Beach*, 62.
24. Ellmann, *James Joyce*, 508.
25. Quoted in Riley, *Sylvia Beach*, 84.
26. In October 1922, eight months after the first edition, Darantiere would use the same plates to print an edition for Weaver's Egoist Press.
27. Entry for 16 August 1922 in Woolf, *Diary*, 2:189.
28. "Aramis," "The Scandal of Ulysses," *Sporting Times*, no. 34 (1 April 1922): 4.
29. Gillet, *Claybook*, 31.
30. Spoo, *Modernism and the Law*.
31. Ellmann, *James Joyce*, 504.
32. Fitch, *Sylvia Beach*, 108.
33. Fitch, 78.
34. Fitch, 69.
35. Fitch, 127.
36. Ellmann, *James Joyce*, 512.
37. Ellmann, 499.
38. See figure 6.5 in Maria DiBattista's essay in this volume.
39. Larbaud, "James Joyce," 259.
40. Fitch, *Sylvia Beach*, 75.
41. Ellmann, *James Joyce*, 541.
42. Joyce to Bruni, 7 June 1921, in Joyce, *Letters*, 3: 44.
43. Quoted in Ellmann, *James Joyce*, 517.
44. Joyce to Weaver, 21 September 1920, in Joyce, *Selected Letters*, 271.
45. See Baron, "*Strandentwining Cable*," and Creasy, "Inverted Volumes."
46. Ellmann, *James Joyce*, 516.
47. Ellmann, 516, 521–22.
48. Flynn, *James Joyce*, 211–12.
49. Fitch, *Sylvia Beach*, 106.
50. Fitch, 106.
51. Beach, "*Ulysses*," 29.
52. Ellmann, *James Joyce*, 530.
53. Fitch, *Sylvia Beach*, 97.

CHAPTER 6

1. The scandalous "beginnings" and epic travails of *Ulysses* from inception, through publication up to the present day has been told many times, most recently, fully and entertainingly in Birmingham, *Most Dangerous Book*, especially his chapter "Power and Postage," 107–125.
2. Birmingham, *Most Dangerous Book*, 127.
3. Beach, *Shakespeare and Company*, 47. The story of Beach's selfless devotion to Joyce's (demanding) genius is appealing, but like all legends simplifies and takes liberties with complicated circumstances, motives, feelings. For a detailed, fair-minded assessment of Beach's version of this fateful offer, see Bishop, "Garbled History."
4. Birmingham, *Most Dangerous Book*, 274.
5. Arnold, *Scandal of Ulysses*, 30.
6. *United States v. One Book Called "Ulysses,"* 5 F. Supp. 182 (S.D.N.Y. 1933).
7. Cerf, "Publishing *Ulysses*," 2.
8. Eliot, "Ulysses, Order, and Myth," in his *Selected Prose*, 175.
9. Joyce's own calculation. See Ellmann, *James Joyce*, 310.
10. Terence Killeen sorts through the conflicting evidence in "Myth and Monuments."
11. Ellmann, *James Joyce*, 230.
12. Ellmann, 230.
13. Joyce, *Selected Letters*, 83.
14. Ellmann, *James Joyce*, 265.
15. Ellmann, 383.
16. Groden, "*Ulysses*," 3.
17. Groden, 3.
18. Joyce, *Ulysses*, 165.
19. Joyce, 527.
20. Lewis, *Time and Western Man*, 89.
21. Lewis, 89.
22. Joyce, *Ulysses*, 154.
23. Joyce, *Selected Letters*, 248.
24. Joyce, *Ulysses*, 28.
25. Budgen, *James Joyce*, 124–25.
26. Stuart Gilbert tracks this runaway story from its inception to its furious conclusion in *James Joyce's "Ulysses,"* 263–66.
27. Herring, *Joyce's Notes*, 7. All references to the early notebooks are from this edition.
28. Herring, 23–25.

29. Ellmann, *James Joyce*, 416.

30. Budgen, *James Joyce*, 178–79.

31. Joyce, *Ulysses*, 31.

32. See Litz, *Art of James Joyce*, appendix C, 142–45, for a chronology of the novel's stages of composition and serial publication.

33. Joyce, *Selected Letters*, 270. Joyce later elaborated the schema in a version he supplied to Herbert Gorman, his first biographer, and to Stuart Gilbert. See Ellmann, "*Ulysses*," 187 and following unnumbered pages for a history and comparison of the Linati and Gorman-Gilbert schemas.

34. Litz, *Art of James Joyce*, appendix B, 132.

35. Joyce, *Portrait*, 209.

36. Joyce, 213.

37. Joyce, 179.

38. Joyce, *Ulysses*, 3.

39. Budgen, *James Joyce*, 18.

40. Joyce, *Ulysses*, 6.

41. Joyce, 273.

42. Joyce, 98.

43. These changes were first noted by Litz, *Art of James Joyce*, 49–52.

44. Joyce, *Selected Letters*, 246.

45. Joyce, *Ulysses*, 291.

46. Joyce, *Selected Letters*, 246.

47. Joyce, *Letters*, 1:126.

48. Joyce, *Selected Letters*, 238 and 242.

49. Ellmann, *James Joyce*, 528; Gilbert, *James Joyce's "Ulysses,"* 16.

50. Joyce, *Selected Letters*, 241.

51. Ellmann, *James Joyce*, 507.

52. Kenner, *Dublin's Joyce*, 242. I quote the relevant passage, from Aristotle, *Politics*, Book 1, Part II, more extensively to stress Joyce's determination to develop *Ulysses* into the best (that is, the most self-sufficing) work imaginable.

CHAPTER 7

1. Menand, "Silence, Exile, Punning."

2. Pound to Anderson, 17 January 1918, in Pound, *Pound/The Little Review*, 173–74.

3. Anderson, *My Thirty Years' War*, 174–75.

4. Margaret Anderson, "Announcement," *Little Review*, March 1914, 1–2. Issues of the *Little Review* are available at https://modjourn.org.

5. *Little Review*, March 1920, 60–62.

6. Hassett, *"Ulysses" Trials*, 58–65; Hutton, *Serial Encounters*, 7–8 and 100.

7. Vanderham, *James Joyce*, 11–12 and 17–18.

8. *Little Review*, July–August 1920, 42 et seq.

9. Joyce, *Letters*, 1:145.

10. *Little Review*, July–August 1920, 46 and 48. John Quinn included these lines among those Sumner considered obscene in his 16 October 1920 letter to Ezra Pound. University of Southern Illinois Carbondale Special Collections Research Center.

11. Nabokov, *Lectures on Literature*, 1:345–46.

12. Hassett, *"Ulysses" Trials*, 101–2.

13. L.R. 3 Q.B. 360 (1868).

14. *United States v. Kennerley*, 209 Fed. 119, 120–21 (S.D.N.Y. 1913).

15. John Butler Yeats to Quinn, 14 October 1920, in John Quinn Papers, Manuscripts and Archives Division, The New York Public Library, Astor, Lenox, and Tilden Foundations, printed in Torchiana and O'Malley, "Letter."

16. E.g., a letter of 16 October 1920 to Pound, which Pound forwarded to Joyce via a letter circa October 1920, in *Pound/Joyce*, 184.

17. Joyce to Quinn, 17 November 1920, John Quinn Papers.

18. Joyce to Weaver, 10 November 1920, British Library.

19. Quinn to Pound, 2 March 1918, John Quinn Papers.

20. Quinn to Pound, 21 October 1920, University of Southern Illinois Carbondale Special Collections Research Center.

21. Quinn to Pound, 21 October 1920, University of Southern Illinois Carbondale Special Collections Research Center.

22. Margaret Anderson, "*Ulysses* in Court," *Little Review*, January–March 1921, 24.

23. "*Ulysses* Adjudged Indecent; Review Editors Are Fined," *New York Tribune*, 22 February 1921.

24. Quinn to Joyce, 13 April 1921, John Quinn Papers.

25. Reid, *Man from New York*, 455.

26. Hassett, *"Ulysses" Trials*, 102–4.

27. "Mr. Sumner's Glorious Victory," *New York Tribune*, 23 February 1921. Joyce's transcription of the editorial, which he sent to Harriet Weaver, is in the Beinecke Rare Book and Manuscript Library, Yale University, James Joyce Collection, Box 17, Folder 325. Lawrence Rainey identified the location of Joyce's transcription in *Institutions of Modernism*, 49 and 189 n. 23.

28. Joyce to Weaver, 3 April 1921, in Joyce, *Letters*, 1:160; Fitch, *Sylvia Beach*, 77.

29. Fitch, *Sylvia Beach*, 62–64; Pound, *Pound/Joyce*, 181.

30. Joyce to Weaver, postmarked 30 March 1921, British Library.

31. Beach, *Shakespeare and Company*, 47; Ellmann, *James Joyce*, 504.

32. See, e.g., *A. Heymoolen v. United States* (Treasury Decision 42907, Cust. Ct. August 1, 1928).

33. Beach, *Shakespeare and Company*, 201.

34. 19 U.S.C. §1305. Reference in the *Ulysses* decisions to the terms "libel" and "libellant" arises from the fact that, by analogy to the name of the initial pleading in a proceeding in admiralty to seize a vessel, the proceeding to confiscate an obscene book seized by the customs authorities was called a "libel."

35. Cerf, *At Random*, 92–93.

36. See, e.g., Groden, *"Ulysses" in Progress*, 77.

37. Ellmann, *James Joyce*, 519–30.

38. Joyce to Budgen, 16 August 1921, in Joyce, *Selected Letters*, 285.

39. Joyce, *Ulysses*, 299.

40. Ernst's brief is reprinted in a useful compendium of Ernst's files and related documents in Moscato and LeBlanc, *United States of America*. The original

Ernst firm files are located at the Harry Ransom Center at The University of Texas at Austin.

41. Moscato and LeBlanc, 267, quoting Thomas Babington Macaulay, *Essay on Milton*, 1825, reprinted in *Macaulay's Essays on Addison and Milton*, 60.

42. Moscato and LeBlanc, *United States of America*, 267.

43. *United States v. One Book Called "Ulysses"*, 5 F.Supp.182 (S.D.N.Y. 1933).

44. *United States v. One Book Entitled Ulysses by James Joyce*, 72 F.2d 705 (2d. Cir.1934).

45. Joyce to Constantine P. Curran, in Joyce, *Letters*, 1:338.

46. Weaver to Joyce, 13 May 1932, cited by Ellmann, *James Joyce*, 653.

47. Joyce to Eliot, 22 February 1932, in Joyce, *Letters*, 1:314–15.

48. Huddleston, *Back to Montparnasse*, 195.

49. BNA, H.O. 144/20071. See Birmingham, *Most Dangerous Book*, 335–36.

50. 354 U.S. 476, 484.

51. "Trump Renews Pledge to 'Take a Strong look' at Libel Laws," *New York Times*, 10 January 2018.

52. *New York Times*, 9 July 2020; *Washington Post*, 25 June 2020; *Washington Post*, 21 June 2020.

53. Joyce, *Ulysses*, 273.

CHAPTER 8

1. Quinn, *Catalogue*, part 2, lot 4936.

2. Joyce to Weaver, 24 May 1924, in Joyce, *Letters*, 1:214.

3. Quinn to Joyce, 26 June 1919, Rare and Manuscript Collections, Carl A. Kroch Library, Cornell University.

4. John Quinn Papers, MSS Col2513, box 23, files 5-7, Manuscripts and Archives Division, The New York Public Library, Astor, Lenox, and Tilden Foundations (see Barsanti, *Ulysses in Hand*, 43).

5. Joyce to Quinn, 24 June 1920, John Quinn Papers.

6. Joyce to Pound, 1 January 1918, APCS,

Manuscripts and Archives Division, New York Public Library.

7. Pound to Quinn, 27 August 1917, John Quinn Papers.

8. Joyce to Quinn, 13 May 1917, John Quinn Papers.

9. Barsanti, *Ulysses in Hand*, 7.

10. See Briggs, "Full Stop," for the confusion caused by this punctuation mark. To this day, it is still lacking in copies of the "Gabler Edition," despite the best efforts of Hans Walter Gabler.

11. Barsanti, *Ulysses in Hand*, 9.

CHAPTER 9

1. A full finding aid for the collection is available at the UB James Joyce Collection website: https://library.buffalo.edu/jamesjoyce/.

2. See the accompanying catalogue Faucheux, Noël, and Friedlander, *James Joyce*.

3. Oscar Silverman provides a firsthand account of these events as part of his description of the La Hune, Huebsch, and Beach acquisitions in "Why Buffalo? James Joyce: Paris-Buffalo: The Joyce Collections at the Lockwood Memorial Library" in Maynard, *Discovering James Joyce*, 19–27. The essay was first published in 1964.

4. This and the following letters between Bernard Gheerbrant and Charles Abbott are part of XVI. Other Correspondents, PCMS-0020, James Joyce Collection, The Poetry Collection of the University Libraries, University at Buffalo, The State University of New York (hereafter cited as James Joyce Collection).

5. Melissa Wickser Banta, daughter of Philip and Margaretta Wickser, later worked as assistant curator in the Poetry Collection in the late 1960s and early 1970s and coedited, with Oscar Silverman, *James Joyce's Letters to Sylvia Beach, 1921–1940*.

6. For a full listing of the items in Joyce's Paris library, see Connolly, *Personal Library*.

7. Thomas E. Connolly describes these portraits and examines Joyce's dubious attribution of his paternal grandparents and great-grandparents as well as the artist who painted them in "Home Is Where the Art Is."

8. Lucie [Léon] Noël provides more information on the relationship between Léon and Joyce, including her husband's efforts to preserve the Joyce family's Paris belongings in *James Joyce and Paul L. Léon*. See also her 22 June 1967 letter to Oscar Silverman including a manuscript titled "How My Husband Paul Leon Saved the Joyce Books," XVI. Other Correspondents, PCMS-0020, James Joyce Collection.

9. Sam Slote, "Buffalo Wakes," in *Discovering James Joyce*, 64; Crispi, "ReCollecting Joyce at Buffalo," 16.

10. See Silverman's letters to Beach in XIII. Correspondence to Sylvia Beach and/or Shakespeare and Company and Beach's letters to Silverman in XII. Correspondence from Sylvia Beach and/or Shakespeare and Company, PCMS-0020, James Joyce Collection.

11. Silverman, "Why Buffalo?," in Maynard, *Discovering James Joyce*, 24. For more on Beach's version of these events and of her negotiations with Silverman, see her letters to Jackson Matthews in Beach, *Letters*, 266, 271–74, and 284–85.

12. Spielberg, *James Joyce's Manuscripts and Letters*. Finishing in August 2010, Luca Crispi revised, updated, and corrected Spielberg's catalog based upon subsequent additions to the collection, contemporary Joyce scholarship, and his own research to create the current finding aid for the UB James Joyce Collection. See Crispi, "ReCollecting Joyce at Buffalo."

13. Beach, *Shakespeare and Company*.

flowers all a woman's body yes that was
one true thing he said in his life and th
sun shines for you today yes that was wh
I liked him because I saw he understo
or felt what a woman is and I knew
I could always get round him and I
gave him all the pleasure I could leadin
him on till he asked me to say yes and
I wouldn't answer first only looked o
over the sea and the sky I was thinking
of so many things he didn't know o
Mulvey and Mr Stanhope and Hester an
father and old captain Groves and the
Alameda gardens and Gibraltar as a
girl where I was a flower of the mountar
and how he kissed me under the Moorish
wall and I thought well as well him a
another and then I asked him with my
eyes to ask again and then he asked m
would I to say yes my mountain flowe
and first I put my arms around him
and drew him down to me so he could
feel my breasts all perfume and I said
I will yes.

———————

Trieste - Zurich - Paris
1914 — 1921

BIBLIOGRAPHY

Anderson, Margaret. *My Thirty Years' War: The Autobiography, Beginnings and Battles to 1930*. New York: Horizon Press, 1969. First published 1930 by Covici-Friede (New York) and Alfred A. Knopf (London).

Arnold, Bruce. *The Scandal of "Ulysses."* London: Sinclair-Stevenson, 1991.

Attridge, Derek, ed. *The Cambridge Companion to James Joyce*. 2nd ed. Cambridge: Cambridge University Press, 2004.

Barnes, Djuna. "James Joyce: A Portrait of the Man Who Is, at Present, One of the More Significant Figures in Literature." *Vanity Fair* 18, no. 2 (April 1922): 65, 104.

Baron, Scarlett. *"Strandentwining Cable": Joyce, Flaubert, and Intertextuality*. Oxford: Oxford University Press, 2012.

Barsanti, Michael J. *"Ulysses" in Hand: The Rosenbach Manuscript*. Philadelphia: The Rosenbach Museum & Library, 2000.

Barta, Peter I. *Bely, Joyce, and Döblin: Peripatetics in the City Novel*. Gainesville: University Press of Florida, 1996.

Beach, Sylvia. *The Letters of Sylvia Beach*. Edited by Keri Walsh. New York: Columbia University Press, 2010.

———. *Shakespeare and Company*. New ed. A Bison Book. Lincoln: University of Nebraska Press, 1991. First published 1959 by Harcourt, Brace and Company (New York).

———. "*Ulysses* à Paris." *Mercure de France* 309 (1 May 1950): 12–29.

Bennett, Arnold. "Review, *Outlook*, 1922." In *James Joyce: The Critical Heritage*, vol. 1, *1902–1927*, edited by Robert H. Deming, 219–22. London: Routledge and Kegan Paul, 1970.

Bérard, Victor. *Les Phéniciens et l'Odyssée*. 2 vols. Paris: Armand Colin, 1902–3.

Birmingham, Kevin. *The Most Dangerous Book: The Battle for James Joyce's "Ulysses."* New York: Penguin Books, 2014.

Bishop, Edward L. "The 'Garbled History' of the First-Edition *Ulysses*." *Joyce Studies Annual* 9 (1998): 3–36.

Borach, Georges. "Conversations with James Joyce." Translated by Joseph Prescott. *College English* 15, no. 6 (March 1954): 325–27.

———. "Gespräche mit James Joyce." *Neue Zürcher Zeitung*, May 3, 1931.

Brady, Joseph. "Dublin at the Beginning of the Twentieth Century." In *A New and Complex Sensation: Essays on Joyce's "Dubliners,"* edited by Oona Frawley, 10–32. Dublin: Lilliput Press, 2004.

Brändle, Rea. "Sich treffen, lernen, verweilen. Die Zentralbibliothek als öffentlicher Raum." In *Wissen im Zentrum: 100 Jahre Zentralbibliothek Zürich*, edited by Rea Brändle et al., 19–72. Zurich: Chronos, 2017.

Briggs, Austin. "The Full Stop at the End of 'Ithaca': Thirteen Ways—and Then Some—of Looking at a Black Dot." *Joyce Studies Annual* 7 (1996): 125–44.

Buckland, Patrick. Review of *Patrick Pearse: The Triumph of Failure*, by Ruth Dudley Edwards. *History* 64, no. 211 (1979): 334.

Budgen, Frank. *James Joyce and the Making of "Ulysses" and Other Writings*. London: Oxford University Press, 1972.

Cameron, Charles A. "Notes from the Reports of the Medical Officers of Health: The Dublin Poor." *Journal of the Royal Sanitary Institute* 26, no. 8 (1905): 457–65.

Cerf, Bennett. *At Random: The Reminiscences of Bennett Cerf*. New York: Random House, 1977.

———. "Publishing *Ulysses*." *Contempo* 3, no. 13 (15 February 1934): 2–3.

"The Citizen Army of Switzerland." *National Geographic* 28, no. 5 (November 1915): 503–10.

Connolly, Thomas E. "Home Is Where the Art Is: The Joyce Family Gallery." *James Joyce Quarterly* 20, no. 1 (Fall 1982): 11–31.

———. *The Personal Library of James Joyce: A Descriptive Bibliography*. University of Buffalo Studies 22, no. 1 (April 1955). Buffalo: University of Buffalo, 1955.

Creasy, Matthew. "Inverted Volumes and Fantastic Libraries: *Ulysses* and *Bouvard et Pécuchet*." *European Joyce Studies* 19 (2011): 112–27.

Crise, Stelio. *Epiphanies & Phadographs: Joyce e Trieste*. Milan: All'Insegna del Pesce d'Oro, 1994.

Crispi, Luca. "ReCollecting Joyce at Buffalo: Revising and Completing the Catalog." In *Genitricksling Joyce*, edited by Sam Slote and Wim Van Mierlo, 13–26. European Joyce Studies 9. Amsterdam: Rodopi, 1999.

Crivelli, Renzo S. *James Joyce: Itinerari Triestini / James Joyce: Triestine Itineraries*. Translated by John McCourt. Trieste: MGS Press, 1996.

Cronin, Anthony. *A Question of Modernity*. London: Secker & Warburg, 1966.

Curtis, Maurice. *To Hell or Monto: The Story of Dublin's Most Notorious Districts*. Dublin: The History Press Ireland, 2015.

Daly, Mary E. *Dublin, the Deposed Capital: A Social and Economic History, 1860–1914*. Cork: Cork University Press, 1984.

Davison, Neil R. *James Joyce, "Ulysses," and the Construction of Jewish Identity: Culture, Biography, and "the Jew" in Modernist Europe*. Cambridge: Cambridge University Press, 1996.

Delaney, Frank. *James Joyce's Odyssey: A Guide to the Dublin of "Ulysses."* London: Granada, 1983.

Döblin, Alfred. "*Ulysses* by Joyce." In *The Weimar Republic Sourcebook*, edited by Anton Kaes, Martin Jay, and Edward Dimendberg, 514. Berkeley: University of California Press, 1994.

Eliot, George. *Daniel Deronda*. 4 vols. Edinburgh: William Blackwood and Sons, 1876.

Eliot, T.S. *Selected Prose of T. S. Eliot*. Edited by Frank Kermode. London: Faber and Faber, 1975.

Ellmann, Richard. *The Consciousness of Joyce*. New York: Oxford University Press, 1977.

———. *Four Dubliners: Wilde, Joyce, Yeats, and Beckett*. London: Hamish Hamilton, 1987.

———. *James Joyce*. New and rev. ed. with corrections. New York: Oxford University Press, 1983.

———. *"Ulysses" on the Liffey*. London: Faber and Faber, 1974.

Fairhall, James. "Colgan-Connolly: Another Look at the Politics of 'Ivy Day in the Committee Room.'" *James Joyce Quarterly* 25, no. 3 (Spring 1988): 289–304.

Faucheux, Pierre, André Noël, and Johnny Friedlander. *James Joyce: Sa vie, son œuvre, son rayonnement*. Paris: La Hune, 1949. Published in conjunction with *Exposition en hommage à James Joyce*, organized and presented at the La Hune gallery, October 15–December 10, 1949.

Fitch, Noel Riley. *Sylvia Beach and the Lost Generation: A History of Literary Paris in the Twenties and Thirties*. New York: W. W. Norton; London: Souvenir, 1983.

Flynn, Catherine. *James Joyce and the Matter of Paris*. Cambridge: Cambridge University Press, 2019.

Foster, R.F. "Yeats at War: Poetic Strategies and Political Reconstruction from the Easter Rising to the Free State." *Transactions of the Royal Historical Society* 11 (2001): 125–45.

Gifford, Don, with Robert J. Seidman. *"Ulysses" Annotated: Notes for James Joyce's "Ulysses."* 2nd ed., rev. and enl. Berkeley: University of California Press, 1988.

Gilbert, Stuart. *James Joyce's "Ulysses": A Study*. Rev. ed. New York: Vintage Books, 1958.

Gillet, Louis. *Claybook for James Joyce*. London: Abelard-Schuman, 1958.

Gorman, Herbert. *James Joyce: A Definitive Biography*. London: John Lane, 1941.

Griffith, Arthur. *The Resurrection of Hungary: A Parallel for Ireland*. Dublin: James Duffy & Co.; M.H. Gill & Son; Sealy, Bryers & Walker, 1904.

Groden, Michael. *"Ulysses" in Progress*. Princeton: Princeton University Press, 1977.

Gunn, Ian, and Clive Hart with Harald Beck. *James Joyce's Dublin: A Topographical Guide to the Dublin of "Ulysses."* New York: Thames and Hudson, 2004.

Hartshorn, Peter. *James Joyce and Trieste*. Westport, CT: Greenwood Press, 1997.

Hassett, Joseph M. *The "Ulysses" Trials: Beauty and Truth Meet the Law*. Dublin: Lilliput Press, 2016.

Hemingway, Ernest. *A Moveable Feast: The Restored Edition*. New York: Scribner, 2009.

Herring, Phillip F., ed. *Joyce's Notes and Early Drafts for "Ulysses": Selections from the Buffalo Collection*. Charlottesville: Published for the Bibliographical Society of the University of Virginia by the University Press of Virginia, 1977.

Huber, Anja. *Fremdsein im Krieg: Die Schweiz als Ausgangs- und Zielort von Migration, 1914–1918*. Zurich: Chronos, 2018.

Huddleston, Sisley. *Back to Montparnasse: Glimpses of Broadway in Bohemia*. Philadelphia: J.B. Lippincott, 1931.

Hutchins, Patricia. *James Joyce's Dublin*. London: Grey Walls Press, 1950.

Hutton, Clare. *Serial Encounters: "Ulysses" and "The Little Review."* Oxford: Oxford University Press, 2019.

Igoe, Vivien. *The Real People of Joyce's "Ulysses": A Biographical Guide*. Dublin: University College Dublin Press, 2016.

James, Henry. *Letters*. Edited by Leon Edel. 4 vols. Cambridge, MA: Belknap Press of Harvard University Press, 1974–84.

Jameson, Fredric. "*Ulysses* in History." In *The Modernist Papers*, 137–51. London: Verso, 2007.

Jolas, Eugene. "My Friend James Joyce." *Partisan Review* 8, no. 2 (March–April 1941): 82–93.

Joyce, James. *The Critical Writings of James Joyce*. Edited by Ellsworth Mason and Richard Ellmann. New York: Viking Press, 1959.

———. *Dubliners*. Introduction and notes by Terence Brown. Penguin Twentieth-Century Classics. London: Penguin Books, 1992.

———. *Finnegans Wake*. London: Faber and Faber, 1939.

———. *Giacomo Joyce*. Edited by Richard Ellmann. New York: Viking Press, 1968.

———. *James Joyce's Letters to Sylvia Beach, 1921–1940*. Edited by Melissa Banta and Oscar A. Silverman. Bloomington: Indiana University Press, 1987.

———. *Letters of James Joyce*. New ed., with corrections. 3 vols. Volume 1 edited by Stuart Gilbert. Volumes 2 and 3 edited by Richard Ellmann. New York: Viking Press, 1966.

———. *Occasional, Critical, and Political Writing*. Edited with an introduction and notes by Kevin Barry. Translations from the Italian by Conor Deane. Oxford: Oxford University Press, 2000.

———. *A Portrait of the Artist as a Young Man*. Edited by Jeri Johnson. Oxford World's Classics. Oxford: Oxford University Press, 2000.

———. *Selected Letters of James Joyce*. Edited by Richard Ellmann. New York: Viking Press, 1975.

———. *Stephen Hero*. New ed., edited by Theodore Spencer, John J. Slocum, and Herbert Cahoon. New York: New Directions, 1955.

———. *Ulysses*. Edited by Hans Walter Gabler with Wolfhard Steppe and Claus Melchior. Afterword by Michael Groden. New York: Vintage Books, 1993.

———. *Ulysses: A Facsimile of the Manuscript*.

With a critical introduction by Harry Levin and a bibliographical preface by Clive Driver. 3 vols. New York: Octagon Books; Philadelphia: The Philip H. and A.S.W. Rosenbach Foundation, 1975.

Kenner, Hugh. *Dublin's Joyce*. Bloomington: Indiana University Press, 1956. Reprint, New York: Columbia University Press, 1987. Page references are to the 1987 edition.

Kiberd, Declan. *"Ulysses" and Us: The Art of Everyday Living*. London: Faber and Faber, 2009.

Killeen, Terence. "Myths and Monuments: The Case of Alfred H. Hunter." *Dublin James Joyce Journal* 1 (2008): 47–53.

———. *"Ulysses" Unbound: A Reader's Companion to James Joyce's "Ulysses."* 3rd ed. Gainesville: University Press of Florida, 2014.

Laing, Olivia. *The Lonely City: Adventures in the Art of Being Alone*. Edinburgh: Canongate, 2016.

Larbaud, Valery. "James Joyce." In *James Joyce: The Critical Heritage*, vol. 1, *1902–1927*, edited by Robert H. Deming, 252–62. London: Routledge and Kegan Paul, 1970.

Latham, Sean, ed. *The Cambridge Companion to "Ulysses."* New York: Cambridge University Press, 2014.

Leaf, Walter. *Troy: A Study in Homeric Geography*. London: Macmillan, 1912.

Lenne, Francine. "James Joyce et Louis Gillet." In *James Joyce*, edited by Jacques Aubert and Fritz Senn, 151–75. Paris: Éditions de l'Herne, 1985.

Lernout, Geert, and Wim Van Mierlo, eds. *The Reception of James Joyce in Europe*. Vol. 2, *France, Ireland and Mediterranean Europe*. Athlone Critical Traditions Series: The Reception of British Authors in Europe. London: Thoemmes Continuum, 2004.

Lewis, Wyndham. *Time and Western Man*. Edited by Paul Edwards. Santa Rosa, CA: Black Sparrow Press, 1993.

Litz, A. Walton. *The Art of James Joyce: Method and Design in "Ulysses" and "Finnegans Wake."* London: Oxford University Press, 1961.

———. "The Author in *Ulysses*: The Zurich Chapters." In *James Joyce: A New Language: Actas/Proceedings del Simposio Internacional en el Centenario de James Joyce*, edited by Francisco García Tortosa et al., 113–21. Seville: Publicaciones de la Universidad de Sevilla, 1982.

Luddy, Maria. *Prostitution and Irish Society, 1800–1940*. Cambridge: Cambridge University Press, 2007.

Macaulay, Thomas Babington. *Macaulay's Essays on Addison and Milton*. Edited by Herbert Augustine Smith. Boston: Ginn, 1902.

Mahaffey, Vicki. *States of Desire: Wilde, Yeats, Joyce, and the Irish Experiment*. New York: Oxford University Press, 1998.

Manganiello, Dominic. *Joyce's Politics*. Routledge Library Editions: James Joyce 5. London: Routledge, 2016.

Maynard, James, ed. *Discovering James Joyce: The University at Buffalo Collection*. Buffalo: The Poetry Collection, University at Buffalo, State University of New York, 2009. Published in conjunction with an exhibition of the same title organized by the Poetry Collection of the University Libraries, the University Art Galleries, and the School of Architecture and Planning and presented at the UB Anderson Gallery, June 13–September 13, 2009.

McCarthy, Jack, with Danis Rose. *Joyce's Dublin: A Walking Guide to "Ulysses."* New York: St. Martin's Press, 1991. First published 1986 by the Wolfhound Press (Dublin).

McCormick, Edith Rockefeller. *The Library of the Late Edith Rockefeller McCormick*. New York: American Art Association, Anderson Galleries, 1934.

McCourt, John, ed. "Joyce and Trieste." Special issue, *James Joyce Quarterly* 38, nos. 3/4 (2001).

———, ed. *Roll Away the Reel World: James Joyce and Cinema*. Cork: Cork University Press, 2010.

———. *The Years of Bloom: James Joyce in Trieste, 1904–1920*. Dublin: Lilliput Press, 2000.

McManus, Ruth. *Dublin, 1910–1940: Shaping the City and Suburbs*. Dublin: Four Courts Press, 2002.

Melchiori, Giorgio. *Joyce's Feast of Languages*. Rome: Bulzoni Editore, 1995.

Menand, Louis. "Silence, Exile, Punning: James Joyce's Chance Encounters." *New Yorker*, July 2, 2012, 70–75.

Moloney, Brian. *Friends in Exile: Italo Svevo and James Joyce*. Leicester: Troubador Publishing, 2018.

Moravia, Alberto. "Omaggio a Joyce." *Prospettive* 4, no. 4 (15 April 1940): 12–13.

Morris, Jan. *Trieste and the Meaning of Nowhere*. London: Faber and Faber, 2001.

Moscato, Michael, and Leslie LeBlanc, eds. *The United States of America v. One Book Entitled "Ulysses" by James Joyce: Documents and Commentary—A 50-Year Retrospective*. Frederick, MD: University Publications of America, 1984.

Nabokov, Vladimir. *Lectures on Literature*. Edited by Fredson Bowers. 2 vols. New York: Harcourt Brace Jovanovich, 1980–81.

Nicholson, Robert. *The "Ulysses" Guide: Tours Through Joyce's Dublin*. Dublin: New Island Books, 2015.

Noël, Lucie. *James Joyce and Paul L. Léon: The Story of a Friendship. A Proceeding of the James Joyce Society Delivered in Part at the Meeting of November 18, 1948*. New York: Gotham Book Mart, 1950.

Nolan, Emer. *James Joyce and Nationalism*. London: Routledge, 1995.

Pappalardo, Salvatore. *Modernism in Trieste: The Habsburg Mediterranean and the Literary Invention of Europe, 1870–1945*. New York: Bloomsbury Academic, 2021.

Potter, Matthew. "The Rise and Fall of Local Democracy." *History Ireland* 19 (March/April 2011): 40–43.

Pound, Ezra. *Pound/Joyce: The Letters of Ezra*

Pound to James Joyce, with Pound's Essays on Joyce. Edited by Forrest Read. New York: New Directions, 1967.

———. *Pound/The Little Review: The Letters of Ezra Pound to Margaret Anderson, The "Little Review" Correspondence*. Edited by Thomas L. Scott, Melvin J. Friedman, and Jackson R. Bryer. New York: New Directions, 1988.

Power, Arthur. *From the Old Waterford House*. London: Mellifont Press, 1949.

Quinn, John. *Complete Catalogue of the Library of John Quinn, Sold by Auction in Five Parts*. 2 vols. New York: Anderson Galleries, 1924.

Rainey, Lawrence S. *Institutions of Modernism: Literary Elites and Public Culture*. New Haven: Yale University Press, 1998.

Reid, B.L. *The Man from New York: John Quinn and His Friends*. New York: Oxford University Press, 1968.

Robinson, Richard. "A Stranger in the House of Hapsburg: Joyce's Ramshackle Empire." *James Joyce Quarterly* 38, nos. 3/4 (2001): 321–39.

Rose, Danis, and John O'Hanlon. *The Lost Notebook: New Evidence on the Genesis of "Ulysses."* Edinburgh: Split Pea Press, 1989.

Spielberg, Peter. *James Joyce's Manuscripts and Letters at the University of Buffalo: A Catalogue*. Buffalo: University of Buffalo, 1962.

Spoo, Robert E. *Modernism and the Law*. London: Bloomsbury Academic, 2018.

Stoppard, Tom. *Travesties*. New York: Grove Press, 1975.

Svevo, Italo. *James Joyce: A Lecture Delivered in Milan in 1927*. Translated by Stanislaus Joyce. New York: Printed for New Directions, 1950.

Tobin, Robert Benjamin. "The Minority Voice: Hubert Butler, Southern Protestantism and Intellectual Dissent in Ireland, 1930–72." Ph.D. diss., University of Oxford, 2004.

Torchiana, Donald J., and Glenn O'Malley, eds. "A Letter: J.B. Yeats on James Joyce." *Tri-Quarterly* 1 (1964): 70–76.

Vanderham, Paul. *James Joyce and Censorship: The Trials of "Ulysses."* New York: New York University Press, 1997.

Woolf, Virginia. *The Diary of Virginia Woolf*. Edited by Anne Olivier Bell. 5 vols. New York: Harcourt Brace Jovanovich, 1977–84.

Yeats, William Butler. *Autobiographies: Reveries over Childhood and Youth and the Trembling of the Veil*. London: Macmillan, 1927.

———. *The Collected Poems of W.B. Yeats*. Rev. 2nd ed., edited by Richard J. Finneran. New York: Scribner Paperback Poetry, 1996.

Zabel, Morton Dauwen. "The Lyrics of James Joyce." *Poetry* 36, no. 4 (July 1930): 206–13.

CONTRIBUTORS

RONAN CROWLEY is a postdoctoral researcher on the ERC-funded project Classical Influences and Irish Culture at Aarhus University in Denmark and the vice president and president-elect of the International James Joyce Foundation.

MARIA DIBATTISTA is Charles Barnwell Straut Class of 1923 Professor of English at Princeton University, where she teaches *Ulysses* every year. Her latest work, coauthored with Deborah Nord, is *At Home in the World: Women Writers and Public Life, from Austen to the Present*, a study of women's political writings.

DERICK DREHER served as the director of Philadelphia's Rosenbach Museum and Library, the home of the *Ulysses* manuscript, from 1998 to 2021. He received a Ph.D. in art history from Yale and speaks and publishes frequently about *Ulysses* as well as broader topics of interest to the world of rare books.

CATHERINE FLYNN is Associate Professor of English at University of California, Berkeley. She is the author of *James Joyce*

and the Matter of Paris and editor of the forthcoming *New Joyce Studies: Twenty-First Century Critical Revisions* and *The Cambridge Centenary Ulysses: The 1922 Text with Essays and Notes*, both to be published in 2022.

ANNE FOGARTY is Professor of James Joyce Studies at University College Dublin. She was the president of the International James Joyce Foundation from 2008 to 2012 and has been director of the Dublin James Joyce Summer School since 1997. She has written widely on twentieth-century and contemporary Irish writing. Her edition of *Dubliners* will be published in 2022.

RICK GEKOSKI is a writer, rare books and manuscripts dealer, former university lecturer, and Booker Prize judge. He has published numerous nonfiction and fiction titles, his latest being *Guarded by Dragons: Encounters with Rare Books and Rare People*.

JOSEPH M. HASSETT is a trial lawyer based in Washington, D.C. He is the author of *The "Ulysses" Trials: Beauty and Truth Meet the Law* and *Yeats Now: Echoing Into Life*.

JAMES MAYNARD directs the UB James Joyce Collection as curator of the Poetry Collection of the University Libraries, University at Buffalo, The State University of New York. In 2009, he helped organize the exhibition *Discovering James Joyce: The University at Buffalo Collection* and edited the exhibition catalogue of the same title.

JOHN MCCOURT is Professor of English Literature and Dean of the Department of Humanities at the University of Macerata. President of the International James Joyce Foundation and author of *The Years of Bloom: Joyce in Trieste 1904–1920*, McCourt will publish *Consuming Joyce: 100 Years of Ulysses in Ireland* in 2022.

COLM TÓIBÍN is the author of ten novels, including *Brooklyn* and *The Magician*, and two collections of stories. His work has been translated into more than thirty languages. He is a contributing editor at the *London Review of Books* and the Irene and Sidney B. Silverman Professor of Humanities at Columbia University. In 2017, he cocurated *Henry James and American Painting* at the Morgan Library & Museum.

INDEX

CREDITS

THE PENN STATE SERIES
IN THE HISTORY OF THE BOOK

PREVIOUSLY PUBLISHED TITLES IN THE PENN STATE SERIES IN THE HISTORY OF THE BOOK

Peter Burke, *The Fortunes of the "Courtier": The European Reception of Castiglione's "Cortegiano"* (1996)

Roger Burlingame, *Of Making Many Books: A Hundred Years of Reading, Writing, and Publishing* (1996)

James M. Hutchisson, *The Rise of Sinclair Lewis, 1920–1930* (1996)

Julie Bates Dock, ed., *Charlotte Perkins Gilman's "The Yellow Wall-paper" and the History of Its Publication and Reception: A Critical Edition and Documentary Casebook* (1998)

John Williams, ed., *Imaging the Early Medieval Bible* (1998)

Ezra Greenspan, *George Palmer Putnam: Representative American Publisher* (2000)

James G. Nelson, *Publisher to the Decadents: Leonard Smithers in the Careers of Beardsley, Wilde, Dowson* (2000)

Pamela E. Selwyn, *Everyday Life in the German Book Trade: Friedrich Nicolai as Bookseller and Publisher in the Age of Enlightenment* (2000)

David R. Johnson, *Conrad Richter: A Writer's Life* (2001)

David Finkelstein, *The House of Blackwood: Author-Publisher Relations in the Victorian Era* (2002)

Rodger L. Tarr, ed., *As Ever Yours: The Letters of Max Perkins and Elizabeth Lemmon* (2003)

Randy Robertson, *Censorship and Conflict in Seventeenth-Century England: The Subtle Art of Division* (2009)

Catherine M. Parisian, ed., *The First White House Library: A History and Annotated Catalogue* (2010)

Jane McLeod, *Licensing Loyalty: Printers, Patrons, and the State in Early Modern France* (2011)

Charles Walton, ed., *Into Print: Limits and Legacies of the Enlightenment; Essays in Honor of Robert Darnton* (2011)

James L.W. West III, *Making the Archives Talk: New and Selected Essays in Bibliography, Editing, and Book History* (2012)

John Hruschka, *How Books Came to America: The Rise of the American Book Trade* (2012)

A. Franklin Parks, *William Parks: The Colonial Printer in the Transatlantic World of the Eighteenth Century* (2012)

Roger E. Stoddard, comp., and David R. Whitesell, ed., *A Bibliographic Description of Books and Pamphlets of American Verse Printed from 1610 Through 1820* (2012)

Nancy Cervetti, *S. Weir Mitchell: Philadelphia's Literary Physician* (2012)

Karen Nipps, *Lydia Bailey: A Checklist of Her Imprints* (2013)

Paul Eggert, *Biography of a Book: Henry Lawson's "While the Billy Boils"* (2013)

Allan Westphall, *Books and Religious Devotion: The Redemptive Reading of an Irishman in Nineteenth-Century New England* (2014)

Scott Donaldson, *The Impossible Craft: Literary Biography* (2015)

John Bidwell, *Graphic Passion: Matisse and the Book Arts* (2015)

Peter L. Shillingsburg, *Textuality and Knowledge: Essays* (2017)

Steven Carl Smith, *An Empire of Print: The New York Publishing Trade in the Early American Republic* (2017)

Colm Tóibín, Marc Simpson, and Declan Kiely, *Henry James and American Painting* (2017)

Filipe Carreira da Silva and Mónica Brito Vieira, *The Politics of the Book* (2019)

ULYSSES

by

JAMES JOYCE

IS SOLD OUT